MW01489932

GUIDANCE,

GOOFS,

&

Dave Lutes
with Sanet Stander

UNDER NEW MANAGEMENT LLC
Helping you find His Purpose in your career and life

Edited by Sarah Fraps Editorial Services - sarahfraps.com
Email: info@sarahfraps.com
Cover design by Dave Lutes, Rachel L. Hall
Cover Layout and Interior by Rachel L. Hall, Writely Divided

Unless otherwise noted, scripture quotations are taken from The Holy Bible, New International Version ® NIV ®. Copyright © 1973, 1978, 1984, 2011 by Biblica, Inc. Used with permission. All rights reserved worldwide.

Credits, acknowledgements, and permissions are located on page 407.

This book depicts actual events in real locations in the USA and South Africa in the life of the author as truthfully as recollection permits. We have done our best to retell things as honestly and accurately as possible. In some accounts the author's opinion, and the author's opinion only, is stated. We accept that those opinions may not be shared by all readers. No offense is intended. While all persons in this book are actual individuals, some names and identifying characteristics have been changed to respect their privacy or where permission to appear in this book was not granted.

DEDICATION

The following people, through their love for God, devotion and commitment to Jesus, and faithfulness in being His servants to others **helped change my life forever.** *They have all gone to be with the Lord, but their love for God lives on in hundreds, if not thousands, of others—including in me. This book celebrates their lives and service and God's Grace and Power demonstrated through them.*

Noel George Wood

1939 – 2017

For more than 47 years, my mentor, coach, best friend, and most authentically Christian man I have ever known. Faithful and flawed. Inspirational and insufferable. Perfect and imperfect. Passionate and opinionated. Professional and often prepubescent. He was charitable, charming, and competitive—and a chronic and unapologetic cheater at lawn tennis, darts, Ping-Pong (table tennis) and eight ball pool. He was my most special dad in the Lord.

Because he was faithful to God and the Gospel, I have eternal life. I will never forget him and will dance in Heaven with him one day, after I kick his (harp) at lawn (cloud) tennis.

Johnny Weber

1949 – 2007

My brother, friend, flat mate, best man at my wedding, prayer buddy, copastor, smile creator, and constant inspiration.

Sadly, in 2007, Johnny was hit and killed by a drunk driver in Durban where he was attending an evangelism conference.

Pastor "Brother" John S. W. Bond

1920 – 2007

My first pastor, mentor, and inspiration. He taught me the Word of God faithfully and well. I could not have asked for a better, more solid spiritual foundation in my life.

Revd. Canon David Prior

1940 – 2021

David taught me, mentored me, inspired me, and believed in me. He lovingly directed me into my first full-time ministry role at St Katherine's, Uitenhage in South Africa and then sought me out and urged me to come to the UK to do the same there. Without question, David was one of the truly great teachers of the Bible. He inspired me to always try to excel at teaching and preaching the Word of God. He was my friend.

Dave Valentine

1933 – 2011

Our solid rock and steady, mature hand, dedicated mentor, and "uncle"-friend. Those early days of the Jesus Revolution in Cape Town benefited greatly and eternally from the faithful, loyal, and total devotion of Dave to our knowledge of and growth in the Lord. I was among those who were tremendously encouraged and blessed by his friendship and leadership.

Faans "Brother" Klopper

1925 – 2020

Brother Klopper loved, taught, sacrificed, served, and so patiently discipled us young guys so faithfully in the Lord and laid such a sure foundation in our lives that will certainly stand the eternal test of time. He left a truly sound, good, and godly mark on my heart, soul, and life.

Paul West

1948 – 2020

Paul was one of the most authentic, passionate, and "alive" Christians I have ever known. We talked not long before he died from COVID-19, and all the memories came flooding back. From the time I discovered him praying under his desk during lunchtime at the Old Mutual, to the times we shared a stage proclaiming Christ to soul-hungry and searching young people, to the times we ministered together to guide someone to peace and deliverance, and to the times we just hung out while I basked in his beautiful musical talent. Paul was my brother, my inspiration, and my so very special, good friend.

Mike Coleman

1948 – 2002

Mike was a rock in my early days and years as a Christian. He was so utterly faithful, very present, incredibly consistent, and totally committed to sharing and living the Word of God and bringing the reality and power of Jesus' love and salvation. When I think and share with others about when and how God got a hold of me and saved me and began to transform me, Mike is in the conversation.

Chrisman Stander

1943 – 2015

Chrisman was one of the main anchors that kept things focused. He was a member of the Narnia Committee, which brought together the heart, passion, and focus of so many who wanted God's Word to spread and for Jesus to be seen and experienced throughout Cape Town. I am so grateful for his servant heart.

CONTENTS

PREFACE   *xiii*

INTRODUCTION   *xxi*

The Beginning of the Beginning...1

A Step Back in Time...6

"The Search" – Scribblings 15

Interview with Noel Wood – "Camp Commandant" – My Spiritual
Father 21

Uncle Davie, You Don't Know Jesus?...24

Early Wake-Up Call..30

Second Wake-up Call – Blessed Bucket of Cold Water...............................38

Back Home – Bring the Music or Face It?...45

I Insist That You Come to Dinner!..50

Life Upside Down...62

Brian O'Donnell – His Salvation Story and the Hippie Revival.............68

My Own Introduction to the Jesus Revolution 74

Please Lord, Heal My Pitching Arm 78

The Jesus Movement – Put Simply, We Dared to Believe God.................87

Dear Family, Let Me Prove to You Miracles Are Real Today...................93

The Jesus Revolution Heats Up..98

All Over Town! 101

Truly God-Blessed Music in Those Days 105

Then There Was Bernie...109

Bernie Auditore's Salvation Story 120

If God Loves the World So Much, Why Doesn't He Do Something?!..127

The God Who Doesn't Leave You 135

The Conform or Be Cool Dilemma 140

God Just Was..146

Where He Leads Me, I Will … Glug, Glug, Glug....................................155

The Sound of Spit and Grace 158

If You Don't Learn to Pray, I … Will … Shut … You … Up....................166

The Hunger for Miracles – Part 1 178

It Was Not All Rosy with the AOG 182

Other Things Going on in the Cape – Testimonies from Others 189

The World Needs a Revival Like This Again!....................................196

I Believe in This Cup of Coffee 201

Memories of the Jesus Movement 207

You Didn't Go to Vietnam..211

Prayer Boxing IS a Christian Sport!....................................224

Sharing and Praying with People – Growing AOG Resistance............233

When Your Spiritual Ego Hits a Speed Bump 247

But I Saw You at Cape Town Station!....................................253

Do These Two Things, and God Will Change Your Life 259

Now WHAT IS Your Problem, Mr. Lutes? 273

Huge Changes and the Pastor Nipper Miracle Show....................284

Talk About a New Dawn! 296

Done! – Part One, Miracle No. 5..307

Done! – Part Two, Miracle No. 7 & 8 (Sort of…)....................................314

Then All Heaven & Hell Broke Loose – Michael Buckland – Part I.....319

Timothy and the Scorpion 327

Then All Heaven & Hell Broke Loose – Michael Buckland – Part II ...333

Hunger for Miracles – Part 2 – Then There Was William.....................342

Banned by the Assemblies of God – Part 1..351

Banned by the Assemblies of God – Part 2..363

Spiritually Diagnosing My Own Heart Problem....................................371

God is All In! Warts and All! 378

A White Horse, Lengthening a Leg, and Prayer Giggles........................385

Leaving South Africa 391

Leaving South Africa – The Things Only God Knew About................397

Mom, It's So Simple..400

Copyright Permissions and Acknowledgments   407

Authors' Contact Information   409

PREFACE

Over the years, the last 15 years in particular, my sermons, presentations, and teaching sessions have been full of stories. No surprise to anyone who knows me. Many people have urged me to write some of it down and to mix in with the stories some of the practical, down-to-earth, normal people applications of The Faith that have become part of my sermon and teaching style. In other words, to write about the authentic struggles and successes, the victories and the failures, the discoveries, and the insights, as well as the painful (but learning-filled) disappointments that have been part of my own sometimes purposeful, sometimes meandering, sometimes idiotic, walk of faith—and doubts—over the years. This book is about *Guidance,* or the lack thereof, and God's Mercy, tolerance, and *Grace* in spite of me—and my many *Goofs.*

So, I'm calling it *Guidance, Goofs, and Grace (GGG),* and I have tried to ensure it will have a strong, punctuated emphasis on the Grace, patience, Mercy, and sense of humor of God—down-to-earth, transparent, honest, practical, human, and "unglossed"—but of course, honoring God who has remained faithful in spite of my best efforts to guide and run my own life.

You will notice that the phrase *run my own life* is just one *I* short of "ru*i*n." As I am alliteration prone, in short, the rest of the book will be mostly an honest, humorous, and hopefully "hymn-spirational" autobiographical account of my Christian journey, including the faith, fumblings, failures, and forgiveness along the way. There is another hyphenated *f* word I could use, but that wouldn't be very Christian; however, it would also aptly describe some really huge actions, regrets, and mistakes that I got up to and brought on myself in those days.

The real discovery and journey began for me in the early '70s in South Africa. Some of you reading this introduction were there and will agree that that time was incredibly important to us all. Life altering, world shattering, and revolutionary would be more apt.

I want this book to be very much about the Lord ... and not about me. But I also want to weave in contributions from others who have been part of my life from those early days to share their own recollections about our—theirs and mine—contact, relationship, and experiences together (sad, happy, good, bad, funny, momentous, miraculous) or just a comment about an event we shared in. I'm a willing and easy target for gibes and digs, and I welcome them.

Me

1970 & 1975

My first five years in South Africa

Guidance, Goofs, and Grace begins and is written from my perspective as the 18-year-old, ultraconservative, small village Yankee and international exchange student who "rocked up" in Cape Town in the Southern Hemisphere winter of 1970. It tracks a journey of discovery at a time *when God was truly, truly present, active, powerful, and historical – the Jesus Revolution.*

Thanks,
Dave Lutes

~ In Loving Memory ~
Bernie Auditore

1951 – 2023

To my covenant brother in Christ, best friend, inspiration and source of so many wonderful memories that always bring a smile to my face and heart: you will be deeply missed.

***

Dear Old Friends!

Whether you're at the high or low end of the spirituality spectrum at the moment, or somewhere in between (or not on the spectrum at all), I would still love to reconnect, reminisce, and receive your insights, memories, and comments as old, dear friends who shared in those historical times. If it is easier, it could also be great just to hang out for a while online and catch up.

See the contact details at the end of this book if you're interested.

GUIDANCE, GOOFS,

We were Guided.

We really Goofed up ... often!

And we really knew His Grace ...

Oh my God, it was a good time to walk with You, Lord!

Not that it isn't now ... well, ok, you know what I mean.

The Jesus Revolution

1 John 1:1–4 (Prayer-a-phrased)

From the very beginning He spoke, we heard His voice, and we listened. We had to! He showed up in our lives and called us by name—He knew our names! His purpose was to reveal Himself to hungry hearts, our hearts. Every day we saw with our own eyes the amazing things He was doing ... how He touched us, changed us, touched others ... and He even used us to reach out to others to bring them His Life. We lived, breathed, talked—no, proclaimed —everything He told us and showed us—everything! We held nothing back; He gave Himself completely so that people could know Him and have a relationship with Him, and share God's fullness of Life offered through Jesus. The joy we felt and knew in our hearts and souls was amazing, and we absolutely could not help sharing it with others, so they could know Him too. There was no greater joy!

INTRODUCTION

THE CHAPTERS IN THIS BOOK contain many extracts from others who lived in, and then wrote about, the period of 1970–1975 in blogs, books, and other media publications. Their contributions are pretty much left untouched (i.e., as they were originally written with only minor editing) and with full acknowledgment at the end of the book.

Even audio and video sessions, which have been recorded in recent times, have been largely unedited when transcribed. We've retold their accounts and stories almost verbatim—in their style and in their own words. We have not edited British or South African spellings of words and only sometimes transliterated, translated, or explained the meaning of Afrikaans words (some of them a bit crude).

In the name of total transparency, you should know that there are numerous accounts of supernatural events and experiences—including references to Divine healing (and not), encounters with the demonic and details about the Gifts of the Holy Spirit—and their use. Some accounts are disturbing and/or amazing—and may not have been what we thought they were. But we share them as being absolutely true events and as wonderful learning experiences and a demonstration of God's love and power to save, touch and restore the whole of our lives—and others'. And guide us back on the right path when we may have got it wrong.

What is amazing to us about this book is that *all* of the people we have interviewed or asked for extracts from *can and want to* share their stories from those days as still being very real, life transforming, *and utterly memorable*. An incredible level of bless-ed detail still lives in their memories and hearts. We trust He will use this book to create some amazing blessings in your life as well.

Be Blessed!
Dave Lutes and Sanet Stander

WESTERN CAPE PROVINCE, SOUTH AFRICA

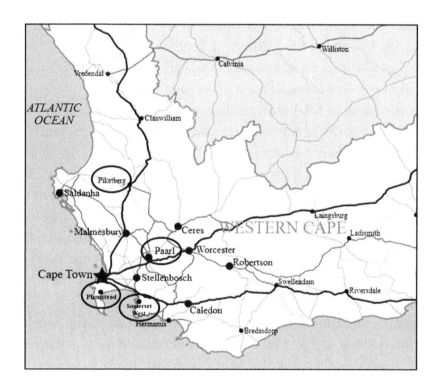

CHAPTER ONE

The Beginning of the Beginning

MAYBE IN MY OLD AGE things have become fuzzy or glamorized over time, or the years and moving countries so many times—and kids—have managed to wipe the struggles and unpleasant stuff during those Jesus Movement days from my memory. But still, 50+ years on, I remember the early seventies as momentous, positively tumultuous, history-shaping , and life-changing times. Personally, and for many wonderful people along the way and in so many other ways, the world got turned upside down by Jesus and the power of His Spirit.

He invaded our histories!

He rocked our worlds!

He changed our destinies and reason for living!

From the moment dear ol' Sister What's-Her-Name, with a mantilla on her head, prayed with a dramatic, quivering voice, "Looorrrdddd, saaaave the hippies!" at the Harfield Road, Kenilworth, Cape, Assembly of God Church's Friday night prayer meeting sometime in the late sixties, lives were changed eternally. (I made that up ... sort of ... by other accounts, it was actually Pastor John "Brother" Bond, Head of the Assemblies of God (AOG), who prayed something similar ... but less quivery.)

* * *

But I can't continue with this story without first bringing Brian O'Donnell into the frame. In those days, I had no idea about how it all —the Hippie Revival and the Jesus Revolution in Cape Town—began. Brian would never want to own this label, but I only know that Brian, for me, was The Main Guy. He was The Man. He was the one who followed the Lord with passion. He led it all, gave it life and visibility, and he had a profound and eternal impact on thousands of lives— including my own. I'll let the late Dave Valentine, one of the early leaders, and one of those that this book is dedicated to, tell some of the story below.

Excerpt from Dave Valentine:

In 1970, Brian O'Donnell had a surf shop and decided to open a flea market on Loop Street (in Cape Town). The Market had small stalls, which were let to producers of artistic clothing and handmade articles. Brian was influenced by the Hippie movement and named it "The Hippie Market." He also had a nightclub called

The Factory, which catered as a dance and meeting place for young, hip people. The Hippie movement was a result of reaction against established values in society and the war in Vietnam, and their motto was "Make Love Not War."

During this time, a new movement from America called the "Jesus People" swept across the land, starting in 1969 with Teen Challenge's Narnia Club in Hillbrow, Johannesburg and Nelson Nurse's underground club called The Downstairs. Some of the hippies that got saved there moved to Cape Town and started working in The Hippie Market—amongst them, Chrisman Stander, Johnny Weber, and Mike and Denise Coleman.

In the same year, Brian (O'Donnell), who comes from a Baptist family involved in missionary work on the railways, got convicted about the life he was living and recommitted his life to the Lord. Brian was married to my sister Sandra who also committed her life to Christ. I was a leader in a nominal church for seven years and was so impressed by their testimony that I followed them to Harfield Road Assembly of God, which had welcomed the hippies.

We were amazed by the singing in tongues and the Gifts of the Spirit—speaking in tongues, prophecy, and healing that were practiced in this Pentecostal Breaking of Bread service. We were impressed by the open ministry where anyone who had an inspired message could stand up and preach. The Lord was in this awe-inspiring place.

Harfield Road Assembly of God, a conservative Pentecostal church in their dark Sunday suits and head coverings for women, was in the throes of a revival after a prophecy that God would bless them with men "like a flood." They were located in Kenilworth and expected a flood of businessmen.

Imagine their surprise when these long-haired, barefooted hippies dressed casually and colourfully started flooding into the church. Initially they resisted, but then John Bond stood up and said, "We prayed for revival, and these are the people that God has sent us; let's welcome them," and they did—and it wasn't long before the church was overflowing."

– Dave Valentine, 1985

* * *

The Hound of Heaven

I'm getting ahead of myself. More later, but wonderfully and eternally put, God heard whoever prayed the prayer mentioned previously and got busy speaking to and laying His hand on and touching people's hearts and lives everywhere.

The most unlikely, completely unexpected, and surprising folks got nabbed and saved. The "Hound of Heaven" (poem by Francis Thompson –1890) stalked and patrolled the streets of Cape Town and the Western Cape—actually, the whole of Southern Africa—looking for hungry hearts and lost and messed up lives in need of rescue and transformation.

He found them. We were there. And not just the hippies.

We were all among the ones He stalked and found.

While a conservative, high-profile Cape Town lawyer was hardly a recognized face among the hippie crowd, God used Noel Wood to grab ahold of me in those days—more than 8,000 miles from home. More later.

I was among those He found.

I never saw Him coming.

His light broke through—into my life.

CHAPTER TWO

A Step Back in Time

TO SET THE SCENE FOR THIS PSEUDO-MEMOIR, I will take a step back in time and share something more of my own personal history and early spiritual journey. You can read more detailed accounts about my journey after those days (and then some!) in the sequel to this book, *Guidance, Goofs and More Grace* (out sometime this century, I hope).

The whole of village life in Trumansburg, New York, where I grew up, revolved around school, sports, crops, hunting and fishing, seasonal tourism cycles, and other community activities. We had a beautiful lake and an amazing waterfall (*"The highest falls east of the Rockies"*), and we were surrounded by history; it was a beautiful, wonderful place to grow up.

We were replete with extended family and thick with cousins and variously connected relatives. My mother was born in the farmhouse of my great-aunt and uncle. There were eight (I think) churches, but obviously, the congregations were quite small. I know that the Presbyterian and Baptist churches eventually closed up shop and shared a church building, and they even merged their names into something like First Presbo-Baptist Church. I was, apparently, baptized / christened as a baby in the Presbyterian Church.

But I had no interest in, and no one I knew well had an interest in or connection with, church whatsoever. I had not a single friend or classmate or relative who talked the Christian language or mentioned church as a significant aspect of their lives. I only remember, in 6th grade, the day President John F. Kennedy was assassinated, that the Episcopal minister's daughter burst into tears. I insensitively scoffed at her for caring so much about a politician, which was typical of my wise-guy persona.

I think I went to a Sunday school class once with my best friend when I was about 13, but that's only a maybe and a very vague memory. In my final two years of high school, I attended the Trumansburg Youth Fellowship, but that was exclusively to get good snacks, hang out with friends, and meet girls … always the same girls. I don't recall ever discussing anything remotely Christian-like or "Bible-y."

I had never opened or even held a Bible in my hand and didn't know even the most common or simplest of Bible stories (except maybe the Christmas story-ish). I prayed hard numerous times in my teen years, mainly of the bargaining type, asking to not get caught or in trouble over something I had done. I didn't have a definition of who I was praying to, and if God ever did rescue me from my sin and stupidity, I never acknowledged it or thanked Him. I just carried on being, well, me.

Other than getting a little weepy whenever I heard the Christmas song, "Little Drummer Boy" (which was weird), the full extent of my religious perspective was sketchy at best but largely nonexistent. It was really a bit odd, looking back, that from age 6–12 I was the designated "Blessing Sayer" at Thanksgiving and Christmas day dinners, which were normally at either my Great-Aunt Mary-Louise's or my Great-Aunt Evelyn's house. All the relatives gathered—maybe 30–35 people, including a huge group of cousins. My great-grandmother, Granny McCluen, my grandma, and my own mom put pressure on me from a young age and assigned me to say grace. I don't think I ever changed the words below, not once, in all those years:

> *Father, we thank Thee for the night,*
>
> *And for the pleasant morning light;*
>
> *For rest and food and loving care,*
>
> *And all that makes the world so fair.*
>
> *Amen.*

Tears running down their cheeks, Granny, Grandma, Aunt Whoever, and Mom would say, "Oh my, he said that so nicely and beautifully."

Cousins, fingers symbolically shoved down their throats, or rubbing their forefingers along their noses, would say under their breath, "Brown nose!" (Which was the mid-twentieth century equivalent of "Suck up!").

Other than that, as I mentioned, I attended the Youth Fellowship mainly to have a laugh and hang out with friends. At the only session that I remember where we had even a sort of serious spiritual discussion, we spent time dissecting the symbolic meaning behind the dual, parallel lyric tracks of Simon and Garfunkel's song, "Scarborough Fair." Not really deeply meaningful, now, was it?

* * *

Senior (and Junior) year in a US high school could be a scary and stressful time, as so much of your future life's success hinged on college entrance exams, Scholastic Aptitude Tests (SATs), and quite a bit of clarity about what you wanted to be when you finally grew up. The jokey, more pessimistic alternative quote, "What do you want to be when you give up?"—was lurking at the back of many minds. Escaping small village life was blended in with that thought somewhere.

There was a lot of pressure—on me at least.

I was president of the Student Council, in the Varsity Club, Boy's State Senator and Governor nominee, Model United Nations representative, District Student Council rep, Teen (Community Service) Council rep, captain of several teams, president of a few clubs, an Honor Student and Thespian award winner; and in a school system where my parents were long-serving and very popular teachers.

You get the idea.

But I was so busy performing, doing, achieving, and showing the world **ME** that I began to struggle academically and mentally. *I simply could not fail in anyone's eyes!* The community in many ways looked up to my family, actually extolled us somewhat, and to let them down would be horrific and shameful in the extreme. I wanted my mom and dad, along with cousins and other relatives (and many friends) to be impressed and proud of me. *I HAD to succeed!* I had to be accepted by teachers, community, coaches, jocks, hippies, girls, and well … everyone.

A simple example of something that happened then that, oddly, still bugs and shames me to this day. I was 17, traveling with some friends to a basketball game in a neighboring town. On the way, we decided to buy some beer, but none of us was 18 (the legal age in those days). We stopped along the way, and I went into the country store, chose a couple of six-packs, and took them to the counter to pay. The lady asked me for ID. I lied and told her that I had left it at home. She asked me my age, and I lied again and told her I was 18. She asked me my name, and when I told her, she immediately said, "Oh, you're Elgie Lutes' boy. Happy to sell you beer, Dave. Elgie Lutes' son would never lie."

As I drank, guilt robbed the beer of any possible flavor or pleasure, and these 53 years later, as I write, I still cringe at my lie and the way that simple act dishonored my family—especially my dad.

The pressure to excel and succeed really got to me. To maintain my image as a scholar-jock, I began cheating on tests and homework, borrowed a stolen and duplicated master key to steal midyear exam answers, started shoplifting (to be "one of the guys"), and neglected the kinds of things you needed to do to succeed legitimately. When I failed Chemistry in my Junior year (the first subject I had ever come close to failing)—and failed badly—it rocked my world. I was fallible after all.

Worst of all, I was a fake. And I knew it.

On top of all this, my brother and best friend, John (two years older and, at that time, in college) was the epitome of all-sports success, including scholarship offers, with a bright superstar future—plus, he was a "babe magnet". I was known inside and outside of our school and village as "John Lutes' brother" —and to add to those self-image woes, even when asking a cute girl to dance at a neighboring school, after looking at me closely would say something like, "You're John Lutes' brother aren't you?! Is he here?!" Plus, my parents were both regarded by many as the best of the best teachers—**EVER!**

The whole family's shadow was very long and very present.

I knew I needed more discipline in my life, so to force my own hand, I applied to attend Annapolis Naval Academy when I eventually left high school. My academic record was almost good enough, except that I had done three years of Latin instead of a modern language and combined with the fact that I was legally blind in my left eye due to a baseball beaning injury. This all meant I was rejected.

So, that particular quest for order, discipline, and focus—and an un-fake life—was out the door.

Apart from applying to a number of colleges in the region, I also put my hat in the ring to be considered as an International Rotary Exchange student and, thus, began to go through the long qualification process. It was a good and bad option, not least because I hadn't done very well on my SATs and because I had the truth and consequences of a huge, stupid mistake hanging over me that could bring off-the-charts shame to me and my family—and would more than likely close the door on the exchange student option—and bring that idea crashing down.

* * *

Huge, Stupid Mistake

I share this next section not to shock and certainly not to embarrass anyone or to start gossip again after 53 years, but my girlfriend, age 15, became pregnant. It rocked her, my, and our families' worlds. We scrambled to find a place and way for her to get an abortion. To *not* do this never entered our heads, and to keep it secret in a small village like ours was absolutely critical, but of course, impossible. She and her parents went to England at my family's expense, of course, not least because she was legally a minor, and therefore, technically, I was guilty of rape. This sin and mistake haunted me and my family for many years —and still does.

Guilt and failure began to cripple me. Whatever prayer I prayed, however earnestly, unsurprisingly, didn't work. At risk was the possibility of me being rejected as a Rotary Exchange student candidate. The village was tiny, and everyone knew everyone else's business. Word would get out in no time, and news of my citizenship, character flaws,

11

and moral deficiencies was likely to reach the Rotary Club decision-makers.

If anyone in the Rotary Club knew or found out, we didn't hear about it; and remarkably, I was selected. So, off I went to Cape Town in July 1970.

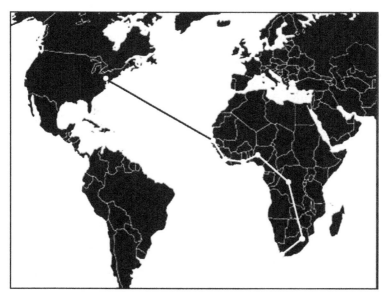

As you can imagine, I carried a lot of that personal (much of it secret) guilt-baggage with me. Part of me felt like I had escaped well-deserved societal and reputational punishment; another part of me was terrified that I could never discover who I really was or who I wanted to become—much less learn some important life lessons. Worse, I continued to carry the feeling deep inside that being a fake was somehow locked into my future's DNA.

I knew my escape to South Africa was only a temporary reprieve and that I had to face the music, my family and community with my failures and flaws on my return in less than a year. I certainly wasn't "free" in my heart and mind, and in so many ways for the first couple of months, I remained in major fake it mode.

* * *

It was midwinter (Southern Hemisphere). I was truly cold to the bone, and frankly, I did not like my first family much at all (the feeling was mutual, apparently). I was desperately homesick and really had trouble coping from the get-go.

Did I make a huge mistake? Did I really have a choice?

It didn't take me long, however, to let my very short, conservative hair down and become a wise guy, pain in the butt nuisance to all who connected with me. The high school authorities, and my first family, apparently complained about my attitude, and the Rotary Club actually contemplated sending me back home (or so I found out later—the first time in their history!). Instead, they decided to give me one last chance to come right and to succeed in the exchange program.

Without consulting me, they arranged for me to go to a Christian Schools and Varsities (S&V) weeklong camp on Stark's Farm in Piketberg, Northern Cape. It was their equivalent of spring break, but really it was also a last-ditch effort to "sort me out." My host family broke the news to me over dinner one evening.

I tried to listen to the idea (well, sort of), but when they showed me the camp pamphlet describing the activities at the camp, including devotional times, ('scuse my French), I got really pissed off, and I made it quite clear to them that I was not happy about going to a religious camp. That said, I really didn't have a choice.

My host father, John (who had spent some time in the US and was therefore keen to have a Yank in the home), witnessed firsthand my in-your-face tirade when I told the camp Commandant (leader) at the bus station in no uncertain terms, that he and the other camp leaders must keep their religious mitts off me. The Commandant (Noel) described me to a friend many years later as "an angry young man."

I won't go into the details now, but suffice it to say, I got introduced to the God who I knew zilch about, who I couldn't care less about, or who I didn't even really believe existed—as well as to His Son who I didn't know or believe was historically, or in any way, relevant or real.

On Thursday night at the camp, after a moving talk given "just for me" (of course), I went to Noel outside the meeting tent to simply say, "Thank you,"—but instead, tears streaming down my face, I grabbed Noel's shirt and shook him quite violently and screamed with heart-wrenching emotion right up in his face:

"Why has no one ever told me about this before?!"

"It's the most amazing thing I've ever heard!"

"Why ... has ... no ... one ... ever ... told ... me ... this ... before?!"

He drew me aside, shared some Bible verses with me, and prayed with me—and so, my new life with God began. The date was October 7, 1970.

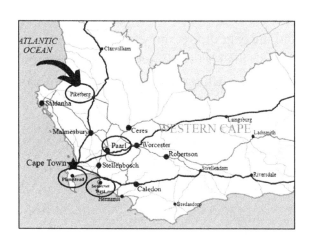

PICKETBERG, NORTHERN CAPE

CHAPTER THREE

"The Search" – Scribblings

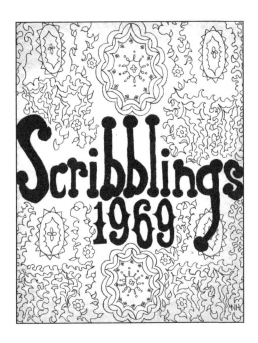

WHAT IS INTERESTING—and really quite ironic—is my first-ever short story, "The Search," that appeared in a school publication called *Scribblings* in 1969, had an unintentional, sort of Christian-themed ending. I have included a copy here, which, looking back, illustrates and gives a small clue that God was already working below the surface in my heart and life.

The Search

--*Dave Lutes*

If it weren't for the "crick" in his neck, Lee would probably still be looking up. He'd been awed by the towering buildings ever since he stepped off the bus. This was something he was entirely unprepared for and was struck completely dumbfounded. And so many people. "Lord, were there a lot of people! How on earth would be find his way around?"

He picked up his bags and began to walk down the crowded thoroughfare, glancing often at the wide variety of items displayed in the windows. He was enjoying it immensely, however, when he came to a sign in front of a restaurant, PETE'S RESTAURANT. The sign read: SUPPORT NORTHERN STATE UNIVERSITY FOOTBALL SAM BROOSTER STYLE He walked on in.

The place really wasn't very big and no one seemed to be in. He walked up to the counter and slopped his bags down on the floor, glancing at the wide variety of snack bar necessities.

"Hey boy! What do ya want?"

Lee spun around. A small bald man, undoubtedly Pete, for the name fit him, was just putting away a broom in the back. He walked toward Lee with a funny look on his face.

"Well?"

"I need some information, sir, about how to get to the university."

"You plan on going there?" he questioned, his bald head glaring.

"Yes, sir."

Pete jerked his thumb. "Four blocks down and on your left." He turned and went into a back room.

Lee, set back a bit, strode out.

The walk to the Administration Building was long and tiresome. He was anxious to get settled so he skipped the tour of the campus and went directly to the counter where it said ADMITTANCE. The clerk was busy writing and didn't notice him until he set his bags down. Her face reflected astonishment, and she said nothing. She just stared, her glasses glaring.

"Is this where you find out about where you

stay, and such, if you're a freshman and all?"

"You'll have to wait over there," she said pointing and looked down.

As he turned two other boys came up. Her response to them was, "Yes, what can I do for you." He continued walking over to some chairs where he set down his bags. He turned to go back in line. By now there were about seven boys in line. He took his papers out of his pocket, glancing in the corners of paper where it said, ATHLETIC GRANT. Getting that $900.00 Scholarship was the greatest thing that ever happened to him. Pa was really pleased too.

He could hear the lady stamping the papers and telling the boys what they wanted to know. Evidentally the boy in front of him was on a scholarship too because she told him to wait with

the group of boys standing "Over there." Lee looked in the direction of the boys' stare, Lord were they big, A few sized up to better than six and a half feet.

"Well?"

"Well! she said again, but this time more impatiently.

Lee turned quickly.

"Yes ma'am. . . oh, uh, on a scholarship too."

"Fill out these and wait with that group of boys over there."

After he filled out about nine sheets and asked for information at another desk, Lee walked on over to the group. He noticed a couple of the boys sizing him up, and that didn't take much, because he was only 5 feet 9 inches, 155 pounds. He heard a few Hi's and Hello's, but that was about it. Someone said something about adding a little color to the team but Lee let it ride.

"All right, let's have your attention."

Lee turned around.

"I'm Coach Kelley. Welcome to N. S U. All right get your stuff and I'll show you to your temporary dorms."

Practice was the next morning at 6:00 A.M.

5

16

and it was real rough. They were clocked in the mile and the forty. They had about an hour straight conditioning. Lee placed fifth in the forty and second in the mile. From looking around the he decided he was the smallest man there. They broke up into groups; himself going with the quarterbacks. Out of twelve in the group, eight were on scholarship; and he was the smallest, the next tallest being 6 foot o inches. Lee wasn't one to be discouraged easily, but it wouldn't be long unless he really produced.

Practice broke up about 9:30 A.M. It was a tough practice and the players had the usual moans and groans. Lee walked back to the dorms by himself. Things weren't looking too good.

He certainly was going to have a hard time holding his own on the field. He'd just about gotten himself into a thinking spell when the blast of a truck's horn jolted him out of it.

"And that's another thing! All that noise."

"You're right. It does get on your nerves, doesn't it?"

Lee startled turned around.

"You don't like it either huh?My name's Lee Howley. What's yours and which way you headed?"

"Donnie Brooks and I'm your new roomate, so I guess we're heading the same way. I got my room assignment from Coach. Nice to know ya." Donnie stuck out a big hand.

"Where you from?"Lee inquired.

"Wellsboro, Pennsylvania. I take it you're from a small town too. Otherwise you wouldn't hate the noise. Where you from?"

"Ridgeport, Ohio. We only have about two thousand people, but you couldn't find a quieter and more friendly place. That's more than you can say for here."

Donnie didn't quite understand, but he didn't press it. Lee wasn't one to complain so he didn't either.

"We're in room 24, so this slip Coach gave me says. I guess all the players are in·one dorm. What say we get settled in and then go out and get some eats?"

Lee left some of his stuff packed. He was pretty hungry so he decided to do it later. He glanced over at Donnie.

"Yep, Donnie was O.K.," he thought.

Lee didn't sleep that night. The little incidents were coming back to him. The man at the restaurant, the clerk, the little word from one of the players, all seemed to have something against him. Everything he had done had been confusing. He had to walk here, walk there, stand in this line and that, fill out papers, remember numbers, and listen to the incessant noise of the city. Everything, everything, was a far cry from the quiet fields, the friendly people, and the calm, non-hectic way of doing things he had experienced back home. Back home he had a favorite spot up on a hill in the back of the house that overlooked the valley. Here he could sit for hours and take in the quiet and think out his troubles. Not so here.

"Boy do I miss it," he muttered.

"What'd ya say Lee?"

"Oh, I'm sorry Donnie, I didn't mean to wake you. I was just talking to myself."

"You miss home too huh?So do I. I miss alot of things."

"Do you like to hunt Donnie?"

"...and fish, and trap, and hike, and just plain sit and look,"Donnie continued, "those are things to look forward to when you go home."

"Ain't it the truth."

They told a few lies to each other about their different explorations and expeditions until about 3:00 a.m. Finally sleep came.

Lee was in better spirits the next morning. Practice was a little better but he still began to feel he lacked the qulities of a college quarterback. Contact would start soon, so maybe then he could show the coaches something. However, it looked as though the coaches already had their choice. John Shoebridge, who had arrived earlier than most, was all-state from New Jersey.He wasideal for the job. The coaches knew it and so did Lee.

After about two hours of practice, the group was called together. The Varsity coach, Coach Brooster, gave his lecture about the rules and regulations. He also stressed unity which was needed to make a winning team. He turned the show over to Coach Kelley, who just about repeated everything Brooster had said, only this time just to the Freshmen.

"The success of a team depends on pride, guts, desire, and team unity. We must strive for these things if we expect to have a winning season. We

6

must act as one big happy family. . ."

"Integrated no doubt," was the comment.

Lee didn't know who said it but he was beginning to put some pieces together.

". . .If we acheive this unity," Coach Kelley continued, "I'm sure we can have a very successful and rewarding season. OK!, three laps and in."

Lee trotted around the field alone. He had a pain in his chest. Lee had never experienced anything like this at home. It was a defeating feeling.

"Mind if a friend trots along?"

"No, sure Donnie."

"I heard the comment. It was Shoebridge; Larry Zager and he were right beside me."

"So."

"Don't let it bother you Lee. Some people are just like that."

Lee said nothing.

"Say, what say after church tomorrow we. . ."

"Church?" Lee interupted.

"Yea church."

"I haven't gone to church in so long I don't remember what it's like."

"Well maybe it'll do you some good, get your mind off things and all."

"Yea maybe."

"Well, anyway, after we get back, what say we toss the baseball around a little bit?"

"What ever you say." was his reluctant comment.

The next morning Lee had more butterflies than before a game. He didn't go to church very often. In fact he counted about five years between the last time and now. He figured he was the hard-working, outdoors type.

"What church do you go to Donnie?"

"Episcopal."

"I was afraid of that."

"Why?"

"I'm Prebysterian."

"That's all right, Just do what I do, and you can't go wrong."

Reverend Hannigan was the pastor of the church. He wasn't real tall man, about 45 years of age, well built, and had a firm trusting voice. He spoke on patience and trust in your fellow man. Lee listened very intently.

The sermon was very good Lee thought, and he felt he got a lot out of it. He was still thinking about it when he walked up the aisle. Reverend Hannigan seemed like an all right guy.

"Are you boys from the university?"

"Yes sir," Donnie answered for the both of them. "I thought so. I hadn't seem you here before. I'm glad you could come," he said sticking out a big hand.

Lee had a broad smile on his face and stuck out his hand. Reverend Hannigan gripped it hard. Lee always liked that.

"I'll see you boys next Sunday."

"You bet."

"Now that wasn't so bad now was it?"

"Nope."

"I'm glad to see you're not at a loss for words. What's the matter. Didn't you like the sermon, or are you afraid I'll rub it in?"

"The sermon was good and don't bother rubbing it in," Lee said smiling.

Donnie was glad to see it.

Monday, Tuesday, and Wednesday were three rough days of practice. On Tuesday contact started and this was the day the coaches really watched and when the men were separated from the boys. Up until now Lee had seen no action.

Lee wasn't having one of his better days. His passing was way off. He was just cocking his arm when he heard some confusion behind him. Someone, one of the backs, was lying on the ground. Lee rushed over. The coaches had his helmet off him. Lee peeked in and was shocked. It was Donnie out cold. Lee moved in closer.

"Hey, give him a little air?" Coach Kelley brushed Lee back. "Get the smelling salts. He took a pretty good shot on the head."

The trainer brought Donnie out of it soon. Pistol Pete, better known as Coach Kelley, sent him in and told him to rest and see a doctor.

Lee's passing and general ball handling now went from bad to worse. Finally, after he made a bad pitch out and then threw a bad block he received the comment he'd been expecting.

"Better sit down, Howley, before you get hurt."

He figured Pistol would come through.

That's all the action he saw for the day. He started back to the dorm in disgust.

7

"Hey Howley, come here a minute. The coach wants to see ya."

Lee trotted back to the field and to Coach Kelley's office. Lee knocked and walked in.

"Sit down, Howley."

Lee sat.

"Howley, I'll put it to you straight. In case you're wondering why you're not playing, well, the other coaches and I have decided that, well, you're not the quarterback you were made out to be and just not a football player."

That hit Lee hard. He was suddenly hot.

"Is that the only reason sir?" Lee realized he shouldn't have said it.

Coach Kelley flushed but regained his composure.

"That'll be all Howley."

Lee turned and left. He walked back ashamed. When he reached the dorm he found a note from Donnie saying he was at the doctor's. Lee was worried about him and he hoped it wasn't anything serious.

Lee had so many problems he didn't know what to do with them all. Donnie had a possible head injury; the coaches didn't feel he was worth the time of day for two possible reasons; and member of the team disliked him because he was black. So what, Did that make him inferior? He didn't know what to think. He sat down to think but didn't have much luck. Every time he tried to reason something out, a truck would roar by, or a car horn would sound off. No matter how hard he tried, he couldn't think.

He decided to take a walk and try to think out his troubles. He didn't know where he walked nor cared. Lord, the noise. . . !

After about an hour he sensed the surroundings to be familiar Up until now he hadn't really looked up to notice anything in particular, but now he glanced up.

"That's a joke." He was standing in front of the Episcopal Church he had attended.

He started to walk past.

"What the heck," he thought.

He strode to the door and tried the knob. If it didn't open it would have satisfied his conscience but it opened so he stepped in. The quiet was deafening. He walked down the aisle a little ways and sat down.

"Well what do you know," he whispered.

This was the kind of peacefulness. It took him about a half an hour to resolve the things that needed resolving. However, he still wasn't sure quite what to do.

"Did you lose something or find something?"

Lee stood up to face his questioner. It was Reverand Hannigan.

"Oh, I'm sorry. I didn't hear you come in. I hope you don't mind me sitting in here. I was trying to find someplace quiet to go and think and this was about as quiet as they come."

"That's all right. Sit down. Is something bothering you?"

"Why yea. How'd you know?"

"You greeted me with a smile once before. You didn't this time."

"I have got a few problems, but I don't want to trouble you with them."

"No. It's all right. Tell me what's on your mind. You know sometimes, it's better to tell someone about it."

Lee told him all right. He rattled on for the better part of an hour. He told him about the different people and their attitudes. He told him about the hill back home that he used to sit on and think. He told him about Donnie and what a great friend he was. And he told him about football and all its hidden miseries.

"Oh I'm sorry Reverend. I had no idea how long I'd talked. You're pretty easy to talk to."

"That's OK Lee. You're easy to listen to. You know, I'd like to help you if I could."

"I'm open for suggestions."

"I'll try. You know Lee, God made people different on purpose. If everyone was alike, I don't think we could stand it. So he mace people different, not only in color, or physical aspects, but in personalities and ideals. He made people like the restaurant owner, and the clerk, like young Mr. Shoebridge. But whatever "they" might do to you they're really the ones who make us try to do better. But, you have to be strong. He also made people like Donnie, the ones who are there to give you a pat on the back and for you to give a pat back. You're going to have to face both kinds, Lee, but you're going to have to face up to them and don't ever let them get you down, OK? I realize it's hard and I don't think I've given you much help

8

but use what I've given to you anyway. It could be a key.

"Now about this quarterbacking. Do you feel you're a good quarterback?"

"Yes sir, but only for high school ball. I'm not big enough."

"Well, I'll let you in on a little secret. I wasn't too bad at quarterback in high school either. I went to college with high hopes, but. . . no dice. The coaches wouldn't buy me. So you know what I did. I went right up to the head coach and said, "Sir, I'm not used to playing the bench. Either do one of three things. One, let me play quarterback, two move me somewhere where I can possibly help the team, or three drop me. He liked my guts so he did the second thing. Inside a week, I was snaring passes with the best of 'em at split end."

Lee smiled. His search had ended, for now.

* * *

That I wrote the story at all surprised everyone—I mean *EVERYONE!* My dad, an atheist, and some good friends who knew me well enough to know I had no, none, zero interest in church or Christian things, all cried when they read it. It puzzled me more than pleased me that they cried, but still, it shows something was going on in my life that I really could not connect any dots to or was not even slightly aware of. Even after I gave my life to Christ in South Africa, I didn't connect that decision with some of the heart issues expressed in this story.

CHAPTER FOUR

Interview with Noel Wood – "Camp Commandant" – My Spiritual Father

I MET DAVIE IN THE SPRING [Southern Hemisphere] of 1970. He was an exchange student at Rondebosch Boys' High (which is the same school that I attended years before). We met outside City Hall in Cape Town on the way to Piketberg for the weeklong camp. Our first eye-to-eye introduction was at the Cape Town Bus Station as we were loading up and getting ready to make the three-hour trip to the campsite.

Dave's foster parents (his first host family), and I think the Rotary Club who sponsored him, sent him to the camp to have some peace and quiet with him away, and as a result, he was not very cooperative or happy to be there. Dave was a furious and frustrated young man. He actually told me just before the bus was due to leave to, "Keep my religious hands off him!"

It took about 48 hours at the campsite before he actually started to talk and join in. He started cooperating probably because he saw the ease and naturalness that everyone had at a Christian camp, and he started joining in the activities and games. Dave did not participate in tent quiet times the first few evenings and had no relationship with God that I could tell at the time.

On the 4th night, Dave approached me after the evening devotional talk that I gave and told me he would like to talk sometime. He tried to thank me for the message I had shared with the boys that evening but instead grabbed me by my jacket and began to shake me quite violently. He began to cry and almost shout at wanting to know why no one had ever told him about Jesus before, that it was incredible news to him, and to please tell him more. I have to admit that I was completely shocked by his intensity.

I took him to a spot some distance away and told him a bit about Jesus. He then asked me to "introduce him to Jesus." We prayed together, and I can truly say, (as I watched him for years afterward) that time of prayer was the turning point in his life and an incredible one in my own. I followed up with him the weekend after the camp finished, took him to church, and introduced him to my family. And so, our friendship, and the mentoring began. I always considered Davie as my very dear and special son—even to this day.

– Noel Wood, May 5, 2016
(Interviewed by Wanda Bronkhorst)

* * *

In August 2017, Noel and I spoke on the phone for several very emotional hours for the last time. I was in Saudi Arabia on a work assignment, and he was on his deathbed in Cape Town. Though dying and clearly ready for his journey "home," Noel was full of jokey memories about our connection and time on earth together.

We reminded each other of the day God used him to get ahold of me and change my life. We accused each other, for the thousandth time, of cheating at lawn tennis, darts, and pool (snooker), and we piled memory upon memory of the amazing father-son relationship we had. Throughout all the years previously, and up to his last breath, Noel always called me "Davie, my son." As I couldn't be there, it was my saddest-most-joyful pleasure to write a memorial tribute to him that was read out at his funeral.

CHAPTER FIVE

Uncle Davie, You Don't Know Jesus?

AFTER THE CAMP, I went back to my host family—the Kains—who were the first of four families I would stay with that year. As I mentioned, Noel Wood had spent some private time with me, prayed with me, and guided me to accept Christ into my life. When the weeklong camp ended, the obvious question was, "So, what next?"

I certainly had no vocabulary for what had begun to happen to me or what was going on inside my heart and mind. All I knew was that something remarkable and life altering had begun.

I knew it but had no words for it.

I'm sure my host family was very nervous about my return home to Kenilworth after the camp—a possible storm cloud already nervously forming. But after a couple of days doing normal family things, my host mother (Muriel) came to me a little hesitantly, almost shyly, and said, "You know, Dave, there's something different about you since you came back from the camp."

"Really, what?" I asked, somewhat surprised. As far as I was aware, I hadn't been doing anything differently from before. That said, I was pretty much oblivious to my irritating behavior before the camp.

She said, "I don't know. There's just something softer. The hard, rough edges seem to be smoother. Something's happened to you."

It was a profound moment for me. I had no language for how I was feeling or what I had experienced when Noel prayed with me at the camp.

I said, "I really don't know how to say it or explain it. It was a really good time at the camp! It's neat and strange, but the only way I can explain is that I feel like I've been born all over again. I don't have any other way to describe it."

We didn't talk about it again.

If the Rotary Club leaders discussed me again or consulted with my host family to get their opinion about sending me back to the US, I didn't hear about it. The rest of my time with my first host family was actually quite pleasant.

* * *

The President of the South African Baseball Union, Arthur Berezowski, was a member of the Rotary Club that sponsored me. He introduced me to a team in the area, which would become a wonderful distraction and special focus while I stayed with four different families for the next year and attended Rondebosch Boys' High School. Even though I had finished high school in the US and it was just a token year, I made a real effort to give myself to academics and tried to make things work.

* * *

But then ...

... a truly wonderful and special thing happened.

To most people reading this, it probably won't seem like much, but it illustrates God's patience, determination, timing, and proactive, intentional love so well. Simply put, *He had found me—lost at the bottom of the world—*and the journey to understanding what He had done, or why He had done it, was only just beginning, starting with the help of a young child.

The very next weekend, Noel contacted my host family and told them he wanted to take me to his home in Pinelands, and also, to church. When I got to Noel's house, I met his charming wife, Jenny, and their two very young daughters, Karen, and Susan (Sukie), aged four and five years old.

While we were driving to church, with me in the back seat, Sukie climbed onto my lap, cuddled me a little, put her hands gently on both sides of my face, looked me straight in the eye—and asked very sincerely and lovingly:

"Uncle Davie, you don't know Jesus?"

My heart was bursting with a mix of fear, regret, and total joy; *her words cut me, overwhelmed me, and healed me all at the same time.*

I managed to choke out, "No, I don't. Will you tell me please?"

"Sure!"

She talked about Him like He was right there in the car and with her every day when she played with her dolls or when she was with the family dog or with her friends. Jesus tucked her in at night and laughed at her silliness when she danced around the room with her toys—and with Him. Her sister, Karen, giggled throughout the telling.

I couldn't get my head around this; my heart was breaking with pain and joy. It was pure, beautiful, heavenly agony to listen to her innocence *and* certainty.

What Noel had shared with me at the camp was amazing enough, but up to that point in my life, I had never met anyone of any age who knew, talked with, and lived with Jesus as if He was someone real in the here and now.

My heart and head were asking (in simple kid's language), *You mean you can actually know Him; you can actually talk with Him?! He is that real that He's part of your daily conversation and life?!*

For me, before the camp, Jesus was not even historical, much less real, and personal; the stories about Him were only fables, and the Bible was not a real book you could rely on, which is weirdly ironic considering I had never read one word or discussed any of it with anyone—*no one!*

> But listening to Sukie, I suddenly realized that I had no idea what spiritual thirst, while wandering and dying in the desert was like—until that moment.

This was so completely new to me; *you have no idea how much this was rocking my world!* Nobody had ever spoken to me like this before, and the first person other than Noel, and to some extent, the Baptist minister who led our team tent, was *a five-year-old!*

And Jesus is just her friend ... and He's just there ... all the time ... and He's just great and nice and kind, and He's really funny, too.

"You really gotta know Him more, Uncle Davie! Uncle Davie, you gotta know Him more! Really, really you do!"

I had no words.

* * *

We arrived at the beautiful thatch roofed Pinelands Methodist Church. This was my first time in any church. I was nervous about protocol and procedures … stand, sit, kneel? I didn't know the first hymn and was very sure I wouldn't know any others. I certainly didn't want to stick out like a newly converted sore thumb.

The pastor took up his place behind the pulpit and began to preach.

I don't remember now what exactly he preached about. All I know is that the sermon was for no one else there that morning. *It was prepared and written and shared only for me.* As far as I was concerned, there was no one else even in the room. Everything he said was perfect. It was like he was reading my heart and telling my story out loud—including my secrets, wishes, hopes, and dreams. It ignited in me a love and a desire to know more; an immediate hunger that I sensed could never be fully satisfied.

I wanted it all!

I was truly, truly lost … but now I was well and truly found. Once I was blind, but now I could see … well, a little bit. Show me more!

Those amazing truths from that day bring grateful tears even now as I write 50+ years later.

* * *

Noel continued to follow up with me as best he could. He was a very busy and successful lawyer, as well as being a founder of, and volunteer with *LifeLine* (a crisis counseling service)—and a leader in his local church. So, it was a bit difficult for him to make time for me.

Baseball began to dominate.

I was back at school.

Life happened.

I didn't know any Christians other than Noel and his family. I felt adrift, but strangely calm, on an uncertain, friendly, and periodically turbulent sea with one foot on the beach and the other in a leaky boat. There was restlessness and expectancy that more was yet to come, but I didn't have a clue what that would be or look like. Soon, I would be moving to my second host family, the Steigers, which brought with it a truly wonderful series of events.

CHAPTER SIX

Early Wake-Up Call

A MONTH OR SO AFTER THE PREVIOUS CHAPTER, in early November 1970, as you know, I was a brand spanking new, out of the box Christian. I had no language to describe what had happened to me in the previous month and didn't even possess a Bible or attended a church to help me explain it.

Somewhere inside me, near my brain, was saying, **"So what?"**

Another part deep inside my heart was asking with nervous anticipation, **"Now what?!"**

Push came to shove; I could only describe what happened to me in calendar time—at a specific time and place but not what happened inside me in *eternal time*. As I mentioned before, the best I had been able to come up with was to say, in a completely unaware way, "I feel like

I've been born all over again." I didn't know that similar words existed in the Bible (John 3). Noel hadn't shared that portion of the Gospel with me.

Some people over the years have told me that I was lucky that I didn't need to unlearn, undo, or unravel a bunch of religious, doctrinal, or denominational knots that have been part of many people's tangled, unhappy, or unproductive Christian upbringing.

In short, I was clueless, and looking back, I guess I am glad I was spiritually dumb. Although I had screamed at Noel on the night he shared about Jesus with me, it was, in essence, the best news I had never heard of before.

Apart from beginning to be slightly curious about what it all might mean in terms of life, behavior changes, thinking, my future, education, girls, etc.—and how this change was beginning to affect my time as an exchange student at Rondebosch Boys' High School—all I was focused on was playing baseball and adjusting to living with my second host family, the Steigers.

They were Dutch (not Afrikaans), old, strict, and loved to party! My host father, *Oom* (Uncle) Steph, was an old, groovy, hip character who reminded me of George Burns, cigar and all, and seemed to gracefully tolerate his marital "chains" at home. He was an excellent storyteller. But so strict was my host mom, *Tante* (Aunt) Dien, about things like sugar, that I actually used to sneak into the kitchen at night after everyone was in bed and take a long swig of Coke (straight from the bottle) to help me feel "un-deprived."

* * *

Thanksgiving and Christmas away from home for the first time EVER were fast approaching, and I was becoming desperately homesick, increasingly irritable, and slightly dependent on Coke. (I guess it could have been worse!). I had no friends really, except the

31

baseball team (who were mostly all married men with families), and my social life was nonexistent. I missed my girlfriend back in the US and had not been on anything remotely like a date in the three months that I had been in Cape Town. I had a small silver ring from her that I wore on my pinky finger (which was also my token protest against school authorities who banned such things), but my Class of '70 high school ring had been stolen in transit when I tried to send it to her two months before—at least I knew it had never reached her.

On the morning of November 15, 1970, I was in history class at Rondebosch Boys' High School and was given a copy of the *Cape Times*. On the front page was a headline about the Marshall University (West Virginia) football team plane crash the day before. I was stunned. My brother John was no longer on the football team but was still living in the team dormitory and had told me in a letter three weeks before that he was planning to fly with the team on that flight so he could visit his girlfriend. I assumed he was on the plane. I crumbled and collapsed.

The teacher took me to the office to get permission to drive me to my host family so I could call home. I rushed into the house to call but when I entered, I saw a letter on the table from my parents—written a couple of weeks before—which informed me that John had changed his mind about flying and his seat on the team plane was given to someone else. He was alive. But I knew from the newspaper story that every friend and teammate of his at college was killed.

Letters, but especially cassette tapes, sometimes took 4–5 weeks to reach the US, to be replied to, and to get back to me. International telephone calls were expensive, were made with a 7–8 hours of time zone difference and had to be booked 24 hours in advance with no guarantee anyone would be home or that the connection would be sound and clear. It wasn't like I could send a text to let them know I would be calling at 6:00 p.m. tomorrow. This was 1970. I wanted to try to hug and comfort John but I couldn't. I felt cut off and adrift.

* * *

The league schedule had us Varsity Old Boys (VOB) playing against Van der Stel in Stellenbosch on the upcoming Saturday. We were in first place, and I was scheduled to pitch. A guy named Johan "Killer" Nel was to be the opposing pitcher (nice guy I later found out, and we became good friends).

It was beginning to get extremely hot, and the Stellenbosch Valley was particularly so (that afternoon was about 105°F/40.5°C). I changed into my uniform, put my wallet, watch, and girlfriend's pinky ring into a locker, and went out to pitch what turned out to be the worst game of my young career.

We lost 12–2. I gave up 12 hits, five walks and only struck out two; plus, VOB made six errors, and I personally struck out four times (which didn't really surprise anyone ... just making a painful point).

The team was invited to stay for a *braai* (barbecue) afterward at the Van der Stel Sports Club, something I was loath to do because it would give the other team a chance to gloat. I didn't take losing very well—*at all!* I really hated gloating (except when I did it).

When the game was over, I went back to the locker room and discovered my ring, watch, and wallet had been stolen, which only added to my feeling of loss and growing frustration. Plus, I had always had a problem with the heat and keeping hydrated and had not drunk enough water during the hot game. My head and body were showing signs of real fluid neglect.

My mood began to lighten a bit as we stood and joked around the braai fire and as the 5–6 ice-cold Castle Lager beers that were shoved into my hand began to ease the sense of loss and cool my irritated demeanor.

As a newborn, clueless Christian, I had not developed any sense of, or formulated an opinion about, the rightness or wrongness of drinking or drunkenness.

As I alluded to before, I had never told anyone about my conversion experience or tried to describe myself in Christian terms; I had absolutely no spiritual, ethical, or moral frame of reference or compass for such things. It had never entered my head or heart that you could or should talk about your beliefs, much less have a special vocabulary for doing so. I certainly hadn't shared what happened to me in the mountains near Piketberg with anyone as though I was witnessing or something.

Not even close. And that evening, beer in hand, certainly wasn't the time!

Not long before food was going to be served, someone handed me a bottle of cold, white wine. Stellenbosch was, and is, world famous for its wine, and having never had even a sip of wine before in my life, I had no idea what to expect, much less know that mixing beer and wine was never a good idea ... especially when dehydrated and especially on an empty stomach. It tasted like soda pop—so, chug away!

During the evening, I never ate a mouthful of food, but apparently, I was very funny. At some point, back inside the sports hall, while I was telling a joke, bottle in hand, I fell directly and completely full-stretch backward, bounced off a rolled-up wrestling mat (fortunately), and hit my head on the wall and then on the floor. I was taken outside the building unconscious ... and was left out there on the grass.

Now, here is where an important new-Christian life lesson was beginning to take shape.

No, not how puking your guts out is a spiritual metaphor about being freed from the bad stuff in our lives! And no, not about how lying passed out in dewy grass on the front lawn of a sports club somehow symbolizes the refreshing touch of the Holy Spirit.

As I moaned myself awake with a never before experienced horrible feeling of being turned inside out, a group of young boys, aspiring baseball Little Leaguers, were standing directly over me, staring.

I have no idea how long I had been lying there or how long they had been standing over me.

As I opened my blurry eyes, one of the boys said emphatically, **"You see, it IS Dave Lutes! I told you it was Dave Lutes!"** Then they ran away, presumably to tell others about their discovery.

As I lay there, I asked myself, "Are you Dave Lutes? Is this really you?"

Whoever he was, he was in truly terrible physical shape as my inability to walk or talk proved. Our first baseman, Anty C., and his wife, Pam, diplomatically and sensitively called my host family and explained that "things were going on a little longer and later than expected" and that they would take me to stay at their place that night and bring me back home sometime the next morning. I guessed my host mother didn't believe their story and really suspected the worst about my condition—but still, she agreed.

* * *

Sick as a dog, tired, and with a mouth like sawdust, I had no ability to focus, much less eat the lovely breakfast set before me the next morning. I was not even sure what to feel emotionally, mentally, or spiritually.

Sick, empty, awkward, pathetic, embarrassed, stupid, and loser all came to mind.

35

Anty and Pam took me home, and I was in pain the whole day and longed for some ultra-strong aspirin, a cold ice pack for my head or someone to shoot me and put me out of my misery.

And also, for an answer as to how and why I could be so stupid.

I'm told that post-booze-binge regret is quite normal—especially for beginners like me. You always remember your first time. But then, most people don't have the words of a young Little Leaguer echoing in the ears of their heart:

"You see, I told you it's Dave Lutes!"

Influence, impact, image, trust, followers, integrity, impressions, good example, and being a witness were words and phrases that I wish had shaped my Christian thinking back then. But they didn't. I truly thank God for using that moment, that night, that damp lawn, and those boys to remind me many, many times in the years to come *how people don't read the Bible—they read us.*

Early wake-up call? Oh yes!

* * *

Footnote

About one-and-a-half years later, after I had returned to Cape Town, this lesson again came home to me very powerfully. I was, by then, assuming some level of Christian sportsman celebrity status and was sharing my faith and the Gospel widely in the Western Cape. One day, while going down an escalator in a department store in Cape Town, a teenage guy who was standing in front of me kept looking back over his shoulder. When I reached the bottom, he seemed to pluck up courage and turned around and faced me squarely—not a little embarrassed.

"You're Dave Lutes, aren't you?! You're the Christian baseball player!

"Whoa! Heavy! Far out!"

I acknowledged him with a smile, but before I could say anything, he hurried off … to tell others about his discovery meeting? I kinda hoped.

Enough said.

Anty and Pam C. became dear, special friends in the years following. I owe so much to them and their love and hospitality and steadiness in my early Christian life. They later became extremely dedicated and active Christians and leaders in their local church. But I'm quite sure it wasn't the message that the young boys who found me on the sports club lawn shared with them that helped them find the Lord.

CHAPTER SEVEN

Second Wake-up Call –
Blessed Bucket of Cold Water

THAT MIDSUMMER, and at the end of my time with the Steigers, I went with them on their annual caravan camping break at a place near the tip of the Cape Peninsula called Miller's Point, not far from Cape Point. While I was there, I met a girl—K.

Now, I need to be honest. She was a ridiculously, incredibly, cute blond; I was girlfriendless, my hormones were raging, and I'd done nothing about it for many months (such is the sad commentary on my teenage life). In fact, I had had no personal dating-type contact with girls—*any girl*—whatsoever, since arriving in South Africa.

During the final evening for me at the campsite with my host family, K and I went for a walk. We held hands. We finished our walk and then kissed goodnight. The very next morning, I was due to go by train on a trip to Rhodesia (now Zimbabwe) as part of the exchange student program.

Before I left the campsite, K pulled me aside very seriously and told me about Jesus. She explained to me that she kissed me because she liked me (and liked the kiss) but that I also needed to know that she loved Jesus first and foremost. He was the Lord of her life. He would always come first, and I needed to understand that.

It was a blessed bucket of cold water that I really didn't expect to get doused with.

I had never heard language like this before. *First a four-year-old, now a cute teenage girl?* It was a whole new world, and it was the same message from both of them! We said goodbye, I did the trip to Rhodesia, and when I got back, K and I connected up again.

* * *

By that time, I had moved to my third host family. I got permission from them to visit K and her family in Paarl, Cape, on a Saturday evening after the baseball game—a 75-mile round trip train ride. I met her parents, her older brother, and her two sisters. They were Dutch.

Both sisters were Christians. The brother, mother, and father were not. Family life was a blend of quasi support and quite vocally cynical and critical opposition to Christian things. They were an extremely musical family—*everybody!* This united them as a family in a unique way that I think in some ways helped them avoid conflict on Christian subjects.

I learned very quickly that not everyone welcomed Jesus into their lives and homes; more interestingly, that where believers and nonbelievers lived under the same roof, attended the same school, or participated in common events, there was safe and not-so-safe Christian vocabulary and right and wrong times and places to discuss it.

K and her sisters spoke in a way that was, to my ears, a somewhat jargony Christian language. I'd never heard anything even close to it before. I gathered it was almost like a Christian teen dialect. They talked about being "born again" (I knew something about that … I thought!), about proactive believing, about being led by God, about hearing His voice, about seeing things revealed in His Word, about speaking up for Him and about being His disciple.

Huh? What?!

They talked about Jesus as if He were real and relevant and powerful and **THE** most important person factoring in anyone's life. There was nothing stuffy or boring about it. They spoke of Him as *The King*—not *a* king, but **THE** King and **THEIR** personal King.

This blew my mind!

I'm thinking, not only do I now have a smart, musical, beautiful girlfriend, but she is also teaching me and helping me to discover some basic truths and lay some foundation stones for being a Christian.

I got my first Bible from K.

I had never even held one in my hands before, much less read one. I was almost scared to touch it!

K began teaching me how to love the Bible and how to pray. Up until that time, I had only said a prayer when I didn't want to get in trouble with my folks if they caught me drunk or if I got the car home too late. We prayed together at her home, and also, we held hands during prayer at her Methodist church—which tickled and struck her fellow classmates who were also there as a bit fanatical—but cute.

We went to the youth group whenever I was able to be there, and I began to feel like I was the most blessed and luckiest guy on the planet. I had a beautiful girlfriend who loved God, and she could describe it in ways that I had never heard before. I wanted her, and I wanted what she had.

Thank God our relationship wasn't sexual. It could easily have gone that way, but I really, truly do thank God that that wasn't the path we went down at all. Instead, we headed down a road toward stronger and deeper commitment to Christ—and toward adult believer's baptism. The road had some interesting twists, temptations, turns, and bumps along the way, but it was a ride I will always remember.

* * *

When I was nearing the end of my time as an exchange student in South Africa, and therefore, my return to my small village in the US, our desire to be baptized as adult believers by full immersion (*Afrikaans – gedooped, "dunked under"*) increased considerably.

I didn't know there was a debate about such things: christening, dedication, sprinkling, pouring, and immersion in, with, and by water by a minister or other church leader. I had no idea that the church had been arguing passionately for centuries about how much water, whether the water should be poured or sprinkled on your head, whether your entire body should be immersed below the water completely, or whether a water cross should be applied to your forehead.

More than that, I was gob-smacked to discover that doctrinal debate really heated up over the words used during the ceremony. What happens when you do whatever you or your parents have decided to do? Are you ready for it, and does it matter if you are? And whether or not one form of church initiation (because of the false hope it might give) actually helped send people to hell or prevented it.

When you get baptized, are you born again? Have you become a member of the church? Are you just publicly confessing your faith in some way, getting your sins washed away, receiving the Holy Spirit, guaranteeing your place in Heaven, or just experiencing varying degrees

41

of wet? Can you even call making a cross with water on a baby's forehead baptism?! I mean, after all (so I learned), the word *baptize* in the original language meant "to immerse." But for me, that theo-intellectual debate really only came later.

As neither I nor my parents, in my memory, had ever darkened the door of any church in our village, I never knew that I had been "done" as a baby in the Presbyterian Church. By the time I left home at age 18, because of falling attendance in both congregations, the Presbyterian Church had joined organizational hands with the Baptist Church, and even their building and names were merged into one—the Trumansburg *First* Presbyterian-Baptist Church, or something like that, though it was not *the first*; it was the only one … anywhere, ever, as far as I know.

As I mentioned above, and as I understood it, the debate was as much about what happens spiritually to or within the person (baby or otherwise) as it was about the word formula used and the meaning those words communicated to others. It's not worth getting into here—whether something transformational happens or not. The only thing that was important at the time was that when I spoke with the Full Gospel minister, Ellis A., about being baptized as an adult, he suggested it might be a good testimony for me to do so back in my hometown—and to do so as publicly as possible.

I also discussed it with a local Methodist minister. He was the local lay pastor who was also part of the Methodist preaching circuit team in Paarl, Cape, and he thought that adult believer's baptism was a bad idea. I think he was pretty much required to think like that because it meant that he would have to get permission from someone higher up to do something for somebody in his congregation that his own denomination taught against.

Not that they were only pro-infant baptism (apparently), but they advocated very strongly that to be *"done again,"* as they put it (i.e., baptized or christened as a baby *and then* baptized by full immersion as an adult) was a huge theological contradiction, not to mention a denominational dog dump—probably with stinky implications for the minister who performed the ceremony.

This is all retrospective commentary that makes it seem like I had figured it all out. I hadn't … not by a long shot!

All K and I knew was that we were convinced that it would be important, and more biblically correct, for us to demonstrate our belief in and commitment to Christ that way. We had each hung a sign around our heart-neck that declared *We Are Under New Management*—our new lives were to be lived for Him and not for ourselves.

We believed the best way for us to demonstrate this new life would be in a church before other people as a public witness and testimony that the old person (the old messed up me) had died and was buried and that we could not live this new life that Jesus had given us alone or in our own power and ability.

We believed it was important and right to declare that we needed to be raised again into a new life by the power of the Holy Spirit. The old guy was dead and buried; the new guy was alive and ready to live for Him (whatever that meant—I still really didn't know exactly).

Reading what I just wrote makes me think I was using a Baptist Church baptism pamphlet as a reference guide.

So now, let me be totally honest here.

What I have written above was not even close to what I was able to articulate to ministers, friends, or family back then. It sounds like I really had my thoughts and feelings all neatly bundled up into a nice, tidy theological package. *No way! Not even close!* I didn't really know or understand any of the theology behind it all.

My/our decision was based solely on this:

1. Death and burial and rising up alive were strong images.

2. It seemed obvious in the New Testament that that was the way it was done.

3. No matter what happened internally or externally when you were baptized, we knew we needed all the help we could get … whatever that might mean in real life.

4. It was as good a place as any to start.

As I said, I didn't really know what the debate was all about. I only knew that my life had begun to change, and that God was working in me. I only knew that I wanted to declare this new life publicly and that I wanted my family, I wanted my friends, I wanted the whole world, anyone who would care to look and listen, to know *that the old Dave Lutes was "dead" and that he was now a new person.*

Or at least, he was making a new start and that the new Dave Lutes had been offered a new chance, a new life because of Jesus and that I had taken up His offer with both hands and with all my heart. It was my way of saying that I was alive for the first time in my life—spiritually or otherwise—in a way that I had never known before.

So, when the Full Gospel minister suggested I should be baptized back in my hometown, I agreed.

CHAPTER EIGHT

Back Home – Bring the Music or Face It?

WHEN I ARRIVED BACK HOME IN MID-JUNE 1971, one of the first things I did was contact the Methodist minister in the village, still not really knowing what all the rebaptizing debate and fuss was about. I didn't know him at all but still I put the baptism idea to him. To say the least, he was not keen to do it! Because, again, to do so was going to be a contradiction for the church body, the wider denomination authorities, and other local church leaders.

More religious poop?

When he told me he wouldn't do it in Trumansburg yet invited me to preach three sermons on an upcoming Sunday, at the age of 19 nonetheless, I felt that that was a fair compromise. That said, I didn't really know what I was doing, or planning on doing, on either front— baptism or preaching.

I have no recollection of what I preached about—to a bunch of campers at the park, then a small church in the village of Jacksonville and then in the main village church—but it was a public faith statement of some kind. My parents stayed at home, I believe, wondering how they were going to field questions about what the hell was going on with Dave from at least half of the 1,250 people who lived in our village.

When I expressed in a letter to K back in South Africa that IF I returned to play baseball at the end of August (as I hoped)—after I said goodbye to my previous life and returned to live my own, new, adult life far away from my family—we would then be baptized … together.

She said she would wait. But then...

* * *

Healing Conflict at Home

I wanted desperately, deep inside my heart, for my parents to accept what had happened to me both spiritually and in terms of the radical new direction my life was taking. I wanted them, **needed them,** to "get" me, support me, and understand that all this was a huge thing in my life. It WAS my new life now! I had very little, if any, Christian language at that time to explain what was going on in my heart and head, but I wanted them so much to also try to understand.

The sum total of my knowledge was, *"Once I was blind, but now I can see … and this is how it happened to me when I wasn't looking for it or asking about it. In fact, I knew literally nothing about Christian things and quite honestly didn't care."* This is what I told a couple of friends that summer. Frankly, I was in radically new, scary territory in so many ways; I was making it up as I went along, hoping God would get involved if that's the sort of thing He did. I really wasn't sure.

About three weeks after my return to the US, before I preached, my parents and I tried to talk about the possibility of me going back to South Africa. The baseball team had by now more formally suggested (to my parents as well) that I return to play, coach, and promote baseball in the province—bring equipment, baseballs, and other items—and that my dad could find a new player from our area each year and send them to play with me there.

We ended up having a massive blowup about it. It was vocal and volatile, not least because of who I was by nature (something of a hothead), but also because at that point I had not realized fully that my dad was a hard-core, but nonvocal atheist.

I'll never forget that conversation. I was lying on the couch not looking directly at my folks sitting in their easy chairs (for fear they would give me the very entitled and valid *We're-your-parents-and-know-what's-best-for-you* look). They were both extremely smart, hardworking, dedicated teachers whom I loved and respected more than any two people in the world. I knew without any doubt they loved me and wanted only the best for me, but their life's reference points didn't include an adventure like the one I had begun in South Africa—God involved or otherwise. I seldom, if ever, asked them for advice, such was my self-willed determination to make my own path, even when I was younger.

But I really needed them to hear my heart at that time.

At one point my dad said, "We just don't want you to do this [go back] because you resent us."

Deeply and instantaneously hurt to my soul's core, I exploded off the couch and stood bolt upright in front of my dad; a torrent of tears poured down my face, and a heart-wrenching wail erupted from my heart of hearts. *"I don't resent you! I love you! I love you!"*

I stormed out and went upstairs to my bedroom. I was in absolute shock and turmoil. Part of me believed that returning to Cape Town was the right thing to do, but what did I really know about being guided or led or hearing God's voice?

Another part of me was discovering and better appreciating the tremendous sacrifices my parents had made to get me (and us as a family) to this point in life. By this time, I had said "no" to the Detroit Tigers spring training invitation and an even bigger "no" to a full baseball scholarship at Ohio University. The latter was my parents' dream, especially as there was no way they could afford to put me and my brother through college almost at the same time. My brother John already DID have a scholarship.

Added to this was my complete and utter failure as a son when I had gotten my girlfriend pregnant, resulting in her having an abortion. They had bailed me out, somehow with heads still held high.

It began to actually dawn on me that, along with my desire to leave home, what I was doing amounted to me metaphorically giving my incredible parents an off-the-charts, ungrateful, unappreciative, self-centered, middle finger.

In less than five minutes, I said my first-ever, truly sincere, "*I think I really screwed things up, Lord*" prayer and went back downstairs and straight to my parents who were talking in the kitchen. I hugged them both with heartfelt passion and, still weeping, said that I was sorry I hurt them and asked them to forgive me. Not even knowing what the phrase meant at that stage, they were both completely gob-smacked—utterly stunned.

Full of emotion, my dad said, "I know a boy who less than a year ago would never have come and said he was sorry. Something has happened to this boy."

From that time forward, we worked together to plan for my return to Cape Town and to find another player from the area to also join me there. But unbeknown to us, the military draft for the Vietnam War was just around the corner, waiting to lead me into more turmoil and make me wonder what the Lord was doing. My number came up in the July 1971 military draft lottery, but because of a legally blind eye (baseball injury), I was given a deferment that allowed me to leave the country. It was perfect timing and an interesting turn of events. (See Chapter 34, "You Didn't Go to Vietnam.")

* * *

A Dad and God Moment

While I was home for that short while in the summer, I worked with a local housebuilder—a friend of my dad. It was physical, dirty labor, but it helped put some money in my pocket. But the language all day was just-off-the-ship very salty, sailor, colorful, "blue." I was never a prolific swear-er, so this environment was truly shocking and upsetting to me for some reason. I had never sworn in front my parents—not even a simple, tame four-letter word. One morning, for some reason I decided to let my sense of feeling dirty or contaminated erupt in a conversation with my dad. All the really bad words poured out—many! I was very judgmental and self-righteous in my comments—and angry. My dad let me spew and then said something that has always stuck with me to this day—my non-religious, atheist dad.

> *"Dave, Jesus was the most tolerant man on earth and in history, and He mixed with everyone. Maybe you can find some of what He had?"*

Talk about gob-smacked!

CHAPTER NINE

I Insist That You Come to Dinner!

Early Introduction to the Holy Spirit and the Jesus Revolution

WHEN I GOT BACK TO SOUTH AFRICA, baseball was first, and revisiting the issue of baptism was a very close second. It was only about two weeks into my return to Cape Town when I went to spend time on the weekend with K's family in Paarl and when we had planned with a friend of Pastor Ellis A. to go surreptitiously to the Full Gospel Church in the suburb called Monte Vista, north of Cape Town, to get baptized.

It was to be a semisecret evening service, only in the sense that nobody, other than us and a small group from the church, would be present. The minister was happy to do this because he believed it was the right thing for him to do as a Full Gospel pastor.

So, on a Saturday night in early September 1971, K, one sister, and I all went to the Full Gospel Church. The first thing we had to do was to stand up publicly and give our testimonies. It was the first time I had ever told my story to a group. I hadn't even done so when I preached back home. It was the first time that I had ever connected the dots between the old Dave Lutes who knew nothing about Christian things, about the Bible, about what I believed or what I could believe, or about what was real and was not real.

K and her sisters helped me to find language for what had happened to me and for the decision I had made, but I had never talked about it to anyone publicly. When I had tried to tell my family in the summer before I returned to South Africa, all I could say, again, like in my conversation with my first exchange student host mom was that I felt like I'd "been born all over again" and to describe how it happened. Just the facts.

K and her sisters helped me connect that particular dot to a verse in John 3 where Jesus tells Nicodemus, "You must be born again." Suddenly, the whole thing was becoming alive and real for me. Not that I understood all the theology but that I actually had good historical, biblical, and spiritual reasons to publicly confess my faith by being baptized.

Standing up in front of a crowd was a fairly natural thing for me to do, as I enjoyed doing that anyway, and I was excited to tell my story. That said, I hadn't planned it; all I did was pray beforehand. But I was concerned, even in those days, about whether I was praying the right words; praying "correctly." Besides, this was a whole new ball game. This was crossing into new territory that had eternal implications.

51

This was more real than anything I had ever said or done in my life.

I can't stress this enough. I'm emotional as I write about this 50+ years later. *This was the beginning of something eternal*; this was momentous, utterly real, and deeply heart-and-soul revolutionary. Please think about this as you read my words: *I knew nothing … nothing.* I had no experience of church or Christianity. I didn't even know I was seeking God or needed God or that it was even possible to know Him.

And in His profound Mercy and amazing timing, He sent me to a camp in the mountains in South Africa and spoke to me … whispered my name … wooed and nudged me toward His love. He found me wandering and lost and brought me Home more than 8,000 miles from my hometown and rescued me from my sin and myself.

I prayed a prayer something like this as I knelt on the floor alone before the actual baptism:

"Lord, I just want to do my best for You tonight. I just want to do this right, and I just want it to be a blessing to people. And I just want You, God, to know that I'm grateful that you have changed my life and got your hands on me and turned me around and faced me in another direction and broke this selfish obsession to be the all-American boy, to achieve greatness. Just to be Dave Lutes who's a nobody, really, from a small village, who has now found the most amazing treasure that anyone could possibly find."

I guess that was *just* about what I was trying to say in my prayer. In terms of my prayer life and language, I can see I was going through my *"just" phase*. My *"Ya know, man, like, ya know"* phase came later.

I stood up publicly in front of probably 20–25 people who had been invited specially to come to the Saturday night service. I told my story, and I remember the thrill it gave me to see people's faces light up with understanding that *they knew exactly what I was talking about. That was so cool!*

They could say the same thing in their own way, in their own words, with their own life story, yet I was now connected to them. I was part of them. I was joining this family of local and worldwide believers, *and I didn't really even know we were called "believers!"* I knew that I was crossing a line into something dramatic and powerful and utterly transformational in my own life, and I was heading in the direction that I wanted my life to go—that God wanted my life to go in. And these people celebrated with me!

K testified, her sister testified, and then it was time to be baptized. The leaders sent us to the back of the church to separate rooms, and I changed out of my street clothes and put on the white clothes that they had supplied. It was a cold Southern Hemisphere September 1971, not quite the beginning of Spring.

I only found out later that the white shirt and white pants I had changed into were intentional and symbolic of the fact that my old life was gone; I was being washed clean—as white as snow—and I would symbolically come out the other side (of the baptism tank) a new creation.

More words, symbols, and dots were being connected.

I went down into the water with the pastor, and there he explained to me that I should close my mouth, hold my nose, and he would place his hand over mine. He would hold me upright and then allow me to fall backward—still holding my nose—completely immersed under the water and then help me stand up again. I had never seen a baptism of any kind before. *The water was freezing!* But I couldn't tell if I was trembling from excitement or the cold water. The pastor spoke:

"David, do you confess Jesus Christ as **your** Lord? Do you confess that **you** believe in Him, that He died for **your** sins and rose again from the dead according to the Scriptures to give **you** new and eternal life? Do you declare that you will faithfully live the new life He has freely given to **you**—for Him?"

"Yes, yes, and yes!"

He continued, "Therefore, on your confession of faith in the Lord Jesus Christ, I now baptize you in the name of the Father, Son, and Holy Ghost."

And he did.

When I came up out of the water, cold but smiling, someone handed me a towel, and people were shouting, "Amen! Hallelujah! Praise the Lord!"

Hearing this was weird and wonderful at the same time!

Good grief! Who the hell shouts like that, and in a church, for goodness' sake?!

I had never been in an environment like this before. It felt like a family loudly cheering at someone's birthday party. It felt like I had just awakened from a long sleep, walked down the street, turned a corner, and discovered a whole new world with people celebrating life—*my life!*

This was it! This was now truly the beginning of my new life!

* * *

When I returned to the back room behind the baptismal area, the magnitude of what I had just done more powerfully dawned on me; my life had now changed dramatically—*forever.*

This is it! This was my whole reason for existence! I had a new purpose for living!

My whole life had dramatically changed direction, that much I knew. My life had a new meaning and a new purpose. I felt a call, a deep inner prompting, to spend my life helping others discover this new, amazing thing that I had found. Actually, it dawned on me that God had found me—I didn't find Him. Slightly weirder, I felt I wanted to go into the ministry (whatever that meant).

A sense of calling to be and to do something with my life for Him was there.

I knelt down and prayed something like this:

"God, I'm yours. I belong to you. I give my life to you, and I want to find out what it means to live for you and to serve you forever."

As I prayed, I started to shake, to tremble. I wouldn't say it was electricity-like because it wasn't that powerful. I thought it was because I was cold, which I was. Then, while the trembling continued, a warmth came over me and began to flow in and through me—and I began to jabber.

It's the only way I can describe it—gibberish gobbledygook.

Words began to come out of my mouth, and I had no idea what they meant. It sounded like I was speaking nonsense, but I continued praying and speaking in this strange way that had me completely confused and surprised.

But, oh wow, it felt so good inside! But how can something I can't explain or understand feel so good and seem so natural?!

The more I let it flow and didn't hold back, the more I loved and wanted God. *Is this what heavenly praise is?* It was amazing and powerful and warm and releasing and full of joy and peace—and a bit scary, all at the same time.

* * *

I suddenly remembered an article I had seen when I was traveling back to the United States from South Africa at the end of my year as an exchange student. While on layover in Zurich Airport, I was sitting at the gate, waiting, and I picked up an English copy of *Time Magazine*. The front cover displayed the feature story. It was about the Jesus Revolution. There was a contemporary, kinda cool, and artsy picture of Jesus on the front cover, and there were stories inside about things that were happening among the hippies in California and in the Jesus Revolution in different parts of the world.

It described times of prayer that these people had when they spoke in tongues.

That was the phrase that was used: *speaking in tongues.* They described it as a gift of a language given to believers that they didn't understand but that was great for praying and worshipping and was a sign that they had received the power of the Holy Spirit in some special way.

Now, in the back room at the church, while kneeling on the floor, I remembered that article and wondered if that was what was happening to me. Maybe it was; maybe it wasn't. I had no way of confirming or denying. If it was specifically a hippie thing, then I doubted it was the same as what I was experiencing, ***as I was so* not** *a hippie that it was funny.*

> *All I knew was that something remarkable—albeit very strange*
> *—was happening to me.*

I told K about it that evening, and we prayed again together to thank God for the time we had spent testifying and being baptized and then went to bed. I was sleeping in the camper at the back of the house, and we weren't interested in any kind of romantic time at all. That wasn't part of our experience or relationship.

* * *

The next morning, we went to the local Methodist Church, and as was customary in that part of the world, there were part-time, lay preachers who rotated among the different communities. One Sunday they would preach at one Methodist Church and the next Sunday at another and so on and so on.

On this particular occasion, there was a preacher (Haughton B.) who was very passionate. I'd heard him preach there before. He had fire-red hair, a red mustache, and was very loud and very expressive with fiery eyes. Did I say fiery? To use the word *dramatic* to describe the way he presented the Bible would be to put it mildly, and I was very taken by him as he always seemed to inspire me to find out more, and on this occasion, to tell him more.

After the service was over, I sought him out, and I asked if I could speak with him. K was standing there with me, and I said to him, "Pastor, I need to tell you something and ask you a question. Yesterday evening, K and I were baptized in the Full Gospel Church in Monte Vista—"

As I said this, he reached out and put his hand on my shoulder to stop me.

He cautiously looked around the area and over my shoulder to see if anyone else was listening. He had a surprised look on his face because, I gather, he knew that our baptisms were by full immersion.

Hesitantly he said, "Really? OK …"

I added, "I also wanted to say that I feel a real call to the ministry."

His mood and posture changed noticeably. Patting me on the head and with a somewhat patronizing tone, he said, "That's a nice thing, son. Well done. You know, some time we must talk about that."

Dismissively, he began to walk away, as if what I told him was little more than youthful exuberance or something he'd heard many times before.

Before he escaped too far, I stopped him. "But wait, after we got baptized, I knelt and prayed and told the Lord that I really and truly wanted to live for Him and wanted to serve Him, and then I began to speak in this strange gibberish-like language and to shake and shudder. I felt warm all over. I couldn't stop … It was amazing! Do you know what happened to me?"

He turned quickly, approached, and looked very intently at me—directly into my eyes. He took my shoulders in his hands and pulled me even closer to his face. In slightly more than a whisper, nodding as well toward K, he said, "I insist that you come to dinner—both of you."

We made an appointment to go to his house the next weekend to meet with him and his wife in Somerset West. Off we headed home.

* * *

The next Saturday arrived, and we drove to Somerset West. He and his wife sat down with us, and he took out the Bible and said, "Dave, let me tell you from the Bible what happened to you; inside you."

He showed us a number of verses in the Bible that describe the same or a similar experience to what I'd had. I had never read them before, or if I had, I didn't remember them. We went through numerous accounts in the Book of Acts, stressing that the indwelling of the Holy Spirit in the believer was God's promise in the Old and New Testaments, and we connected the texts to our recent water baptisms, such as following verses:

"Repent and be baptized for the forgiveness of sins and you will receive the gift of the Holy Spirit. And you will receive power after the Holy Spirit comes upon you … to help you to be powerful witnesses for Christ and the Gospel" (Acts 1:8; 2:38–42).

He explained, "What happened to you Dave, is that the Holy Spirit came into you in a very powerful way to equip you, to empower you to be a witness and servant for the Lord. One of the signs that this has happened is the ability to speak in another language—to speak in tongues. It's a gift, a sign, and a prayer and worship language. While it is absolutely true that Jesus lives inside you by His Spirit, He promised a separate and distinct empowering—another experience."

I'm writing this down here now like it was very clear at the time.

It wasn't. At all!

Haughton B. and his wife shared so confidently, sincerely, and clearly that my heart and mind became a willing sponge. He also explained that this particular experience, or belief, was nothing new or strange today. There were many Pentecostal churches, the Charismatic Movement, and the Jesus Revolution on my doorstep in Cape Town where this was a normal Christian thing.

We took it all in, and Haughton B. and his wife explained what was going to happen next. They were going to lay their hands on us, like in the Bible. Then they were going to pray for us and with us to receive an infilling—and overflowing—of the Holy Spirit and to experience His release of power and praise with the ability to speak in tongues. They carefully and simply explained each step of the prayer process. They stressed that we were *not* asking for the Gift of Tongues; we were asking for power to be effective witnesses for Him with our words and lives.

I knelt down next to the couch, and K knelt down in front of a chair, and we all began to pray.

Haughton B. and his wife began to pray for us, and soon afterward, they began to speak in their own strange languages.

They both spoke completely different languages, but if I'm honest, they still sounded a bit "gibberishy" to my inexperienced ears. At one point, Haughton B. put his hands on my head and said simply, without any emotion, "Dave, receive the Holy Spirit." I was so happy to be in that moment! God's touch was immediate and evident inside me.

> *"Thank you, Lord, thank you, Lord, thank you, Lord! Oh wow, God, I love you so much!"*

I began to giggle.

For a moment, I thought it might be inappropriate and even disrespectful. But I couldn't stop. I simply couldn't control my laughter. It wasn't a chuckle or a snigger—it was a near hilarity laughter that came from somewhere deep within my belly, within my heart, within my soul, within my spirit. It was *real gut-level laughing!*

It exploded and gushed from within me, and I began to speak in another language. I laughed even louder, surprised by what I was hearing. I began to sing in another language and laugh in this other language.

It just would not stop! I just could not stop—nor did I want to!

I carried on and on for maybe 10 minutes. I was so full of joy with tears streaming down my face as I laughed and laughed and laughed in the presence of God. The only way I can describe it—it was as innocent and simple as a child's delightful and delicious laugh.

> *Unashamed, abandoned, unembarrassed worship, giggling, and laughing!*

While this was going on, Haughton B.'s wife placed her hands on K's head and said the same words:

"Receive the Holy Spirit."

K started to cry … and cry and cry … and then she began to speak in another language completely different from mine. She raised her hands up with tears streaming down her smiling face; she just loved the Lord!

Eventually we were able to stop, and we sat there broadly grinning at each other with tearstained faces.

Haughton B. explained to us that we could choose to speak and praise with our new languages at will—any time we wanted to—and stop anytime we chose. He explained that we may never feel the same level or type of emotion as we did that night. He also stressed that the more we used our languages, the more it would strengthen us and build us up. ("Anyone who speaks in a tongue edifies themselves …" 1 Cor. 14:4a). He stressed that the language and type of tongue might change over time.

Sure … whatever, I thought. He was proved right in time, but at that moment, we didn't really take in the full meaning and possible impact of his words. This was a totally unbelievable new world. We found out some months later that the whole baptism in the Holy Spirit and tongues thing was a big controversy. But for now, we were very, very glad that a Methodist Pentecostal minister, Haughton B., *insisted that we come to dinner*.

CHAPTER TEN

Life Upside Down
Back to the Beginning of My New Beginning

WHEN I RETURNED TO CAPE TOWN IN AUGUST OF '71, word had gotten out that the American baseball player had returned to SA, and he was now a Christian. Exactly how word got out is a mystery till this day. All I know is that Youth for Christ (YFC) contacted me, and one of the leaders of YFC in Cape Town at the time, Brian Helsby, came to see me on my lunch break with a tape recorder. We sat in his car, and he asked me to give my testimony about not only how it was that I came to hear the Gospel and give my life to Christ, but also how it affected me as a sportsman.

Truthfully speaking, I had absolutely no idea how being a Christian affected me, or others, when I played baseball. *It never entered my head to connect those two things. Baseball was baseball … did Jesus ever play it? Why would He care about it anyway?*

More than that, I didn't know then that I was going to be the cover story of their national magazine—*IN Magazine*—that was published a week or so later called (see article below).

It was interesting that, while sharing with him, it was the first time I was forced to find language to provide historical context and *current relevance* while describing to a wider audience what had happened to me. Thankfully, he coached me a bit. In a sense, the Full Gospel Church group that was at my baptism didn't fall into the same category. Regardless, I had very little vocabulary for this, only what I had shared then. I didn't have a born-again dictionary to hand. I didn't have the language of the Bible as part of my spiritual DNA, apart from knowing that I was a new creation in Christ—and was not much more than jargon to me, and only understood by a specific audience.

As a result of that article, I was then invited to speak at conferences and a lot of youth rallies on behalf of YFC, and then later, with Scripture Union, and then later, with other parachurch organizations. Almost without exception in those early days of sharing, my opening lines were, "I am from a small village in Upstate New York, which is in the top right-hand section of the US map and is about 300 or so miles northwest of New York City on your way to Niagara Falls,"—so people would begin to visualize where I was raised. I would normally say these kinds of words soon after: "We had one main street and no robots (South African speak for 'traffic lights'), not one."

"Everyone knew everyone else's business; there was nothing secret, and there was nothing that could be hidden." As I am saying these words, I see people nodding as if to say, "Yeah, I get it; I can relate to that." Then I would talk about my parents who were both teachers; how I was regarded as the all-American boy with the big future; how I was president of the Student Council, captain of clubs and teams, and played varsity (First Team) sports from my freshman year in high school (I had to explain that because that didn't make any sense for them because Varsity = College—actually short for "University" in SA). I was learning how to tell the story better and better as I was going along.

Long story short, those speeches and talks catapulted me into the public eye, and I realized that people were asking more from me than what I was able to give in terms of substance, especially in terms of biblical content and Christian life experience. "Once I was like this, didn't know anything, and now I'm like this, and still pretty much don't know anything except that I was blind spiritually and now I can see …" That was pretty much the sum total of what I shared.

Quick Note: In the article, "Man of the Match," transcribed below, you will notice that Brian left out the part of my story where described how I cried and screamed at my spiritual father, Noel. In those days, I found out that YFC really tried to play down anything emotional connected with response to the Gospel message.

* * *

"Dave's night as Province cruise in." That's how the headlines went after Western Province's baseball clash with Eastern Province. The article continued, "Pulverising hitting, and deadly blazing pitching gave WP a crushing 9–1 victory over E.P. Undisputed man of the match was New Yorker Dave Lutes who hit 2 firm doubles. Dave Lutes had 12 strikeouts with a fast ball that had Eastern batters groping."

We sent Cape Town based Brian Helsby to find out more about Dave. Here is the result:

Q. How long have you been playing baseball?

A. Fifteen years.

Q. What experience have you had?

A. Well, I started playing Little League baseball from the age of 4 years with my father's team; then I just progressed and as I got older, I went to a higher division until summer Baseball League on a local level. Then professional trial camps experience with eight or nine professional teams until I came over to this country as a Rotary Exchange Student.

Q. How do baseball standards in this country compare with the states?

A. I hope not to offend some of my friends, but I would say that the top baseball teams that I've seen in this country would quite possibly compare two first year varsity maybe or last year high school level in the states.

Q. What in your opinion are your most memorable achievements so far as baseball goes?

A. Winning the championship at home; pitching what they call an "no hitter' and being picked for the Western Province team last year.

Q. What is a 'no hitter'?

A. It means that you throw about 2½ hours of consecutive baseball, and the batters hit the ball but it doesn't go into a place where they can be in a scoring position. There is no safe hit.

Q. When did you become a Christian?

A. October 1970.

Q. Would you like to tell us a bit about it?

A. I sure would! I was at a S&V Camp. I went there a bit dubious. I didn't want to go to a camp, because I was an agnostic before I went, and I had a lot of problems I brought a lot with me from America, and I created a lot of them here because of my stubborn nature and my self-confidence. I went to the camp a bit doubtful about the outcome because I heard that the camp was religious. I went there and one of the Commandants spoke one evening in Q.T. and he told us that the problems weren't so great and that they could be solved, and I accepted Christ.

Q. What Christian work do you do?

A. Well I patronise a local Christian coffee bar. I'm still a young Christian so I just try to learn as much as I can about the Bible and grow in my faith so that I might be able to set an example in my work and on the field of play. But as it stands, I work at the coffee bar in order to be there not only for the spiritual blessings but also for the fellowship and to help the younger people who are searching for Christ that have the same problems that I had. I also conduct Bible study on Wednesday evening at a hostel where I live.

Q. Have you any advice that you'd give a young Christian?

A. Trust God. Don't be afraid to be a fool for Christ. Trust in God that he will breakdown all the barriers of doubt; personality and social conflicts. Other advice for young Christians—just read your Bible that's all. I tell you the Bible has opened a new dimension to me. I'd never read it before but as soon as I did there was the most wonderful experience—it's got an answer for everything. Keep fellowship, read the Bible, and PRAY.

Thank you, Dave Lutes.

* * *

**Then along came the Jesus (Hippie) Revolution into my life—
or I entered it. Either way ... oh my!**

* * *

*Brian O'Donnell, the leader of the Hippie Movement was the
first person I met, not realizing the impact that he and others
in the movement would have on my life. I have recounted part
of his own story in the next chapter.*

CHAPTER ELEVEN

Brian O'Donnell –
His Salvation Story and the Hippie Revival

MY FATHER BECAME A CHRISTIAN at the Billy Graham film at the Jan Van Riebeeck Festival, and from then on, my life was never the same. My father started a Mission in District Six, Salt River and Woodstock, where he preached and led people to the Lord. He took me with him on many occasions. He used to put up huge signs saying "Jesus Saves" in front of our house, which was embarrassing the family; my mother threatened to leave home, so I took down the signs at night. My brother, Miln, and I started attending the Baptist Church when we were older, as this was the only place we were allowed to go to on the weekends and the only place where we could meet girls. We attended the Youth for Christ rallies that were very active at that time.

When I finished school, I went to work and decided that I was not going to go to church again, as I felt that Christianity had restricted my life since childhood. I embraced the world and did what every red-blooded young man would get up to. I met my future wife at a bus stop on a Boxing Day night. I had spotted her at a cinema in Cape Town one night when she and her friend walked past us at interval. Sandy and her friend, Lynette, would not accept a lift in our car, so we followed the bus up to her house in Moulie Point. When she got off the bus, I told her that I also lived in Sea Point so as not to seem too uncool. Anyway, the rest is history. We went steady for a few years and then got married in St. James Anglican Church in Sea Point. We had two children, a boy called Zane and a girl called Lisa, within two years and one month.

I started building surfboards in our lounge, and then my friend, Tom Munro, and I decided to manufacture surfboards for a living (i.e., Viking Surf Boards). We later parted, and he went on to make Munro Surfboards, and I made O'Donnell Surfboards, which became one of the best surfboards around and were very popular. I then opened a surf shop, and besides surfboards, I sold clothing and leather sandals and thongs. My friend, Tony Kitchen, opened a record bar in my surf shop, which was also very popular, and it became a place for people to hang out in.

I had heard about Kensington Market in London, and I decided to open a market in Cape Town. This was the apartheid era in South Africa, but we decided that there would be no apartheid in The Market. People were allowed to mix freely and own shops. There was no segregation in our coffee bar, and the result of this was that we were regularly raided by the security police, especially in our busiest times.

The Market was based on the hippie, antiestablishment, alternative way of life—this was the sixties post-Woodstock: a time of freedom, burn the bra, birth control pills, hallucinogenic drugs, free love, "Make Love Not War," get back to the "Garden."

There had to be more to life than just working in a concrete jungle for eight hours a day and never seeing the sunlight. The established way of life was regarded as plastic [artificial], autocratic, and controlling. This was a time of optimism, a bright new world where people could express their personal style and use their talents to make a living.

The Market consisted of 21 shops and was the first boutique shopping centre in South Africa. Many creative alternative people started shops in The Market, and it became known as "The Hippie Market" because of the way the people were dressing and because the chaps had long hair.

The stalls were run by an interesting and diverse group of people, which made The Market very popular with young people, hippies, tourists, and people who were just curious. On the weekends, it was a teeming mass of people, and we required crowd control. It became the place to be if you were a visiting hippie from another city.

After the success of The Hippie Market, I decided to open up a nightclub with my friend, Tony Kitchen. We took over the Blow Up and renamed it The Factory. When my friend, Alan Flack, a "boffin" with sound and music, joined me, the club was renamed "The Headquarters."

I began to experiment with drugs and tried LSD, which made me more God conscious, and I started off on a journey to find God. I was given a book, Power of the Mind, which I believed would help me find the Truth, but I just became more and more depressed. Chrisman Stander owned a stall in The Market selling his designer jewellery; I spoke to him about the occult and Power of the Mind; he just pointed me to Jesus.

I had succeeded in everything I did but still felt an empty void inside, so I stopped going to my club. I only wanted to be on the beach with my family and watch the sunset. Nothing could fill the emptiness I felt in my life.

On Christmas night 1969, I was sitting in my bedroom, looking at the present my father had given me (a Christian book he always gave as presents), which I never read. I looked at the back of the book, and there was a note saying that if you wanted to be saved you must just accept Jesus as your Saviour and send the card to Canada.

I thought how stupid that was, but I mentally filled in the card and then felt the power of God descend upon me. I knew that Jesus was the Way! I felt clear, and all my doubts, fears, and insecurities just disappeared. I knew there was no other way for me. I had found Truth at last, and I felt a new boldness come into my life.

After my experience with Jesus in my bedroom that night, I knew that I had to tell everyone and was very aware of the implications. I was the leader of the Hippie Movement in Cape Town, a well-known surfboard builder, and a nightclub owner. I had been reported on in many newspaper articles. I wrestled with the idea, but I felt compelled to publicly declare that Jesus was the only Way.

Chrisman Stander invited me to meet a group of Christians from the "Narnia" outreach in Hillbrow. The meetings were at Alan and Trish's home. They were a Pentecostal group, and it was there that we experienced speaking in tongues and interpretation. They wanted to reach out to Cape Town, and it was decided that a "Narnia Committee" would be formed to steer the group. The committee members consisted of Ëve, Alan and Trish Crabtree, Chrisman and Drikkie Stander, Jerome, and my wife Sandra and me.

After the first night of our outreach, at about 1 a.m., I was woken from my sleep by Richard Wisdom who told me that The Market was on fire, saying that the police just watched and said, "Let it burn."

I got dressed and went to see what had happened and saw that the structure was still standing but everything was destroyed. The amazing thing was that Andrew Purcell, our insurance broker, had come to see me two days before to sign the insurance contract. We were devastated, but we knew that God would somehow turn the disaster into good. The insurance company gave us an upbeat Egyptian builder who said that he could rebuild the place in ten days, and he did just that. From that day on, miracles became our standard fare.

We had regular meetings in The Headquarters nightclub twice a week, and people were being added to our numbers daily. Some of the people who used to meet in the group at Alan Crabtree's home were Michael and Denise Coleman, Alan, Jenny, Avril, and others.

When The Market reopened, a few of the previous stall owners left since they had lost everything in the fire. Others decided to finish their studies and go back to university. Yet others had gained the confidence to open up their own businesses elsewhere, and quite a few successful businesses grew from their experience in The Market. New people moved in to take over the vacant shops. Chrisman Stander opened up a Christian bookshop plus sold his handmade jewellery. People were accepting Jesus as their Saviour on a daily basis.

We started outreaches, preaching on the streets and market squares in Cape Town. Our outreach team consisted of anyone who could give a testimony and was mad enough to go with us; as a result, many more came to accept Jesus.

We blitzed Cape Town with Christian tracts, stickers, and painted Christian slogans on walls all over the city. Wonderful, miraculous times were had. So many people were being added that we decided to rent a building at 93 Loop Street for our meetings.

Good God times! I often testify about those days and how on fire we were, and nothing could stop us talking about Jesus!

When our team went to a reformatory for girls in Durbanville, nearly all the girls went forward to accept Jesus as Saviour at the altar call. Fortunately, there were quite a number of us to pray with them in groups. **This was such a wonderful time that we began to think that this was how it normally happened.** God really blessed us in every way. It was a wonderful time just basking in the presence of the Holy Spirit.

— Brian O'Donnell, 1985

CHAPTER TWELVE

My Own Introduction to the Jesus Revolution

WHEN I WASN'T WORKING A JOB (sort of) or doing outreach, attending church meetings, speaking at YFC rallies, going to The Hippie Market on Loop Street or The Headquarters on Longmarket Street, I played baseball. After all, it seemed to be within God's "Wonderful Eternal Purpose" that He used baseball to bring me back to Cape Town to play, coach, and promote baseball with the Varsity Old Boys.

In terms of personality and style, as a young guy of 19 years, I was more at the establishment end of the spectrum and was in no way a hard-core Headquarters hippie brother—not by any means.

I was a newcomer, and in many ways a bit part, but I tried to be a pretty faithful supporter, observer, and visitor there (in my longish hair, suit, and tie after work). Then later, when I was at University of Cape Town (UCT), I arrived in the only pair of nonchurch pants I owned, well-worn brown corduroys and *veldskoen*, (in the US we called them "desert boots" in the sixties)—poor and desperate "hip" but not "hippie."

I reminded myself that I was a really new baby Christian with almost zero context or life experience to connect any dots within the new thing that had happened to me. I barely had any language to talk about it. Now, I was immersed in a realm of spiritual life and vitality and ways of describing the world and people and hopes and dreams completely differently. The hippie scene would never have attracted or interested me—as a scholar sports jock—back at home.

It was totally another planet for me.

It was actually quite intimidating, The Market. The closest thing to an open stall market I had ever been to was my Uncle Herman's farm stall where they sold *"... the best strawberries, sweet corn, butternut squash, and eggs this side of Taughannock Creek."*

If I'm honest, there were quite a few moments of skepticism and quiet criticism about the lifestyle of my Headquarters and Hippie Market brothers and sisters—not judgment, Christian or otherwise. It was just that for me at that time, it was a wild, new, and strange scene for me as a small town, very sheltered, conservative, country boy from a family of teachers in rural US of A. It was *a total culture shock!* Not to mention being introduced to Christian things, which was strangely wonderful enough in that context.

At the same time, I was incredibly envious of, for example, Mike and Denise Coleman and their quiet, determined, rock-solid, passionate faith; Johnny Weber's unbounded, let-it-all-hang-out-there-for-Jesus exuberance; and Brian O'Donnell's faith-strong, while thoroughly grounded, life certainty (while being a groovy, spiritual giant of a guy at the same time).

* * *

I remember clearly in the seventies the anointed power given by God to a handful of hippies who literally turned the city of Cape Town to Jesus! I was a leader of the (pre-Christian) Hippie Movement and also the mouthpiece of the movement when, in 1970, I became a Christian. You can imagine the upheaval caused when the leader suddenly turns round and says, "Jesus is the way!" The whole movement is suddenly plunged into disarray! This in turn got me invites to UCT, Stellenbosch, and all other universities and also to almost all the high schools in the Western Cape, speaking to up to 100,000, and possibly more, students.

Some of this you may know, but much of the story I'm telling, most of you don't know! After being invited, two of us went to a Dutch Reformed meeting in Paarl, and after preaching to what seemed like 600+ students, we were astonished to see over 500 students come forward for salvation and had the wonderful joy of leading them to repentance and to Jesus!

On another occasion, we were invited to Stellenbosch University—this time to the Dutch Reformed Kweek Skool to speak to ministers-in-training. More than 10 of the young ministers (as I found out later) through that talk became Pentecostal and dramatically changed the direction of their lives. Three of those ten became Assemblies of God ministers.

One can only imagine the disruption this must have caused and the consternation of the parents and fellow students on the campus, many of whom were seriously challenged! What a mighty God!

I was also invited to speak to most of the *koshuis (Afrikaans – "boarding school")* on campus. Amazing happenings—probably speaking to thousands of Stellenbosch students! Many came to salvation, and a work was started in that student town. Also, at Rhenish Girls' High School, after addressing the assembly, something which had a remarkable effect on these high school girls, so much so that after that talk, The Hippie Market, that I had opened years earlier, became a meeting place, and many of the girls who were touched receive instruction and grew in God. This was also true for the other students (disciples). The Market became a rallying place. Praise Jesus! God added daily to the growing band of converts.

– Brian O' Donnell, 1985

CHAPTER THIRTEEN

Please Lord, Heal My Pitching Arm

THE VARSITY OLD BOYS CLUB was based in Rosebank, Cape. My role was not only to play, but to promote the game more widely; and more controversially, to coach and train so-called "Colored" baseball players in areas like Athlone, Cape, when the opportunity presented itself.

Additionally, if I made the team again, I would be really chuffed to play again for Western Province (WP – regional All-Star team), which could also mean touring the country for tournaments. I had been selected for WP during my exchange student year, which kind of catapulted me to semi-celebrity status, at the high school at least. In addition, as part of the "contract," VOB arranged for me to get a job (Old Mutual, Pinelands, Cape) and a place to live (at the base of Table Mountain in Vredehoek, almost opposite Disa Park Apartments—also rudely known as "Tampon Towers" (see pic above). What is also very cool is that I was considered for the national Springboks team, but because I was not a permanent resident, I couldn't play.

I was 19 years old and one of the only people in my village back home that I knew of who had "upped" and left and moved to another country on a one-way ticket. Other than fulfilling my baseball contract, little else was required of me in terms of rent, food, or gas. Now, here I was in this strange, new, reborn and revolutionary world.

In short, emotionally, spiritually, financially, socially, and geographically, this was a HUGE deal. I had turned down an offer with the Detroit Tigers, rejected a full four-year scholarship from Ohio University, and an invitation to attend the Kansas City Royals Baseball Academy. All this so I could return to Cape Town and discover what more the Lord had in store for my life.

Try telling THAT to your incredibly loving and supportive, but atheist, father who had sacrificed so much to prepare me for my future life. Throw into the mix the fact that I later went into ministry … well, it took him nearly 10 years to pick up the phone and call me and tell me he was proud of me and respected me. He was an incredible man. That memory chokes me up, even now.

As I described in the previous chapter, the return to Cape Town, getting baptized, receiving the Holy Spirit, speaking in tongues, etc., brought me into contact with the Jesus Revolution, The Headquarters

Christian coffee bar, the Assemblies of God (AOG), and the "Give God a Chance" movement, among other things going on at an extremely exciting time in South Africa.

Soon after the AOG connection was formed, I began traveling with Pastor John "Brother" Bond (head of the country's AOG) to Somerset West to support Bible studies as part of a church planting initiative. It was a kind of internship period for me as someone who knew pretty much nothing about the Christian faith or the Bible. After baseball practice on Tuesdays, I would meet him and go there, actually, to meet at Haughton B. and his wife's home—the folks who *"insisted that we come to dinner."*

* * *

Backtrack for a moment. During a pro baseball tryout in the US for the Kansas City Royals Baseball Academy that summer in 1971, I began to experience severe pain in my right pitching elbow and up into my right shoulder. Having pitching arm pain was really nothing new, but this was something more extreme and more troubling. I had been told at pro tryouts in the past that I was a "short arm" pitcher—i.e., I didn't use my back and legs to help throw the ball faster—and that eventually, it would likely result in permanent damage to my overworked and abused arm.

In fact, for several years before this, I always kept Deep Heat muscle and pain relief cream *and* ice packs on the bench, which I alternated using between innings. My arm was a mix of fiery hot and numbing cold for much of the game. Once, when I pitched two consecutive games back-to-back and threw approximately 230 game pitches (not including warm-up pitches), I could barely raise my arm above my waist.

Stupid, I know ... don't say it.

Very soon after the season began in Cape Town, small bumps or balls of something or other began to appear under the skin, traveling from the outside of my right elbow and winding up through my bicep into my shoulder. They seemed to be intertwined with the muscle or tendons, and the balls, or whatever they were, became so prominent that you could easily feel them and could actually pinch and raise them up with two fingers. It was excruciatingly painful to even touch them. There were probably 20–25 of these very recognizable small lumps.

I continued to pitch and to play, but obviously, I was becoming less and less effective. But much deeper down in my heart and mind than that, to be honest, I was feeling incredibly guilty that I was probably going to be unable to fulfill my contractual obligations to the baseball club who had gone to such great lengths and expense to bring me back to Cape Town.

In mid-to-late-November, on a Friday, one of the team leaders took me to an orthopedic specialist friend of his to have a look at my arm. He concluded that the little lumps were in fact some kind of gristle made of a calcium crystal-like combination (he thought), and while not made up of the same stuff, appeared similar to Dupuytren's contracture nodules (Google it!). The only thing that could fix the problem was to have the lumps surgically removed.

Surgery would likely end my baseball career … for that season, at least. The coach of the team, Brian L., who I stayed with below Table Mountain in Vredehoek, had seen my pain and felt the bumps and knew it was something that could not be avoided or put off.

I was crushed.

Only the guilt I was carrying over letting the team down was stronger than the physical pain I felt. The doctor called on Monday and scheduled me for surgery on the upcoming Thursday.

I didn't throw at practice on Tuesday but still went to Somerset West with Brother Bond. I'd learned that he didn't understand my baseball obsession (and barely respected my commitment to the club, if he did at all), so I didn't bother trying to tell him what was going on during the 35-minute ride. I secretly suspected he would be relieved that I finally had a reason to give up that worldly pursuit and focus on the Lord's work—and maybe cut my hair when I did so.

The AOG, and Brother Bond in particular, really considered such things as parties, dancing, drinking, movies, rock music—and apparently sport for the fun of it—as frivolous and even sinful.

* * *

I didn't know much, if anything, about divine healing. Actually, I only knew that healing existed in the Bible, and the AOG talked about it and taught that miracles were *"for today"*—and that Jesus still healed people today. I was confused about how to make that happen, when and how to ask, who to ask, what words to speak, and how much faith it might take. To give you some idea, how my young, new, naïve, faith mind worked:

"If I only have 50% of the required faith to be healed, does that mean He will heal only 50% of the problem?"

Stupid, I know ... don't say it.

I wrestled with the issue of presumption versus trust versus expecting versus sort of demanding—in a humble, sanctified way. Again, I'm writing now like I actually had theological or Christian language for all this back then. *I didn't.* I'm putting actual words into my head and heart retrospectively. I even thought that asking questions like these would be added to my list of "Lack of Faith" questions, like some kind of test.

But most of all, I was stuck between two competing loyalties and obligations (in my mind)—a baseball contract versus new life lived out in the church and for Him.

And if I could find enough faith and get God to heal me, then I could actually be doing the team AND God a favor.

Don't say it!

* * *

Author's Note: Because of printed articles like the one put out by YFC in *IN Magazine* (see copy in Chapter 10), I was by now known as "Dave Lutes, The Christian American Baseball Player, Superstar Who Plays for Western Province" (I've paraphrased). While I did enjoy the limelight, I also accepted the social-spiritual fact I had a good public platform from which to preach and share the Gospel with young people. Surgery could or would take me off that particular reputational platform, which I carried, rightly or wrongly, in my head and heart as another obligation pressure.

* * *

When I was kneeling in front of a chair at the Bible study meeting in Somerset West that Tuesday night (the same place I knelt when the Lord filled me with His Spirit and gifted me with tongues), no one other than 4-5 guys on the baseball team (mostly Jewish guys, by the way) knew about my arm and shoulder lumps and upcoming surgery.

The depth of my anxiety and my confusion about having my life turned upside down by the Lord, leaving my family behind, changing career and education directions, being eliminated from military service, and moving to another country—**only to be stopped in my tracks like this**—was a spiritual and emotional weight I couldn't handle.

Dare I even suggest to the Lord that He heal me?

*What level of "cheek" does even that thought represent?!
After all, who am I?!*

I had very little experience of the words one properly uses in prayer generally, or when praying for something like this, specifically. I was spiritually a child and totally clueless about such things. I simply began to pray—moan and yearn really—deeply and silently from my heart. I was in tremendous spiritual, emotional, and physical pain and felt utterly helpless and frighteningly dependent on something outside myself. Not a comfortable "*Lutes thing*"—*we Lutes boys liked control!*

"Not telling you what to do, Lord … just letting you know that I could really use your Love and Mercy right now. And if I were to ask you to heal me, what's the proper way to do that?"

Tearfully, I began to speak in tongues quietly and felt, *yes felt*, a wave of love and calm come over me and in me. I "knew in my knower" that He was there with me right then.

In a hushed voice I said, *"Please, whenever you want to do it, if you want to do it, or however you want to do it, whatever you want from me and my life—I'm asking you to heal me, please, **in Jesus' name.**"*

As I said those words, I stretched out my arm full length above my head, which was something that was physically impossible for me to do without extreme pain for many weeks previously. I knew it was going to hurt, and I knew it was going to cause real discomfort, but I felt that was the right thing to do.

There was no pain.

There was no discomfort. I had full use and mobility of my arm and shoulder.

The real shocker—**what was even more amazing**—was when I touched my arm and felt up and down all the way, elbow to shoulder. I couldn't find or feel any nodules or bumps. The little balls of whatever they were, were all completely gone. I moved my arm some more and stretched it full length some more.

I stood to my feet, and I raised my arms and hands to God.

Everyone in the room heard me and saw me smiling and crying and worshipping. Incoherently, I tried to get the words out: "Thank you Lord! I'm healed, I'm healed!" Apparently, I sounded like a drunken sailor talking about "sanking the keel onboard" and something about "seals."

I floated home in the car (well, in my seat anyway), and I told Brother Bond the whole story. My flat and teammate, Brian L., was already asleep, so I didn't wake him and instead, worship grinned myself to sleep.

I kept feeling and massaging my arm with total wonder and amazement. In the morning, Brian asked me, of course, how my arm was feeling and how I was feeling about the surgery the next day.

* * *

Seven Dilemma Questions (There will be a test on Monday morning):

1. Do I tell the baseball team the truth, the whole truth and nothing but the truth? Or do I safely distort the facts about what happened and find safe, non-Christian language to avoid an in-

your-face Jesus message and debate because I don't really know how to explain it anyway?

2. Would similar words like, *"I don't know how it happened or how He did it; all I know is that once I was blind (crippled-ish), but now I can see (throw a fastball),"* be sufficiently God-honoring?

3. Was I brave enough or wise enough to talk about miracle stuff confidently and positively and helpfully?

4. Would they just be glad that their star pitcher could play again, and there would be no excessive medical bills to pay, thus making the cost of my return to South Africa worth it after all?

5. Even though I was healed now, did that mean I should continue playing and maybe run the risk of hurting my arm again? **Would that be testing God?**

6. Would I even be able to throw like I used to?

7. Was the healing for another God-planned purpose? If so, how and when could I know what that purpose was?

All this was rattling around in my head and heart as Brian asked the question. I won't say I avoided the subject completely – I did say we prayed for my arm and that I thanked God for being so good to me. I also decided to let my pitching and my sportsmanship speak for itself. We cancelled the doctor's appointment and celebrated me being okay and standing back on the pitcher's mound again.

CHAPTER FOURTEEN

The Jesus Movement –
Put Simply, We Dared to Believe God

IT WAS REALLY QUITE REMARKABLE and scary and thrilling but also, just plain normal, that *in those days we dared to believe God*. He was active, real, alive, present, interested in, and involved in every second of every day of our lives.

Our lives.

My life.

That's just how we saw things.

The same living, active God who invaded world history also tracked us down, wooed us, called us, found us on the road, wrestled or threw us to the ground in a blinding, loving light or held us close with a gentle whisper and embraced us for and to Himself.

This same God opened doors, lit the pathway, provided jobs and places to live, healed hearts, touched bodies, gave us stories and words of witness to speak to anyone who came across our paths. He intervened, so it seemed, with a constant stream of mini miracles in our daily walk.

This was the same God who healed my pitching arm.

* * *

It was no "Sunday only" lifestyle or mindset. Knowing and walking and talking with Jesus was our life's drumbeat. In spite of how new or young or naïve we were in our faith, we believed that He spoke. He spoke through nature, others, in an audible and a small, still inner voice, in visions and dreams, in "God-incidences," through circumstances (that weren't really coincidences, were they?), and through the Bible, of course. It seemed to be the norm to us that He would do sign-type miracles all the time for us, in us, and through us. It was just the way we thought and saw the world then.

* * *

Extract from Bernie Auditore:

Well, you know it was a very special time because God's Holy Spirit—you know when you're born again into a revival, you don't know anything else. So, you just think that's day-to-day normal. It was really a time of God's visitation, and we were all young, didn't have any real responsibilities other than working and earning some money, but there was great fellowship amongst us, the services were great, the Bible study teaching was wonderful, and when you just get saved, you're hungry for everything and you want to know, and God's meeting you in everything.

Now, I've gone into far deeper spiritual experiences after all of that because, let's face it, we're all babes in Christ (although we don't like to think we were), but we were in like Kindergarten with the Lord, and we were in junior school, but the fellowship was fantastic. It was very simple; there were no agendas, no church politics (at least in the beginning). The Assemblies Harfield Road was wonderful. Downtown was great. We just took Jesus at His word. Life was really simple. I honestly believed that Jesus was coming soon, and so, why bother to do anything else? We just wanted to share the Lord with anybody and everybody.

Brian (O'Donnell) and I used to go pray for people to be baptized in the Spirit, and boy, just about everybody always did. People said, "You've got a gift of laying on hands." Well, I don't know about that. That's putting on a sticker or badges, but God was moving, and people's hearts were open, and I'm encouraged and excited to look forward to this new twenty-first century revival and however we can be a part of that because, at the end of the day, it is only Jesus. I've brushed shoulders with billionaires and pop stars and the bravest of the brave, the weakest of the weak, and it's all the same—only Jesus.

– Bernie Auditore, 2020
(Transcribed, unedited)

* * *

Excerpt from Denise Coleman

Dave [through Sanet], asked how I would describe the Christian "thing" that was going on back then.

It was a special time. There was a bond, a connectedness, among us. Most were "alternative," not mainstream; although, some were. There was a sense of freedom. We would be at braais or meetings, and then it would just happen—we suddenly felt the presence of God. People would kneel, pray. There was a oneness, a sense of the Holy Spirit. No restrictions. Freedom.

Those days were an excellent foundation, a good entry for becoming a Christian. People were getting saved and not necessarily in church. It was as in Acts: Breaking of Bread in homes, fellowship, and prayer.

Some Highlights

I got saved at the AOG. Mike and I got invited by a friend. We took a train to Harfield Road. This was all new to us, and by the end of the service, we were ready to leave. But quite a few people came around us. They were so warm and friendly. We were invited to YP (Young People) on Friday night, invited by John Bond. We went. People were enjoying themselves (without booze and weed). It just grew organically without being influenced— Brian and Johnny Weber—spontaneously through revival.

The Headquarters (owned by Brian O'Donnell) only hosted Christian meetings on Monday and Tuesday in the beginning. On the other nights, it was still a disco. In fact, Mike and I had our first date at The Factory (later The Headquarters). Some nights the music would go off, and suddenly, Johnny (Weber) would start preaching.

There were weekend camps (we were married); it was community as we've never seen it or seen it since.

The Atmosphere at the Time

The Church and the state were separate then. Young people wanted a cause, and Jesus brought meaning. I remember the "Give God a Chance" rally, evangelism on the Jameson Hall steps, and some "debating" with Jack Hartland.

I have no regrets or disappointments about that time but started to feel more constraint going into full-time ministry. Our time in Sea Point was led by Noel Cromhout. There was open ministry, public speaking, discovering, and honing our giftings. There was no Internet, so we had to research ourselves, and we did. We had the Bible and concordance. There was a lot of quiet time. The Holy Spirit led us into truth. I also learnt that context is important.

The AOG was relatively conservative. We weren't originally "church people." The Breaking of Bread was something new to us. At one such service, the bread and wine was passed around. I'm not sure if the guy was hungry and thirsty or if he didn't know, but when the elements were passed to him, he finished the entire goblet and ate all the bread!

I remember there was a man who used to stutter and wore a long robe. Owen wore earrings and was asked to remove them. One of the Elders tried to get Johnny Weber into a suit, but he wouldn't have any of it. On one occasion when the offerings bag was passed around, someone helped himself to the contents.

Johnny Weber was a lot of fun, just full of love. He was evangelistic and simply loved people into the Kingdom.

Mike went into ministry because of the Jesus Revolution. We met on Saturday night open ministry at St. Andrew's Presbyterian Church. We didn't want to miss out, loved getting together. We weren't bound by time at those gatherings.

When Harfield Road became too small, we moved to Loop Street. It was quite rustic—a few holes in the floor, toilet adjacent. Johnny used to go to the toilet within earshot and then come out with a "word."

Only later would politics start playing a role. Maybe we had our heads in the sand, but we didn't get involved in that.

– Denise Coleman, June 2020

(As told to Sanet Stander)

CHAPTER FIFTEEN

Dear Family, Let Me Prove to You
Miracles Are Real Today
("Uncle Dave, Do You Still Speak in That Funny Language?")

THIS CHAPTER WILL DESCRIBE WHAT I CAN ONLY SAY was most definitely not the smartest thing I've ever done in my life. My stupidity and innocence (as in naïve and spiritually immature) will, I hope, be covered by Grace and a good laugh.

As far as I was concerned, my experience of speaking in tongues was a modern-day miracle and proof that Jesus is alive today and roaming the earth to find people, save their souls, and change their lives for good, forever. I know for me, Him finding me at the camp was really a— no, THE—pivotal moment of my life. Being filled with the Spirit and being gifted with speaking in tongues was miraculous confirmation that He was with me to do something amazing in and through my life. It was His doing from beginning to end; I had little to do with it except to be a selfish sinner and welcome Him when He knocked on my heart's door.

Now, I was switched on, pumped up, gung-ho, psyched, and ready to rock the world for Jesus!

Baseball, Christian things, job, and girlfriend ... baseball, Christian things, job, and girlfriend ... I was on a *holy roll.*

I had such a deep hunger, yearning, and almost unquenchable thirst to see my own family back home come to the Lord. I was generally a lousy letter writer, but I kept the sports clippings flowing and dropped in the occasional Gospel tidbit in the hope it would do two things:

1. Help my parents not worry about me because I was surrounded by people who were looking after me, and I was being cared for by God.

2. Sow Gospel seeds and water them with prayer. I hadn't learned many of the subtleties and much of the tact of diplomatic witnessing or sharing of my faith, so I just said it as sincerely and naturally as I could.

In terms of style and Christian personality, I was pretty much out there with positivity and stories and joy about my new life. I spoke bluntly and plainly to young people about my former life, which they seemed to relate and respond to. I wasn't completely oblivious to some of the doctrinal and denominational debates, but basically, I didn't really care that much. Tell "His True Story," that was all.

For me, the simple truth was this: "Once I was blind, but now I can see. He found me when I wasn't even looking for Him, and He opened my eyes! And it's really, really cool!"

That was my only story, and I was sticking to it, not least because I didn't have much else to say ... except ...

...my experience of the Holy Spirit and speaking in tongues at my adult believer water baptism.

Was it a mistake what I did next?

* * *

What I will recount now I do with a blushing face. When my second Christmas away from my family was fast approaching, I decided to give them a personal Christian Christmas message on cassette tape. The whole family was going to spend Christmas with my brother and his wife and daughter (about five years old at the time) near Del Rio, Texas. Bear in mind, to send a cassette tape by airmail in those days, from South Africa to Texas, would take about three weeks. So, I had some time to seriously question the wisdom of what I was planning to do—*a lot!* But I didn't listen to my own questioning.

They received the tape on time and purposely saved listening to it until all the presents had been opened on Christmas morning. Then everyone excitedly sat around the tape player to hear what I had to say. My mom was already emotional, and my dad, while normally able to hide it, was (so I'm told) beginning to lose it as well. My brother, John, my closest friend, sat on the perimeter of the group—alone—so he could keep his emotional distance. My other brother, Skip, was in the military, and his wife, Ginny, took charge of the tape player.

They were all set, and Ginny pushed "Play."

I remember telling them how much I missed them all, something about baseball, work, the weather, the two oceans, the beauty of the mountains, and the people and food. I then proceeded to tell them anything and everything about the Lord that I could think of. It wasn't exactly a sermon, as I wasn't equipped for that level of message, but I did pretty much unload on them ... *"from Genesusis to Revolutions"*—which is ironic considering I really knew zilch biblically.

I told them about my baptism in September and how the Holy Spirit *"did something"* to me. My words were deeply personal, somewhat tearful, utterly sincere, but a tad preachy with a judgmental edge to them. It was a desperate but honest attempt to convince them they needed God and Jesus in their lives. I wanted them to realize that the Gospel was, and Jesus is, *"Really, real! It wasn't philosophy or a fad or a figment of my imagination; it was, He was, really, real!"*

Near the end of my cheery season-of-goodwill Christmas message I said, basically, these words:

"And just to show you, to **prove to you**, that all that I've been telling you is real, that Jesus is alive and that He does miracles today—"

I spoke in tongues for nearly a minute.

Go on (dear reader), *time yourself ... try it*. Begin to speak nonstop right now, in any language you choose, no pauses, very few commas, no hesitation—just an energetic outpouring of words—and *then realize how long a minute is*. It's an eternity, especially to the listeners, *and especially when you're scaring them half to death!*

Now, imagine you're listening to your brother, daughter, son, or a close cousin rambling in a language you couldn't understand and that they couldn't possibly have learned in a country at the bottom of the world that you know little to nothing about. *For a minute!*

I can imagine my dad saying, "He's been kidnapped by a cult!"

No one from my family commented or replied after that—*not one word*—nor did anyone make a dramatic commitment to Christ.

My point and recommendation? Don't do that.

* * *

In 1975, when I was back in the US for Christmas (having been to NO family Christmases or Thanksgivings in between), my niece, then nine years old or so, came and sat on my lap and asked with all sincerity, *"Uncle Dave, do you still speak in that funny language? It was really funny!"*

CHAPTER SIXTEEN

The Jesus Revolution Heats Up

THE FOLLOWING IS AN EXCERPT from Pastor John "Brother" Bond (AOG National President):

One night, the Lord gave me a prayer to pray. It must have been the Lord, for left to myself I might have prayed for Him to send in nice people who could help the church: the rich, the powerful and the good. As it was, I prayed that night, "Lord, send in the needy, the drunkards, the drug addicts, and the broken!"

God certainly answered that prayer. In they came, the hippies. One of the first was Johnny Weber, converted in prison when a friend hitchhiked all the way from Salisbury in Rhodesia to the prison in Beaufort West in the Middle Karoo to tell Johnny that Jesus loved him. Johnny had never before ever been told that anybody loved him. To this day, I have warm fellowship with Johnny, a man with a blessed ministry and a sweet spirit.

Johnny was in prison awaiting trial for stealing petrol out of a car. On the day appointed for the trial, the businessman who laid the charge against him did not bother to show up in court. The case was quashed, so Johnny walked free.

Another early convert in that revival is Brian O'Donnell. Brian owned a nightclub, The Headquarters, a place banned to army and navy personnel because of its bad name for purveying drugs. When Brian got converted, The Headquarters changed, too. We had meetings there. What an experience to preach there to young people and have crowds of them surrender to Christ and then get filled with the Holy Ghost.

Brian also owned The Market, a sort of flea market conglomeration of clothing stalls and the like. Crowds of young people frequented it, and they all were challenged with the Gospel.

Brian proved to be an entrepreneur. He used his talents for the Lord by arranging a number of "Give God a Chance" events held in places like the Green Point Football Stadium. Several thousand people would gather to hear Gospel concerts and the preaching of the Gospel there.

The whole of Cape Town was made aware of spiritual things. In the town centre, walking on the pavements, one could notice every lamppost bore a little sticker, "Jesus Loves You." One person even climbed up a bare wall on a multistorey building and expertly, in beautifully done lettering, wrote, "Jesus saves" for all the office workers in Cape Town to see.

Ultimately, our assembly followed suit by having a parade and a lengthy massed meeting in Greenmarket Square one Saturday. In the morning, a thousand people marched through the city carrying placards: "Jesus loves you," "Christ unites," "Turn or burn," "Repent." At least one indignant citizen found the Gospel hit her right in the eye when a careless marcher accidentally poked her with his placard. In the afternoon that day 5,000 people gathered in Greenmarket Square to hear the Gospel.

When I prayed, "Lord, send in the needy, the drunkards, and the drug addicts," I had no idea the Lord would use our assembly to launch such a series of stirrings in Cape Town.

– John Bond, 1985

CHAPTER SEVENTEEN

All Over Town!

AND HE GAVE US PARKING SPACES!

Well, He gave **ME** parking spaces anyway—a very special anointing!
Yes, no, (Ja, nie) really, He did!

If Johnny Weber was still with us, I just know he would confirm it!

He was in my very uncool, apricot colored 1960 VW Beetle (called Annabel) with me once when it happened. We shared an apartment in Plumstead. Needing to draw some money in Claremont, I prayed for the parking space as we were leaving Kenilworth … and literally a heartbeat after my "Amen," a space appeared right in front of the Standard Bank, Main Road, Claremont, Saturday morning, 10 minutes before closing.

Even Johnny was gob-smacked, which was saying something!

I was seriously spiritually chuffed.

* * *

We Used "Jesus Speak"

The Lord's name, or reference to Him, in some way or other, seemed to punctuate every sentence; He was part of most conversations. He was the focal point, or compass heading, for living our bigger lives, sharing our faith in front of a crowd, or simply going to the corner store. A brief "hello" with a brother or sister was quickly followed by sharing about what the Lord showed us in our quiet times that day or what the *"Lord has been saying to me ..."*

Planning and organizing (which was often characterized as lack of faith—or being irresponsible—by our older, more established brothers and sisters) didn't really seem to factor into things very much for a lot of us. As impetuous as we were sometimes, **we were living on "Blessing's Edge,"** in God's moment, flowing with whatever stream He was pouring out. The thrill of walking on the water far outweighed the thought of possibly drowning.

We consumed teaching tapes and books ravenously ... indigestible bones in the fish **be damned!**

Bible references were a big part of our vocabulary, and I often wonder, looking back, what normal people on the street and in our other lives thought of our eagerness and unabashed freedom to quote KJV verses and say, *"**Praise the Lord!**"* at every turn.

"Amen!" was a comma punctuating our sentences.

For those other brothers and sisters in town who didn't share our enthusiasm and absolute chapter-and-verse certainty as to what the Truth was, we tended to draw our Bible swords and lop off their spiritual ears. Being right, for me anyway, was much more important than being loving. Sadly, too often, people were "soul-scalps," rather than people in need; witnessing, Bible verse point scoring, and leading people to the Lord was too often so many notches on the handle of those swords.

Someone said to me once, *"People don't really talk like that, you know?! Just listen to me, please, with normal heart-ears!"*

Wise or unwise, sensitive, and loving or not, **yes, we did talk like that!** They were exciting times, life-changing times. Thank God for His Grace that He distributed so liberally to us, while at the same time, I'm almost sure, He shook His head in bewilderment at what He had got Himself into with us.

∗ ∗ ∗

Extract from Comments by Cas Weber (Johnny Weber's Wife):

We fell in love with God, and He used us with lots of Grace thrown into the mix! I was born again at 15 in 1973, met Johnny when I was 16, and worked at The Market for Brian and Sandy O'Donnell. Johnny was a youth pastor up and down the Garden Route at that time on his motor bike and came back weekends to visit me at The Market, and he told everyone that he's going to marry me one day! I was only 16 and super shy! He was nine years older than me!

Johnny lived out loud and believed that God would use him to reach the lost, do the impossible, miraculous, and heal the sick and broken. He was an evangelist to his core and would tell anybody and everybody about the Lord and was a great encourager. He would often have Words of Knowledge in odd places like restaurants for waiters or patrons and pray with them for healing or accepting the Lord, etc.—right there and then.

God would heal them!

It was a journey. When you live by faith, you become blasé about miracles because they literally happened every day. Never boring! I miss him so much. I miss his faith in dire circumstances— I just miss him.

– Cas Weber, 2020

CHAPTER EIGHTEEN

Truly God-Blessed Music in Those Days

THE FOLLOWING IS AN EXTRACT from Paul West:

When thinking about the "Give God a Chance" and Nicky Cruz rallies, it brings back such good and super memories. My band Maranatha played at both of those rallies, and they were amazing. A few things stand out for me:

At the Nicky Cruz rally, the organizers (Go Tell Communications, I think they were called) arrived in two white Mercedes limos. They had apparently been staying in a fancy hotel in Cape Town. They asked us to play while the offering baskets were passed around the field. We did so quite happily. Then they came back onto the platform and said they were going to pass the baskets around again, and we must play again. We refused to play and put down our instruments. I think Nicky was also embarrassed.

The band was made up of a few of the Cape Town hippies (Perry van Staden on bass; Nobby Clark on sax; Pierie Steyn on trombone; Roy "Somebody" on drums). I was on guitar and did vocals with two young lasses, Michelle Sher, and a friend of hers whose name I can't recall. It was wonderful seeing all the people on the Green Point track fields where I had participated in athletics competitions. So, it had special significance for me that we were praising God and hearing His Word there.

The first rally at Green Point taught us some lessons as our amplifiers were not strong enough to reach to seating areas of the stadium. So, the next rally was with Nicky Cruz, and we had a problem as even more people were expected to come.

So, Cedric Buffler (who normally did the preaching when we played at youth meetings like YFC, etc.) worked out a solution. If as many people as possible brought their FM radios with them—if they were going to sit in the stands and tune into a certain frequency, then all the people on the stands sitting near to them would be able to hear. We then connected a transmitter to our homemade mixing desk, and apparently, it worked OK.

* * *

Going back a few years, as an introduction to this tale, I had played guitar in a rock 'n' roll band from the age of eleven until the time when I became a believer in Standard Nine at school (I didn't sing, as I was told I had a terrible voice). Due to the memories I had of some of the places we played, I had decided to get rid of all my band equipment and had not played any musical instrument for a few years.

Just prior to the band forming and the first "Give God a Chance" rally, I had been praying about what I should be doing as a young, married man. Did the Lord want to use me in any way? I had just finished praying and went to check if there was any post. There was a letter from a UCT student slightly older than me whom I only knew vaguely from talks he gave when I was still at school. You may remember John Broster as he was at

Rondebosch and may have been a senior when you (Dave) were there or spoken at functions there.

In the letter was a cheque and a note saying that he had been praying and "felt led" to send me the money for music equipment. I was so amazed that the Lord had answered my prayer (from my perspective, immediately; from John's perspective, about a week before I had even prayed). I got very excited and suddenly was singing in a strange language. On occasions I would sing harmonies to what I had been singing but not understanding a word of it all. My wife thought I had gone totally mad, so [she] phoned the headmaster of my old school to ask what she should do. He told her not to worry; it would soon wear off.

This singing continued wherever I had a private place, as I was driving or preparing a training room, but I had no idea what it was. I just felt wonderful and knew it had something to do with God having answered my prayer in such an amazing way. (And by the way, this encouraged me to build some speakers and a mixer and buy some microphones and an amplifier.) I started writing songs and singing them. My voice must have changed because nobody complained, and I have been writing and singing and leading bands ever since.

Now, coming back to the weird hippie band members that so many knew: Perry and the other band members were at Harfield Road Assembly of God and kept asking me if I spoke in tongues. My answer, being a good Baptist (although I was a Metholated-Much-Reformed-Anglo-Bapti-Cost-alarian) was, "No ways—I don't even know what that is!" One day, Perry invited me to a service at Harfield Road, and after the choruses, the congregation broke into singing in tongues. I got such a thrill when I realized what had happened to me was the same thing mentioned before.

– Paul West, 2020
(Shared with Sanet Stander not long before he died;
see Dedication)

CHAPTER NINETEEN

Then There Was Bernie

BERNIE AUDITORE IS MENTIONED in a number of places in the different blogs, testimonies, and stories quoted elsewhere in this book by many people and leaders from those days. He came into my life as a completely startling, but refreshing, surprise. I wasn't cool or hippie-like by any stretch of the imagination—just straitlaced, suit and tie, with a bit longish hair.

That was me.

That most definitely wasn't Bernie.

Bernie was, in my mind, the epitome of leading-edge coolness and hipness.

Totally groovy!

Energy, winning smile, hair to die for, funny, a great storyteller, colorful (and semi-crude)—his spiritual awareness and boldness expressed itself in an utter freedom to talk about Jesus as present, real, powerful, and ready to change lives—*right now!*

He was self-aware but not self-absorbed. Utterly present and "there," but not egocentric in any way. He didn't really care what people thought of him; he didn't mince his sometimes-colorful words and demonstrated a humble boldness for the Lord that was magnetic and infectious.

He'd hate for me to say this, but to me, he was a true inspiration and a real joy to hang out with. He lived the Christian life with intense, joyful abandon, always talking, "Amen"-ing, and "Praise the Lord"-ing. He was theologically close enough to the Truth to touch lives and didn't care one iota if he misquoted a Bible verse.

Authentic—that's the word. He was authentic, utterly transparent, and all out for the Lord.

I was working and living in the hostel at the Old Mutual in Pinelands, Cape—and as I've mentioned in other places—involved in The Headquarters and with the crowd from The Hippie Market. Most of the super active, outspoken types (like Bernie) filled the world with spiritual energy, power, and fun in the Lord.

I cannot state it strongly or loudly enough—God just "was."

We all woke up and lived each day with the expectation that Jesus was alive, real, and stalking people by His Spirit so they could know Him. He chose to include us in His work. It's just how it was. We were caught up in it—gladly, actively, and unstoppably. Bernie was always there, at most meetings and events, ready to speak and be bold beyond belief.

* * *

Sometime in those days, we became connected more closely, if I remember correctly, through Peter Stott who shared a room with me at the Old Mutual. Even though Bernie worked a full-time rep job for EMI Records, and I also worked full-time at the Old Mutual, then later at another job while playing baseball regularly, we found time to be witnessing on the streets, talking with youth, and sharing our personal salvation stories whenever and wherever.

> *We had so much fun and enjoyment and excitement from being fully abandoned to and all out for Jesus. There was no other life that could conceivably come close. It wasn't what we did for kicks or just on Sundays.*
>
> *IT WAS OUR TOTAL LIFE—OUR ONLY LIFE!*

* * *

Before I share Bernie's full, unedited, unadulterated, and tell-it-like-it-was testimony in the next chapter, I want to share a couple of true, humorous, and personal stories that illustrate Bernie's style and my somewhat-more-than-fringe involvement with his life. In a million years, I would never have thought his stories would be part of my story, but I am blessed beyond measure that God saw fit to connect us and include me in what He was doing in Bernie's life.

Story No. 1: It was early 1973. I needed to pick Bernie up from a youth hostel in Tamboerskloof (suburb of Cape Town, on the mountainside) because we were going together to a meeting at The Headquarters. When I got there, he introduced me to a young girl who he had been sharing about the Lord with, and that he'd persuaded to go with us to the meeting.

When the meeting was over, quite late, I drove them back to the hostel. When we got there, out front, the girl's boyfriend was waiting for her (us). We got out of the car, and the guy had a broken bottle in his hand and crossed the street to confront Bernie about "*... messing around* *with his bird ....*" He took a step closer. Bernie stepped toward him and raised up his "stop" hand. They both stopped.

Bernie said in a strong, direct, but very cool way, "Mate, I'm a Christian, and I'm supposed to love you, but you're making it really difficult."

The guy dropped his bottle and backed off and went back to his car. That was it. The girl hurriedly went inside. I stood there, gob-smacked, and totally impressed.

Now why don't I say neat stuff like that, and why can't I be that cool?

Stories No. 2-4: In 1973, Bernie, Johnny Weber, Peter Stott, Billy Davies, and I shared an apartment in Plumstead for a short while. I had been with Bernie on a couple of occasions walking down the street when some guy coming toward us stopped dead in his tracks—the dilemma about whether to run away in fear or not contorting his face. Each time this happened, they virtually squealed out similar words: "I didn't do it, Bernie! It wasn't me! I didn't do it!"

I felt like I was in incredibly good hands unless someone with a gun took a potshot from a moving car or something!

* * *

Not long after this, I don't know where we were exactly, but Bernie was on the phone to his younger sister in Bulawayo, Rhodesia. He was listening carefully to what she was telling him. I gathered it was something about her new boyfriend (we'll call him Leon). Bernie clearly wasn't pleased with what she was telling him. He took a deep breath, searched for words, and spoke very, very coldly to her, "Sis, when you see Leon again, just tell him this: Bernard knows." Bernie was informed about a week later that they had broken up.

* * *

Then, to top them all, during one full week that same year, we had three official visits at the apartment, one day after another:

1. The Tax Revenue Service

2. The South African Police

3. The Department of Home Affairs (Immigration/Passport Control)

Each of them wore an official, military-type uniform. Each of them had a formal legal document in hand. Each of them was looking for Bernie. He wasn't there at the time, so each of them asked me to prove my own identity and to sign for and promise to give the official documents to Bernie. They were very Afrikaans, very cold, very insistent, and very direct. How they knew Bernie lived there was a complete mystery.

Long story short, if I remember correctly, Bernie was in possession of (I thought at the time) an illegal South African passport, had some suspicion hanging over him about some prior criminal activity somewhere else in the country; and either was not properly in the tax department's records or had failed to pay his taxes. *Whatever the case, apparently, he was in trouble.*

If Bernie had a plan to deal with these three (in my opinion) huge problems, he didn't tell me about it. I took him into Cape Town and dropped him off at the police station and waited. He was in there for ages. Next day we went to Immigration. Same deal. Then a day later to the Tax Office ... same result. Each told him they would get back to him. But when Bernie told me what he'd said to them, I was completely nonplussed and utterly staggered by what the Lord did *and the courage and trust in the Lord that Bernie showed.*

Essentially, starting at the front desk or reception, Bernie told them —each official or officer—that he was there to turn himself in or to admit he was guilty or to surrender to their judgment. Each official didn't know what to do, so they passed him on to the next person higher up. When Bernie had each new person's attention, he told them the truth about his crime or error and then described how he had been saved by Jesus and now followed Him. He shared his testimony and threw himself on their mercy. He was passed on up the organizational ladder where he shared, again and again, in full, how the Lord had changed his life.

As I remember it (but I may have some of the details wrong), when they eventually got back to him, each guilty slate was cleaned, and each debt was forgiven, and they even issued him with a fully legal South African passport.

* * *

Author's Note – Leap Forward: In 2010, I was working and based in Dubai and Bernie was living and working in Bahrain. We had stayed connected in previous years over other possible business collaborations but finally managed to get him to visit me in Dubai for a day or so. It was incredibly emotional and meaningful for both of us. We picked up right where we'd left off when we shared a flat together in South Africa back in 1973.

What we realized after only a few hours was that we were truly "covenant" brothers. We said as much to each other. We were knit together in a deeper, more significant way than just brothers in the same fellowship or church—or flat mates. We were eternally part of each other's lives then and still. Whatever positive or negative experience either of us might have, we shared it. Joy, pain, worry, care, expectations, hopes, and dreams—we shared them. We pledged that day to not neglect each other anymore. I'm weeping as I write these words in September 2022.

* * *

Chest Wounds

I've mentioned before that Peter Stott, a new Christian according to the hostel matron, was assigned to share my room with me around December 1971. According to the matron, he had a rough history that, she implied, involved drugs but that he was making an effort to change. How she knew this, I had no idea and didn't ask.

After a couple of days of getting to know each other, I gathered Peter was interested in learning more about the Lord and meeting some other Christians. Peter was pretty uptight and older than me, and while only 19 myself, I felt a bit protective of him as a new brother. I wanted him to get exposure to The Hippie Market and The Headquarters crowd as soon as possible. I felt he would fit in. On a Tuesday night (Bible study night), we took the train into Cape Town and walked over to Longmarket Street to The Headquarters.

The main room where the meeting was being held was quite dimly lit and about 10–12 people were there watching and listening intently to Mike B. who had displayed on the wall numerous weird and wonderful posters that he interpreted and drew from the Book of Revelation: e.g., seven-headed monsters and strange creatures the meaning of which he dramatically described and explained to everyone. It was kind of complicated by the fact that on the wall behind the flip chart posters was a huge psychedelic face-like painting that had always creeped me out. Mike B. was passionately explaining the End Times; I knew Mike, sort of—a bit of an odd character, very academic and opinionated—but his intentions, I believed, were good.

We entered at the back, watching Mike speak before moving to sit in one of the donated church pews used for seating. Peter stopped dead in his tracks and stared, looking down. I followed his gaze and saw the local drunk and addict, Lionel, passed out on a pew. His shirt was open, and on his chest was a bleeding cross that had been carved into him with a knife. There was no way of knowing if he or someone else had done it. It was a tragic and disturbing sight.

Welcome to the family, Peter.

We left and went back to the train and then to the hostel. I made a mental note to do … well, actually, I didn't know what to do! This was all new to me—a whole, strange, new world. One thing that the evening did was draw us closer together; honest questions and personal discussions followed over the weeks ahead and a special level of trust and transparency was born in our new friendship. I have to admit, Peter's insights into this other hippie and drug-connected world were as helpful as they were disturbing. We both grew spiritually through our friendship.

* * *

Extract from Cedric Cross:

My dad was involved in the original AOG Cape Town. James Mullan was appointed in PE (Port Elizabeth). That was in the 1940s. I grew up in the AOG and got saved at the age of eight. Different branches of the church grew as the years went by.

My dad and I started a home church in Worcester. My involvement with the church as a child was very much growing up spending time in the houses of different evangelists.

I went to medical school in Cape Town and joined a youth group. It was charismatic—very different and ridiculed by other churches at the time.

The youth group was led by John Bond. Having said that, it was never a one-man ministry. There was not a single pastor, but rather, joint pastorage. There were paid full-time workers, but no one was more elevated than the other. The open ministry and working with the Holy Spirit were a feature of God's Breaking of Bread table at that time. The church grew from 50 to 400 members.

I was one of a few guys who would bus "broken people" from Town to Harfield Road AOG. The Elders used to sit back and encourage the younger ones to minister, speak, and testify and teach. The one prerequisite for being involved in open ministry was being saved. Responding and speaking as the Spirit led, exercising the Gifts for hours on end, it was so healthy, so good, growing in that.

I remember, for example, Johnny Weber sitting next to an older congregant who just looked at him strangely. He had rancid hair and was just out of jail. Many people were very radically saved. We were boring; they were vibrant and alive, and they could communicate and testify to others in a very unique way (without the theological background).

I remember at one communion service, there was a table in the middle of the building on which the communion elements were held. The chairs were placed all around the table. We were sitting in the back row; Dave (Lutes) and I were next to each other. The Spirit moved so powerfully that night; it was like a wave. There were so many tongues and interpretations all over the place. As the one would speak in tongues, someone else would give an interpretation. There was a freedom to utter—complete unity in Spirit. I can remember giving an interpretation that night. The Spirit just kept putting the words in my mouth, and it just flowed out of me.

Since this is Dave's book, I probably should say some things about him.

Dave stood out. He was gifted. I remember wishing that I was like that. He had a blonde girlfriend, K. Dave arrived at the pinnacle of the Jesus Movement. I would refer to him as Tom Cruise in contemporary form. He had the looks, the walk, the talk ... the girls went gaga! How can I say this? He was not too interested in anything frivolous. He was able to focus on things—one thing. He was VERY focused on Jesus. Some folk found that degree of intense focus difficult.

An example of this was those that had just given their life to Christ (like the hippies from very different backgrounds) versus us who have grown up in the Faith. He was very mature, very confident. He carried himself very well. We were a bit envious; we grew up differently to him. Dave didn't commit completely only to the AOG. He just committed to it all, all that God was doing ... full stop.

There is one thing that Dave said back then that I remember to this day: **"We Christians have to grow teeth."** I have always remembered that quote.

— Cedric Cross, 2020

CHAPTER TWENTY

Bernie Auditore's Salvation Story

SANET STANDER (my cowriter from Somerset West, Cape Town) and I met with Bernie on a Zoom call at the end of 2021. Our discussion is transcribed and is minimally edited below. It's just as he told it—raw, direct, and from the heart … and very cool (but don't tell him I said that)!

While I have a soft spot for my dear brother, and his own story is amazing, there were many, many others from those days—thousands actually—who can tell similar accounts of how the Lord wonderfully and powerfully invaded their lives with miraculous love and intervention.

> *Oh my God! He touched so many of us so beautifully, so powerfully, so eternally—and He wants to do so again these days! I hope Bernie's own story will capture your attention and heart; and will move you to radically step out in faith and serve Him.*

* * *

I was in a motorcycle group in Bulawayo; I started it. Because I left school young, I used to date all the birds that were older than me and lied to them about my age. All the guys I used to hang out with were guys older than me who were already working. I wasn't allowed to work being that young, but I lied about my age, and the boss kind of knew. Listen, his old man died, and the family in the *kak (Afrikaans – "crap")* so we just shut up. But he said to me, "Behave, and don't get out of hand."

It was a really heavy place where I worked. It had all the ex-Congo mercenaries, the gays, the perverts, the alcoholics, the guys that they let out of the jail, [and] the guys from the mental hospital; all those kinds of crowd were there, so it was kind of rough. And I had to sort of live by my wits there a bit, but motorbikes were my release. I was a very good rider. My dad used to race motorbikes at one stage, and so I got involved. Actually, 18 of my associates were killed on motorbikes before I left Rhodesia. We were a mad motorbike country, and it's interesting, but in the group that I was in, the one guy became the world champion, Gary Harking. He's in the record books. He used to ride for MB Augusta.

* * *

When I was a kid, I went camping in the bush, and I landed up about five kilometers away from a very big terrorist presence. The police and the army came in, and they completely freaked out when they found us there. They insisted we left the area and carried on.

We weren't going anywhere; we'd ridden 120 miles on our bicycles through the bush, and these guys could go and eat peanuts, you know? We were going to stay. So, we went back about 500 meters ahead in the bush and long grass. When they pushed off, we just went and followed their track and saw that they had left. So, we set up a camp. And that night, I remember, we shot a buck, and we made some meat, and I was dancing around this massive, big bonfire on this *koppie (Afrikaans – "hill")* looking out over the bush.

And a voice said to me: "God will look after you."

And I thought, *I don't need You to look after me; I brought my .22 rifle single-shot, and if there's terrorists*—and I was shouting out, "If there's any terrorists, come and get us. We wanna kill you!"

Anyway, we were basically camping and partying, having a boys' camp in the middle of a terrorist and a war zone.

So, somewhere along the line (I was young, about 10), we had drama in our country for years before it started. Anyway, you know, I grew up an outdoor fishing, hunting, shooting, camping, rowdy, motorbikes, and that was my life. I was never a hippie.

Soon as I got a chance, soon as my dad died, I thought, *Time to chuck everything out of the window and go overseas and raise hell,* you know. I used to say to my friends: "We're going to go down to hell; we're going to put out the fires and have the biggest party we ever had!"

And that was my kind of rebellious, whatever, free spirit although it wasn't free at all.

When I got to South Africa, and I'll talk about it later, my passport was an illegal passport. Illegal in that the South Africans issued it to me by mistake. So, when they found out about it, they came looking for me. They took it away. I was illegally in the country, but I had a letter telling whoever asked, so I was stuck.

And that's how I started hanging around South Africa for a while, and I teamed up with a couple of other Rhodesians. You know, we really had a bad attitude. We thought we were like the chosen race. It was quite a tough crowd and a rough crowd. Basically, we were just young guys, you know, in our late teens. We just had a good time and just lived according to our rules.

* * *

I got to Durban, and one Sunday night, we looked for some chicks, and there was, like, this youth church service there. So, my friends went in there. I said, "Hey, come on, man, we're not going into a church." Anyway, it was my friend Billy. They grabbed Billy, and they started casting demons out of him. They threw me out of the church, and here's all these church guys, and I thought, *I can't start boxing these little young guys with suits and brill cream in their hair, white shirts.*

And they said: "No, man, you're not allowed in here. You're a problem."

Anyway, they got hold of Billy, and they put him on the ground, casting demons out. I was watching, and I thought, *You know, I need to rescue my mate. But what do I rescue him from? They're giving him tea and biscuits.*

Anyway, a guy came and witnessed to me. It was Charley Payne. He was the director of Youth for Christ. He said to me: "Are you a Christian?"

And I remember, I got so cross. I actually lost it with him. I cussed him out and said, "You stupid idiot! Do you think I'm a nigger or something? I mean, look at this form; it's got a Christian name on it. What do you think I am—a Buddhist or Muslim or something? *Voetsek (Afrikaans — "get lost")*! Don't you talk to me, or I'll give you a *klap (Afrikaans — "hit you; thump you")*."

So, he said, "You can stop me talking to you, but you can't stop me praying for you."

I said, "Don't pray for me; you'll put some curse on me; things will go wrong. Just voetsek and bugger off!"

Anyway, we carried on going, and I got down to Port Elizabeth. That's where things really got rough. It was a tough port town in those days, and we did all sorts of crazy things. In the end, the police were after us. We hadn't actually done anything wrong, but three foreign white guys had gone in and hit a bank and robbed a factory, and they thought it was us. And we hadn't done it.

So, you know, I decided to cool it a little bit, and I went to get a night job. Some famous American surfer pinched my surfboard, and I was very irritated, but I couldn't find him. So, I went to work at night in order to afford a new surfboard, 'cause we had no money.

And there, a guy witnessed to me, and I said to him, "Hey, I don't do this religious thing, you know. I'm not giving my life to anybody, and I'm not repenting. I'm having too good a time; I'm free."

I was part of a Catholic Church when my dad was alive. He used to force us to go to church. I hated every minute. In fact, a friend and I tried to beat up the Catholic priest, but what we didn't know is that he was an ex-German professional boxer, so that didn't end too well. I wasn't too cool with the religion thing.

Anyway, one day, to cut a long story short, all my friends had gone partying and surfing, and they were going to do some drugs and birds and just have a wild time. I stayed in my room. I thought, *Same ole, same ole.*

And then it happened, something I've always had problems talking about, but I had this vision of Jesus on the cross dying for me. And I remember looking up and saying, "Hey, get off, man. Come down. Like, what are you doing?"

So, He said, "Because I love you so much, I'm dying for you."

And I said, "You're crazy. I'm not following you. I'm not bending any knee to anyone."

And He said to me, "Well, you know, even if I have to bleed, and you stand in it, and you rub your feet in my blood on the ground and make mud puddles out of it, I'm dying for you anyway."

It hit me hard. I thought, *Yeesh, OK—*

So, I gave my life to Christ. And I got saved. That was it.

* * *

And the amazing thing was shortly after that, I got a job in the music industry. I was like a sales rep and a talent scout and a promotions guy, and I got in early, and funnily enough, I became a top guy in South Africa (EMI Records).

And I don't know how that worked, but I think I was just reliable. I did a lot of things, and one day, I was down in a discothèque in the Holiday Inn doing a promotion, and these two birds were really wanting me to have a scene with them, so I didn't want to, you know, 'cause I was a Christian now.

So, I went to my room, and I locked the door, and I lay on the bed, and I thought, *Yeesh, Lord, I've read in your word that You said that I didn't choose You; You chose me. And You showed Yourself to me, like it wasn't about anything I did.*

But now, how am I meant to live this life? I mean, I'm 19 years old, and I've got this big car. I've got long hair, Chelsea boots, pink shirt, floral tie; I'm in the music industry; I've got all these people trying to get a piece of the action, and it's too hard.

And then Jesus walked into the room.

Dave, this one experience has been my Magnetic North. Whatever I wanted to do, and no matter how dark the night is, Jesus walked into the room.

Man, I shut my eyes. I thought, I'm not worthy to look at Him. He came and stood next to me and baptized me in the Holy Spirit. And oh my goodness, you know, I was shouting out, "Praise God! Praise God! Thank you!"

But I didn't know anything about talking in tongues. That happened later. From that day on, for twenty years, I never had one temptation. No more sex, no more this, no more that … It just never entered my head. He took my spirit, and He put it in heavenly cement where I could just live above all of that, and yes, it was incredible.

So, anyway, I went to a Baptist minister in PE and said, "Hey, listen, I was in a Holiday Inn room in Oudtshoorn at the discothèque, and Jesus walked into my room, and what do you think happened …?"

And he said to me, "You were demon possessed."

And I grabbed him and said, "Listen, chum, I will break your head open. Don't talk kak like that. Where did you get your license? Let me see your certificate. Maybe you didn't go to college."

And I walked out and thought, *So, that's a line from the Baptists.* Anyway, I just trust that he didn't commit the unforgivable sin, but he was a real dipstick.

– *Bernie Auditore, December 2021*

CHAPTER TWENTY-ONE

If God Loves the World So Much, Why Doesn't He Do Something?!

WHEN I WAS AT THE UNIVERSITY OF CAPE TOWN (1973), I wasn't a particularly good student. I was on a bursary from the Cape Provincial Administration but had a very poor sense of responsibility to them, or even to God, to study and learn excellently.

In those days, for me anyway, there was nothing more important than sharing the Gospel whenever and wherever the opportunity presented itself. My studies came second and even third.

Nothing was more important than witnessing for Jesus!

The way I saw it, my job in life was to be prepared and equipped with language and willingness, to stay open to opportunities, and to walk through open doors to witness or preach.

Even if I saw my studies as maybe somewhat essential to my life or career, such was my limited spiritual world view that completion and qualification in some field of study or other was only a stepping-stone to the "real" world of work—*witnessing and preaching or being a pastor.* Being armed to the proverbial teeth with a variety of Scripture blades for my Gospel sword was what it was all about.

There were a number of us who used to preach a lot on Jameson Hall steps, which was at the heart of the campus. It was quite a famous place, very popular for political rhetoric, speeches, campaigns, protests, etc. The backdrop to the top steps, Jameson Hall, was an amazing piece of architecture where a lot of public meetings were held, politicians spieled, and celebrities posed. Brian O'Donnell and others who were the key people in the Jesus Movement in those days often spoke on "Jammie Steps." The backdrop to the Hall were part of the Twelve Apostles Mountain Range extending from Table Mountain and running down the spine of the southern peninsula.

Our place and platform were on the top step as students passed by at lunchtime. It was from there that a small group of friends mingled with those gathered to listen to witness to them or pass out Christian tracts. I was a frequent visitor there, a frequent presenter there, and because of my accent and because of my style—my hair, my glasses, etc.—I was fairly well known, I think. It was a nervous and exhilarating privilege for me to be able to do that and use my profile to gain their attention and to draw them in to listen. We weren't allowed to use sound equipment, and the steps were long and wide, but we found a way to shout out the message.

That said, when combined with a rather Scripture-laden *"You're all sinners going to hell"* rant, the louder we shouted, the more people wanted to answer us back. Not a few people told us to "Shut up!" (Or similarly colorful, unrepeatable words).

I must have stood there on the steps at lunchtime maybe twenty or thirty times that year. Often, people responded and came to ask us questions, and if it was the right time, and if there was enough time, then to sit, share more, and even pray with them—occasionally to pray with people to accept Christ. But mostly, it was Gospel seed-sowing and awareness-building, and sadly, point scoring.

As for preaching on the steps, more often than not, my message and the motivation inside my heart was:

I've got to use the Sword of the Spirit, which is the Word of God (preferably the one truly and specially anointed King James Version [hear joking sarcasm]) to stab people and to convict them. The language, content, and tone had to be right. I must share it perfectly and passionately, making sure people get it! Right between the eyes of their heart!

The message that I preached was not one of love; it was one of conviction. It was for me to stab, slice and dice, hack, and lop off ears—in essence, to do the convicting work of the Holy Spirit. It was articulate quasi fire and brimstone—warm but not quite crackling with the smell of burning flesh.

I believed I was on fire for God, but I didn't really know how to convey His message of love when I shared that fire! In the "handbook," it was all about choice—your choice and my choice. Without your right, correct choice, God's hands were tied!

In essence: "You are wrong; God is right. You need Him. You don't need to, you shouldn't, continue to live for yourself. You don't need to be stuck in sin. God can rescue you from that. God can break the chains; He can take you out of the pit. But make no mistake, whoever you are … you … are … wrong. He … is … right … and today you need to choose if you want to be rescued!"

> *"Oh, and by the way, I'm here as His messenger to set you right and help you."*

Technically, theologically, and doctrinally that all may be true (-ish), but my message and tone were one of constant challenge and unrelenting rebuke in an attempt to provoke and to make people feel guilty. I did it loudly and well (apparently).

* * *

One particular lunchtime session, after I and some fellow students had finished preaching and sharing, I was walking through an adjacent building to head to the cafeteria. As I was about to enter the building, a young guy about my age, another student, confronted me at the door. The look on his face was one of rage, of sorrow, of frustration and confusion; and my interpretation of his body language, of course, was that he was searching. Actually, in all honesty, in my opinion at the time, everyone was searching for God but didn't know it.

In many ways, because of my particular motivations and my temperament, *he was a target,* and he, in more ways, could be one of my soul-victims that I was going to stab with my Gospel sword.

Getting into my space and face, he angrily said, "I can't believe you! I can't believe it!"

I asked, "What can't you believe?"

"Why would a loving God, an all-powerful God who has created everything, allow famine, racism, segregation, poverty, divorce, sickness, disease, and war?! Why would He allow all of that?! Why doesn't He care?! Why doesn't He do something about it?!"

As he shouted and screamed at me, tears were streaming down his face. He was frighteningly angry, obviously frustrated, and very concerned about everything going on around him and in the world, and especially, I assumed, in apartheid South Africa in 1973. He wanted answers. He needed hope and purpose and trust and love.

If I had been sensitive to the hurt and pain that he was feeling and crying out about, I would have toned down my internal Gospel rhetoric and tuned into his heart—that he wanted to know salvation somehow; that he wanted to know real love somehow; that he wanted to know God was real and cared for him … him!

Somehow.

But because I was more interested in being right than being loving, I simply whipped out my Gospel sword once again and quoted Jeremiah 17:9 to (no, at) him: "The heart of man is deceitfully wicked and desperate above all things."

Then I wielded my sword again and figuratively cut off his ear and nicked his heart with the sword tip in the process.

"God **HAS** done something about it, but **YOU** won't accept it! He sent His Son! But **YOU** won't accept Him! **YOU** are the reason why God can't work because **YOU** won't choose to let Him into your life and follow Him."

As "right" as ever, I walked away, leaving him standing there drenched in his angry tears … until I got a short distance away. It was then I felt his anguished cry stab me in the back: *"I am not a soul-scalp —I'm a person! I'm a person!"*

As I write, I'm filling up emotionally. I can't believe I was so narrow and calloused and cruel!

All this said about my heartless and unsympathetic swordlike comments to the guy above, while my spiritual snobbery was very real, there is some truth (actually, considerable truth) to the message in the following anecdotal account. Other than sounding like I was too clever for my own good, I wish also that I had somehow, lovingly, shared it with the guy though I doubt it would have helped.

I was a blockage to His love, not the channel for it.

* * *

Author's Footnote: You may have picked up in other chapters on the fact that I had an issue with performance, being seen, loving the platform, being known, etc. In truth, I liked the limelight. While I was studying, I was financially very poor and had only two pairs of shoes (one for normal life, one for church), two pairs of pants (daily and for church), and a few shirts, a tie, and a suit coat, plus two baseball uniforms and spikes.

A friend told me that one day she was talking with another student who attended UCT, and she asked her if she knew Dave Lutes. She didn't. When asked what I looked like, a description of me was given:

"American, medium height, longish hair, dark-rimmed glasses, nice smile ..."

"Nope, don't know him."

"He talks in public a lot, preaches sermons on Jameson Steps at lunchtime ..."

"Nope, don't know him."

"He wears brown corduroy jeans and veldskoen."

"Oh, him! Yeah, I know him!"

So much for my high-profile, spiritual giant image and rep!

* * *

Why Are You Tearing a Page Out of the Bible?!

When my friend, Dale McGregor, and I (in the same Psychology I class) had to come up with a project on human behavior (or something similar —can't remember exactly), naturally we wanted to do something Christian. We stated so up front in the introduction of the project hypothesis as follows:

"That the Word of God is powerful, even in print, and that if someone will open their hearts and minds even slightly and read the words even briefly, then through even those few words on one random page, God can

and will reach them and show them His love. Some of their reactions to His Word will, therefore, noticeably show on their face or actions or through other behavior—(or not)."

Our personal "secret" project intent was really to, yet again, sow Gospel seeds and score more witnessing points.

We used the following method:

1. Walk around campus and select someone at random.

2. Hand the person either a Christian tract (with fairly tame language but still "Gospel-y"), or while the receiver looked on, tear a random page out of the New Testament paraphrase Bible, *Good News for Modern Man* (GNFMM).

3. Follow the person surreptitiously and discreetly for three minutes; if they got up and took the page with them, wherever they went, observe and record their behavior or reaction to the page (e.g., did they read it, put it in their pocket, look curious, wad it up and throw it away, give it to or show it to someone else, etc.?).

4. Switch roles from "hander-outer" to "observer-tracker." We did this with dozens of people.

On numerous occasions, people would be horrified that we were literally tearing a page out of a book.

"Why are you doing that?! What book is that?!"

"Because I want you to read it—it's the Bible."

"You can't (or shouldn't) tear pages out of the Bible!"

"Why, do you read or believe the Bible?"

The conversation would continue on from there—or not. All this went into our project data section and enabled us to prove our point that the Word of God is powerful, convicts of sin, and other stuff. We were on very shaky psychological and scientific ground, but for what it's worth, we got a C- for the project. The professor objected to our opening hypothesis. But what was quite cool, we actually discovered later—too late—that the publishers of the GNFMM made a version with perforated page edges.

CHAPTER TWENTY-TWO

The God Who Doesn't Leave You

Avril (Mills) Meeker, Cape Town

IT WAS SOME TIME IN 1971. *My sister, Jenny, and I met a girl who had got saved and baptized and invited us to one of the services at Harfield Road Assembly of God. We were really shocked to see hippies and people we knew there. Marge (Magic Marge) from Rhodesia who was from a Johannesburg club group was there, and there were quite a few of the hippies staying in Loader Street (upper Strand Street) in so-called condemned housing. Altogether, there were around 15 people, including my cousin David and his girlfriend.*

* * *

Marge (previously involved in the occult) was now a new Christian in the AOG and invited us to The Headquarters on Longmarket Street in Cape Town. On Monday nights, it was a Christian coffee bar. Jenny particularly was interested in going as the Six Days

War had just happened in Israel. She was very anxious about a prophecy that this event will lead to the Second Coming of the Lord and was really afraid of being left behind. She got saved that night.

At the time, I was dating a British boy who was about to embark on a trip through Africa. He warned me not to go to The Headquarters, which of course, me being me, made me all the more eager to go. I used to get terrible panic attacks and night tremors. My cousin, Dave, would watch over me during the night to make sure that I was all right. After some time, Dave's girlfriend didn't want him to look after me at night anymore. I was left alone with the constant panic attacks. I took out a Daily Light [Bible] that my mom had given me and read Psalm 121: "Your God doesn't slumber nor sleep ...." In my dream that night, I repeatedly said the name of Jesus, and I felt how He was washing me in love. All the darkness and moodiness were gone. It was like turning black to white.

One evening, the Vodka Queen of Cape Town (a former prostitute) was the speaker at The Headquarters. The love of Jesus just shone through her face. The reality of Jesus struck me like never before. This was in such contrast to the AOG who would talk about condemnation, hell, and sin. I really got saved that night (well, really, very strongly rededicated my life to Christ).

In those days, I can only describe my faith journey as a process and began to completely believe that God doesn't leave you. Pastor Paul Lange (Sunday communion at the AOG) had the gift of praying for the baptism in the Holy Spirit. That morning I received the baptism of the Holy Spirit, and it was as if the demonic raised its ugly head. The AOG didn't deal with deliverance, and it started feeling like God was peeling my mind back.

I was very shy, which was a huge front. I knew that I had to open up more and be authentic. I went to The Headquarters one lunchtime and asked Johnny Weber to pray for me because I thought I was losing my mind. God ministered to me through the Word and Johnny.

I had a dream that night where I saw myself wrapped up in bandages, completely bound. God started pulling them off, actually ripping them off. I knew I was being delivered. When I woke up, I felt this dream to be very real. I heard God saying: "You will hear a voice—this is the Way, walk in it."

During communion one Sunday, soon after, a woman laid hands on me saying: "You will hear a voice—this is the Way, walk in it."

* * *

I have fond memories of Dave Lutes' *kombi (Afrikaans – "van")* and going to youth meetings and outreach to Somerset West. Bernie Auditore was also a big part of this in those days. Dave and he shared an apartment, I think. There would be prayer when the girls were picked up, and the glory of God just filled the kombi. Sometimes we had to agree not to pray, otherwise it would continue for a long time—the kombi literally shaking as we were praying, singing, and worshipping.

One time, Dave [Lutes] was running late picking everyone up and getting to Somerset West on time to open the coffee bar outreach. We started normally at 7:00 p.m. It was now 6:45 p.m. As we started out from Observatory (about 41km/25 miles), we started to worship and praying in tongues (and English).

Absolutely true, God's glory filled the kombi. We sailed; we floated or glided. Dinkum truth, we arrived at 6:55 p.m. Some people got saved that night.

– Avril Mills Meeker, 2020

* * *

Another Account from Bernie Auditore About the Kombi:

We had some amazing experiences … This might be out of context, but Dave, myself, Avril, and her sister Jenny, we used to go down to Somerset West every Friday night, and we had a funny little place called the August Moon Coffee Shop, and we used to put out all the chairs, and we used to share Jesus, and people would come in and listen. It was like our little outreach; it was before an AOG was fully established in Somerset West.

I used to invite people to come out from Cape Town, and some actually did; some nice-looking birds from the recording industry came out one night. We really shared with them there, but one night, we were going home, and we used to go in Dave's kombi, and it was great. The girls used to sit in the back, and the boys in the front, and we used to sing and talk and joke, pray, and had wonderful fellowship in that kombi.

And that night we went home, and the Lord came into the kombi. We had to go and drop Avril and Jenny at their house. They were staying with their mum in Plumstead, and instead of driving into Avril's gate, we drove into the neighbour's gate, and we landed up in his garden, parked just under his bedroom window. So, I said, "Don't worry. Let's only start the car again

138

when we leave; we might wake the neighbour up. Let's just have a little prayer and thank God for tonight."

And I remember saying, "Lord, thank you so much for your favour ...," and as I said that, the Holy Spirit just came into the kombi, and we started praising God and worshipping God and hollering and speaking in tongues and shouting "Hallelujah!"

And at the time I thought, *I wonder what* (and Avril said, "These people here are spiritualists") *they were thinking in their beds, all huddled up, and a kombi full of loud, mad Pentecostals shouting "Hallelujah" and worshipping the Lord.* I've often thought, *Lord, how does your Holy Spirit work where suddenly His presence, you know, boom, it makes a difference?* Good things like that, we really had some wonderful times.

But you know, we were also quite stupid. I remember reading a Brother Andrew book, and he had a poster of somewhere in communist Russia where he wrote, "My God's Not Dead—Sorry About Yours." So, I thought, *What a cool saying.* I made a big poster up like that, and I stuck it at the back of Dave's kombi. Do you remember that, Dave? And we went to The Headquarters. We parked it, and some guys came in very irritated and said, "Oh, what's this?" They wanted to pull it off, and I said, "Hey, that's my sign. You don't touch it, and you're not pulling it off."

Anyway, they started gobbing off about it, and I think we basically told them, "Look, it's toughies, the sign's staying, and if you don't like it, you can just take a hike." But we cruised around with that sign for a while. And you know, I was thinking the other day, would I put that on my suitcase today and walk through an airport? And I thought, *Hmm, probably not.*

– Bernie Auditore, December 2021

CHAPTER TWENTY-THREE

The Conform or Be Cool Dilemma

LOOKING BACK NOW, I think that we (hippies and nonhippies/ unchurched alike) were constantly tiptoeing carefully along and testing the boundary line between our new freedom in Christ and in the Spirit and the Assembly's nudging us toward its brand of legalism, performance-based holiness, and meeting attendance-based spirituality.

At the same time, we were navigating the minefields of temptation, raging hormones, career planning, jobs (or not), paying rent, values adjustment, the stripping off the old, and discovering how to apply Christian "stuff" in our new, less than normal and imperfect lives.

For me at least, in those days, the spirituality thermometer—a health and pulse test, really—was faithful attendance at and participation in a minimum of eight—**count them, eight**—meetings of some form or other per week!

* * *

A lighthearted example I remember so well was that ill at ease "if I could just quietly sneak out the back door" feeling of having fallen short of the meeting performance standard—when I hadn't said anything during open ministry in the Breaking of Bread (prayed, preached, tongues, or shared a testimony or something) on any given Sunday. Dear ol' Brother (Elder) Swanapoel would nab me at the door asking, "Were you in the meeting this morning, brother?"

Looking back, it was an interesting contradiction—for me at least. On the one hand, because of the absolute certainty with which Brother Bond and other leaders taught the truth of the Bible, I almost felt it was a sinful lack of submission, or woe-betide-me unbelief, if I questioned them—even thought it.

On the other hand, it secretly troubled me that I don't think I ever heard, *not once that I can recall*, any teacher among the local or national leaders ever say, **"I don't know; I'm not sure"** or that there **"could possibly be equally and otherwise true and legitimate ways of looking at or interpreting a portion of Scripture."**

Looking back, putting Scripture in its historical context was hard to come by. If I'm honest, it seemed as if to do so somehow made the Word too "un-powerfully" down-to-earth; or somehow robbed the Gospel of its effectiveness. This dynamic brought with it a rock-solid, and at the same time, extremely shaky foundation. There was a lot of encouragement to read, learn, inwardly digest, and hear from God new insights and revelations—as long as it was doctrinally agreeable—even when the verse was about something we really knew very little about historically or experientially.

A case in point would be the Word of Knowledge (one of the Twelve Gifts in 1 Cor. 12). I never witnessed one and never heard it explained with the Bible, plus practical examples—*not once*. It seemed like a big deal to me, not least because we were a Pentecostal church that believed in "The Gifts" and that God did miracles today by the power of the Holy Spirit in the name of Jesus!

Genuine questioning and truth-seeking was characterized more as unbelief, and Hebrews 11:6 was almost translated and interpreted as, "Without utter acceptance of what you are taught here, it is impossible to please God. Trust us; we know what's good and best for you." There was a sense of, and probably a need for, trying to rein in the free spirit and un-and irreligious exuberance of that time. But for the AOG and other leaders in the Cape, I think it was sort of like lassoing smoke. We were living in and on the edge of incredibly exciting times; energy and emotion and exuberance were standard fare. They couldn't allow it to get out of control. I get and respect that.

The list of memorable, truly historic, and life-changing events seems endless in my mind: the "Give God a Chance" campaign, the Nicky Cruz rally, YFC, and other rallies. We didn't live and survive spiritually because of these high points (unlike, it seems, the highly event, program, and celebrity-focused standard fare of church life today). These events were momentum creators for lives already on the move for and journeying with God. I remember Pastor Noel Cromhout at Harfield Road Assembly of God saying so often, ***"It's easier to cool down a fanatic than to warm up a corpse."***

No wonder Noel looked exhausted!

* * *

In those days, we didn't really try to explain it or theologize it, we just believed it. These days, 50+ years later, I would call it well-meaning but immature Christian presumption and an undisciplined, disorganized new life—on fire but not up in flames. At that time, ***God just was.*** That was good enough for us! Better than enough.

We just did our thing—believing more than hoping—that it was also His thing. He was on our side, and we were on His. Simple but incredibly exciting times. I've thought about it many, many times over the years. If there was such a thing as spiritual adrenaline, then we were high on it in those days—continuously it seemed.

We hadn't yet adopted the perspective that was common in the more balanced and conservatively theological circles: *facts, faith, feelings* and *only in that order.* We got that message, sort of … but when you think about it, here many of us were, going down the road to hell, completely screwed up, totally offtrack, trapped, addicted, and compelled by forces inside and outside ourselves, and *God confronted us and grabbed us!*

He dragged us from our perches, wrestled us to the ground, or pulled us out of the toilet, looked us in the eyes, and told us He loved us and not only that He could, but wanted to and would change us. Forever.

It was an off-the-charts experience, and the feelings of wonder, relief, curiosity, hope, and excitement were all bundled together.

He changed my life!

He did it!

MY life—can you believe it—me?! The feelings were and still are real!

So, of course He can do, wants to do, will *do miracles today!*

* * *

Were we always walking and living morally and ethically and in the Spirit?

No way!

Did we glorify Him in all we said and did?

Not a chance; not even close!

143

Were we actually hurting, struggling, doubting, and crippled secretly inside or in a constant, repetitive cycle of repentance, forgiveness, and trying again? *I know I was.*

> *"Thank you, Lord, for Noel and Merle Cromhout and people like Faans Klopper and Dave Valentine who so patiently and wisely shepherded and anchored us in those days of searching and struggle!"*

Later in life, when I became a youth pastor, and then, a "real" pastor, I had dozens of hormone-laden, confused, troubled and emotionally mercurial young adults and teens under my care. I had to make sure that I didn't pin my own happiness and sense of peace to theirs, or I would have been in a permanently depressed state—at minimum, in therapy. The good news, I suppose, for them was that I remembered what it was like when I was where they were.

* * *

Excerpt from Pastor John "Brother" Bond:

[In 1970] God visited the congregation with a very blessed revival. I feel privileged to have been involved in such a move of God, but I must be the first to confess that it was not my preaching, leadership, or spiritual gifts that brought it about. Essentially, it was a sovereign work of the Holy Spirit. My greatest achievement was to fit in with what God was doing and to cooperate by prayer and preaching and by trying to be obedient to what I saw the Lord wanted me to do and say.

The time came when the place was packed with people. We called it the "Hippie Revival." They sat in the aisles, about the platform, and crowded around the doorways. A visitor once described it as "wall-to-wall people." For about two years, there was not a Sunday when there were no decisions recorded. Sometimes there were as many as 20. Four or five were thought of as just a few.

The whole of Cape Town was moved by the revival at Harfield Road. The blessing passed from us to other churches as their members came to see, got saved, and were filled with the Spirit, speaking in tongues. We never tried to proselytize or persuade the converts to stay as members of our church. Many of them returned to their own churches, full of fire. Even the University of Cape Town was touched through our young people conducting meetings on the campus.

— Pastor John Bond, 1978

CHAPTER TWENTY-FOUR

God Just Was

WE SAW EVERY SPECIAL, COINCIDENTAL TIMING as a sign of God being active and orchestrating our lives constantly, proactively, purposefully. There were times when it seemed as if we were the only people He was working with, spending time with, interested in. WE were what God was doing in the early seventies. We read and heard about other shows in town, but we felt we were really part of the unique purpose of God, and we were gripped with a fever of anticipation of God's continued, and more amazing, working—*nervous, excited, expectant, believing and trusting anticipation!*

* * *

Studies, work, family, and thoughts of marriage or ministry all crowded into many a long conversation and sleepless night. So many of us were a real mess with our struggling romances and relationships and our hearts toward God while our hormones bounced around, while searching for careers and feeling the tug of God's calling.

If I had a buck for every time any one of us talked about going full-time (in ministry), I could have retired long ago! We thought doing so was the ultimate career and life goal. It really bugged me to no end when preachers reminded me that David didn't become king, and Jesus didn't begin His ministry until around the age of 30+.

Wait until I am 30?! Are you kidding me?! There was NO WAY I could wait that long!

At that time, we were discovering an overwhelming desire to be part of something eternal, to give our lives for something that would last forever. Sink or swim, we were poised to step out of any boat that He put us in or called us to climb out of. Guidance was a tricky business, and being led was hardly certain, but we nonetheless expected Him and trusted Him to be there to pull us out soaking wet and take us by the hand and to direct and guide and love us to a place where we could sing the walk-on-water tune again—complete with a collection of "Sorry, Lords" and "Praise the Lords." We knew for sure that there was no other life worth living, no other swim worth attempting; drowning didn't enter our heads!

Boldness is the word that characterized our lives in those days. Some church leaders would describe it as undisciplined, reckless, theologically cringeworthy, and even a flash in the pan fad laced with enthusiasm on steroids. We called it "being bold for Jesus."

* * *

But Then, Baseball ...

When I wasn't working a job to pay for rent and gas, or doing outreach, attending church meetings, or doing other Christian stuff, I of course played baseball. I had never had God on the field, on the pitcher's mound, or in any way with me before when I played ball. I didn't really know if He approved of it. I never really thought about it in those terms. I wanted to honor my family's sacrifices over the years in support of my sporting life and to honor Him with that ability while participating in the war between ego, fame, personal choices, and God-blessed excellence. He had wonderfully healed my pitching arm as encouragement that He was involved. I even prayed between pitches— nearly every pitch—during the game!

I didn't pray that He would help me beat the other team or that I would throw a perfect strike, but rather that my effort, my place, and my status in the sports community would be the best it could be; simply, that I would honor God there and then. He was there with me, active and engaged, even in that aspect of my life. I believed it more and more. I wanted it! But I was completely surprised by it at the same time.

Not that I didn't enjoy seeing my name or photo in the sports section of the *Cape Times* or *The Argus*—even *Die Burger*. That was quite cool. I remember once, when visiting a home for my job where the young kid in the family who played Little League asked me to give him six autographs, which he sold to friends later. I should have asked for commission.

At 19 years old, it's hard for the ol' ego not to be affected. I remember a Christian umpire pulling me aside once after a game, which we won (not that it mattered, of course ... of course) and asking me if I was speaking in tongues between pitches (which I was) and if that was why my curve ball was so good that day.

As you know, a few things happened about the same time in the spring-summer period of 1971 (Southern Hemisphere). Brian Helsby, then a leader in of Cape Town YFC, interviewed me and wrote a story about me in *IN Magazine* (Chapter 10). As a result of that story, I became known as "The Christian Baseball Player." At the same time, I was staying with the coach of the VOB baseball team.

A neighbor who drove me to my job each day at the Old Mutual in Pinelands turned out to be a Christian who knew other Christians at the company, including one of the most prominent, larger-than-life umpires in the baseball league, Alex "Husky" Hutchison.

Husky really knew how to talk about, well, almost everything, including me. (Husky was the umpire who asked me if I was speaking in tongues between pitches.) So, unsought-after fame was the result of knowing Husky, along with a certain standard of play and sportsmanship and all eyes watching me for sinful slipups.

* * *

Two challenges when playing the game:

1. When a pitcher (me) had an opposing player on third base and that guy, along with the batter, attempted a suicide squeeze (Google it), my job was to hit the batter deliberately (often with a fastball), thus creating a dead ball situation. The batter went to first base, sure, but the runner had to return to third base. No run scored, and it also created other ways to get players out without run scoring damage. When I hit a batter in that situation, I would get cheers for being a smart, good Christian and honorable team player and sportsman from my team and bench—and boos and hisses from the opposing bench, along

with, "You call yourself a Christian!?" (They must have been the **Goodwood *Demons!*)

2. If I was on first base (which didn't happen often), and the ball was hit to the infield for a possible double play, my job would be to deliberately slide into the fielder who was trying to convert the double play at second base and disrupt the play, sometimes actually knocking the fielder down or maybe even hurting him. Again, "Yea!" and "Boo, Hiss!" plus the rest of the comments that, eventually, came with the new Christian territory I was journeying through.

* * *

Conversation with Bernie Auditore

Sanet: Bernie, is there anything you'd like to add regarding your relationship with Dave?

Bernie: Yes, I want to tell you a funny story. Dave starts talking to me about baseball. He was like a real hotshot star. I was just some back-street motorbike rider with a leather jacket and riding down the road with just—on a Saturday night to irritate police, but here this dude comes to teach our Springboks how to play baseball.

So, I'm talking to him one day—now in our country, only the girls played rounders. And I thought, *What would a boy want to play rounders for?* So, he starts telling me about baseball. I knew nothing because from the British colonies, we didn't play baseball, we played cricket—cucumber sandwiches and gin and tonic. So, he tells me his thing is he can throw a ball. I thought, *Ja, anyone can throw a ball. I can throw a rock, you know.* So, he said if he really got a good one, he can throw a ball at 100 miles an hour. So, I said, "Let's go downstairs, and you throw a couple of balls to me, and I want to see if I can hit them." Maybe I could be a baseball batter.

So, we go downstairs, and he marks out this area; they don't have wickets in baseball, so I don't know what they call it. So, he says, "You reckon you're going to knock this ball into the middle of next week, but I'll be kind to you. Let's start off with a tennis ball and see how you do with that." So, I stand with the bat, ready, and all I hear is a noise like a bullet going past me. He said, "Strike one." I said, "I wasn't ready." So, we go again. I have fast reactions. Even when I boxed and did martial arts, one of the strange things was that I had remarkably quick reactions. Second ball, the same thing.

So, I said, "David, for the third ball, try and hit the bat." He threw it, and I missed. He can throw a ball. I said, "OK, you've proved your point." I've told many people about my short tryout for American professional baseball league—I didn't get very far.

– Bernie Auditore
with Dave Lutes and Sanet Stander, 2021

* * *

Excerpt from Dave Valentine – "Give God a Chance" Campaign:

The One Way Inn was the meeting place for the "Give God a Chance" committee, also called the Narnia Committee. One evening, we were all gathered at someone's flat. The ladies challenged the men to do more and seek God for a vision. Brian

O'Donnell, Chrisman Stander, Mike Coleman, Johnny Weber, Bernie Auditore, and I'm all newly baptised in the Holy Spirit and not very confident yet, decided to wait upon the Lord in another room. Brian brought a tongue, and I interpreted, "You are all wanting more power, but you have received all the power you need when you were baptised in the Holy Spirit." They were not convinced and asked for confirmation. Then Bernie started seeing a vision: "I'm in a desert and looking for water all over the place then suddenly see that the water is at my feet!"

Then Brian said, "I had a dream last night.... We were all marching with armbands reading 'Give God a Chance.'" At this time of global political upheaval, the war in Vietnam and the struggle in South Africa, hippies were proclaiming "Give love a chance," and we felt that this was our opportunity to proclaim to Cape Town to "Give God a Chance."

– Dave Valentine, 1985

* * *

My Personal Note

I'm not sure Brian O'Donnell will appreciate me sharing this. He may even deny it. I was by no means and in no way a hippie, and I'm sure no one in The Market or The Headquarters saw me like that. I did, however, visit The Market on Loop Street from time to time, not least to connect with brothers and sisters I had come to know, to hang out with Brian who I had come to greatly respect, and to learn what all this beads and incense thing was about.

There was a café spot on the top floor with menus, waitresses, etc. Some non hippie-type visitors were giving the cute waitresses a hard time—teasing, saying inappropriate things, etc. Brian approached them and said something like, "Hey, stop hassling the sisters or leave!"

They didn't stop, so Brian came again and nearly forcibly escorted them from the café. A few minutes later, Brian looked out the window and saw on the street below the same guys continuing to mock, tease, and generally cause a problem, especially with other "sisters" who were there or entering. I watched from the window as Brian approached the leader and said, "I told you to stop hassling the sisters. In Jesus' name …"

And he hit the guy in the face with his fist.

I may have got some of the details wrong, and my Kingdom values and perspective may have also taken a hit that day, but I know I didn't dream it and will always remember it.

* * *

Excerpt from Faans "Brother" Klopper:

(The Beginnings at Harfield Road, Kenilworth, Assembly of God)

Then the hippies came; the Assembly was in a state of shock—their dress, or lack of it, their spontaneous behaviour, their expressive language, some young men with hair reaching far down their backs.

The Elders met. Brother Bond presented the request of the hippies to fellowship with us. Objections were raised: "What about our children? What if they introduce drugs? Etc." A Word of Wisdom followed: "Brethren, what are we here for?" End of discussion but requested that on Sunday mornings they respect us and come cleaned up. On Sunday night, come as you are.

Harfield Road experienced a mini-explosion in numbers. I remember one Sunday night when some 40 followed the Lord through the waters of baptism.

A nightclub in Cape Town became an outreach for the Kingdom of God so did Brian O'Donnell's "Hippie Market." It was not long before a venue was sought in Cape Town for meetings; an upstairs space above a secondhand car dealer in Long Street was hired for midweek meetings. Later, the group meeting there was accommodated in the Presbyterian Church. The work there grew and became the Assembly of God in Sea Point.

The Spirit of God was also at work in Stellenbosch.

A report appeared in the Sunday Times, expressing concern regarding the students, some Dutch Reform Church Theological students, that were being caught up in this Jesus Revolution. We later ministered there, and an Assembly was subsequently established.

In Meadowridge (Southern Suburbs, Cape), a couple became burdened for the young people and got a number of local churches to support a coffee bar. They rented an upstairs room in a shopping complex. The supporting churches cooperated with speakers and funds.

With young people beginning to speak in other tongues, opposition came, but the work grew. With Harfield Road overflowing, the Library Hall in Meadowridge was hired. This was just opposite the "Upper Room," and soon the young people were absorbed in the newly formed Assembly.

– Faans Klopper, 1982

CHAPTER TWENTY-FIVE

Where He Leads Me, I Will ... Glug, Glug, Glug

THE FOLLOWING STORY GOT TOLD, retold, and probably embellished, many times over at youth and other church events back in the day. Looking far to the Northeast in South Africa, at an Assembly of God Church in the Transvaal (back when it was called that), believer's baptisms were scheduled at a nearby river after the morning Breaking of Bread service. An all-afternoon affair, a group met for a picnic, and after eating and a time of fellowship, the baptismal candidates emerged from a tent in long, white nightdress-type clothes. The pastor (John S.) shared a brief word about dying to self, burying the old man through baptism, and being raised up as a new creation in Christ, etc.

Each of the candidates were then asked to share a brief testimony about their conversion and personal journey leading to commitment to Jesus. When they were finished, Pastor John went down the riverbank into the river, which was flowing a little too swiftly for his liking. He decided to go in just deep enough to barely be able to fully immerse each person.

The first five people entered the water; he briefly explained to each that they should hold their nose and he would place his hand over theirs —together squeezing their nose and mouth shut—then he would place his hand on their back between their shoulders, and they should trust him and lean (fall) backward. *("Keep holding your nose tight, sister! Keep your mouth closed, brother! I'm holding your hand, too! I've got you!")*

"Upon your confession of faith in our Lord Jesus Christ, I baptize you in the name of the Father, the Son, and the HOLY Ghost!"

He would guide them fully under the water, burying the "old man" and raising up the "new man." Then he would help them up, standing on their feet. They would then move toward the riverbank, smiling, crying, and laughing as they got out of the river to the sound of "Hallelujah," "Praise the Lord," and the group singing, note swooping, and scooping a well-known ol' time Gospel chorus—on this occasion, "Where He Leads Me, I Will Follow."

The final candidate was a rather big, no ... a very substantial, very large woman. He explained the practicalities, the mechanics, and the ritual routine. She clutched her nose, he clasped his hand over hers, and he said the baptismal words, "I baptize you in the name—*oops!*" Because of the unanticipated extra weight, they both staggered and stumbled backward. Pastor John, trying to maintain his balance, stepped, as it turns out, straight into a deep gully with a much more swiftly moving current.

Now, they were both completely underwater and were being carried along, only their clasped hands sticking out above the water—floating, drifting, and flowing together—like a hands-shaped periscope.

Unfazed and right on cue, the group on the bank sprang into action —not rushing into the river to help, but rather walking slowly along the shore together, watching the floating hands without a hint of panic, not missing a beat, and singing, "Where He Leads Me, I Will Follow."

CHAPTER TWENTY-SIX

The Sound of Spit and Grace

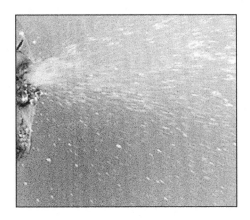

AS A YOUNG, SINGLE GUY IN THE ASSEMBLIES OF GOD, as you know, I was very much concerned about my Christian—my spiritual—performance. Attendance at meetings, speaking out in public gatherings, handing out Bible or Christian tracts on the street, witnessing to people, doing my own devotions faithfully and intensely every day, praying for a certain length of time, and memorizing and quoting King James Bible texts like a parrot, were all part of my spiritual thermometer.

Participating in a visibly active way, taking the initiative, tirelessly discussing Evangelical beliefs and rhetoric, and obeying the rules [e.g., no smoking, no drinking, no swearing, no sexing, no dancing, no Beatles, and no bioskop *(Afrikaans – "cinema, movies")*] were all part of the formula for holiness and spirituality as mandated by the leaders of the church.

I was utterly sincere, and I very much wanted to be truly committed. In my heart, I wanted this output to be really Christian, and I would do whatever it took to keep the new spiritual law (although I would have never called it that, since we are saved by Grace through faith and not by keeping any kind of law). Subtly, maybe secretly, I really wanted others to see that I was a young man of God who was destined for full-time ministry.

Attendance at 8–12 meetings per week was something that was important to me. Added to this was a subtle attendance and participation pressure from the leadership, which acted as a burden of sorts placed on our backs as a form confirmation of our commitment to heart-filled walking and living in the Spirit.

Here's what my self-compulsory typical week looked like:

- Saturday morning—handing out Bible tracts and preaching on the street corners in the local shopping area.

- Saturday afternoon—playing a baseball game (sometimes in another suburb).

- Saturday nights—leading or attending church senior youth group.

- Sunday morning—attending Breaking of Bread (communion service) with open ministry opportunities, testifying, speaking in tongues, enthusiastically saying "Amen"—all lasting up to two and a half hours sometimes.

- Sunday afternoon—meeting with other young people at the pastor's house (and a free lunch!).

- Pre-Sunday evening Gospel service—praying and prepping pre-service.

- Sunday evening—participating in the Gospel service (maybe singing in a group).

- Immediately post-Gospel service—meeting for counseling or coffee, witnessing to visitors or meeting with leaders to talk about the day's or week's Gospel "successes."

- Later post-Gospel Service—taking girlfriend back to her school boarding house.

- Monday—working a job or studying (and day off).

- Tuesday—practicing baseball until 7:00 p.m., then traveling with the pastor (John "Brother" Bond) to Somerset West, about twenty-five miles from Cape Town, to help support the outreach for and the establishment of a young new church.

- Wednesday—participating in pre-Bible study prayer meeting, Bible study, post-Bible study prayer for others or hyper-spiritual discussion with other young aspiring, single men of God.

- Thursday night 1—practicing baseball.

- Thursday night 2—meeting at The Hippie Market or The Headquarters.

- Friday night—attending AOG prayer meeting.

- Saturday—meeting at The Headquarters or lather, rinse, repeat the previous Saturday's activities.

If the film *Groundhog Day* had been out in those days, I would have rivalled Bill Murray.

* * *

In the middle of all of this, I began to speak at numerous Youth for Christ or Student Christian Association (SCA) rallies or groups, youth camps, youth clubs, etc. and worked a day job or studied.

> *I mention all this again because, to put it mildly, I was eager, opinionated, King James Bible-quotey, and high on in-your-face, intense Holy Ghost adrenaline. Oh, and of course, I was absolutely and always right—even about the things I knew nothing about. But to be honest, I was utterly sincere and convinced it was the right way to live my life. The was nothing fake or phony about it all—intense, yes—but absolutely sincere.*

* * *

One Saturday morning, six or seven of us had gathered on the train station platform in a suburb of Cape Town called Wynberg. Our task for that morning was to hand out tracts and invitations for a special church service that was coming up on the following weekend in the adjacent suburb, Kenilworth. When the trains pulled up along the platform, we would hand out tracts and invitations to people through the train windows to those who were continuing their trip. We also did the same for those getting off the train there. Big smile, big smile ... *Praise the Lord!*

Leading the team was a married couple, Riaan and Margie (pseudonyms), who were notable because we, our group, hung out with very few married couples. They didn't really attend our young adult group, but they wanted to support us in the advertising and the promotion of the forthcoming event the following weekend.

As they spoke Afrikaans, they helped at the tail end of the train where the cars were exclusively for so-called "Coloreds" who generally (as far as I knew as a fairly clueless American) spoke Afrikaans. Our services were "officially" open to anyone, and we wanted to give invitations to people in the area from all races and backgrounds. That said, we were all **very** white, and we didn't have a single non-white attending our services normally. That would have been against the law, I think (actually, I'm not really sure) or at least very awkward or uncomfortable on both sides.

This activity at the train station was rare but sincere—or maybe it was a token exercise where we symbolically declared all people equal under God. We said it, but I'm not sure we really believed it. After all, government policy said "non-whites" must live in a different area, and *we* must obey the government (as per Romans 13:1-5).

* * *

Here I was, very much into thrusting as many tracts or invitations through the windows as quickly as I could, trying to smile sincerely and spiritually. But to be honest, for me, it was more about the number of tracts and how aggressively (sorry, I meant enthusiastically) I could hand them out "In the name of the Lord!" *("Take it you sinner!")*. It was very unloving, but utterly sincere, and at least I was being seen to be active and committed, and that's all that mattered. I could repent of this attitude later. That said, I really **did** want people to come to meetings, come forward and be saved, and you could count on it that if they walked down the salvation aisle, I would know the exact number that did!

After an hour or so, Riaan was standing very close to the edge of the platform waiting smilingly for an approaching train. As it stopped, a guy pushed down the window, cleared his throat, and spat directly into Riaan's face. Then he put the window back up as the train pulled away.

When I saw this, I speed-boiled to livid!

I wanted to reach through the window, grab the guy, drag him onto the platform, and beat him senseless or throw him onto the tracks (in the name of the Lord, of course). It so incensed me that this surely damned sinner didn't appreciate the good Christian work that we were doing in trying to invite him, a "Colored" guy nonetheless, to one of our services or events.

Riaan, on the other hand, with spittle running down his face, threw his hands in the air and began to worship in Afrikaans (roughly translated as follows): "Thank you, Jesus, for the privilege and honor of having spit on my face. Thank you, Jesus, that you were spat upon and that you were beaten beyond recognition. Thank you, Jesus, for the honor and the privilege of being able to suffer even just a little bit for You. Please bless that guy! Please bless him and call him to Yourself. Let him see Your Light and Your love."

While he stood with his hands in the air and his eyes closed, worshipping, Margie, his wife, strolled over with a handkerchief. Calmly and slowly, without any comment, without any concern, she wiped off the spittle. Then they both stood there waiting for the next train as if nothing had happened.

The anger knot in my stomach turned sour. The heat on my shamed, red face could have fried an egg.

For the rest of that day, and for several days following, His hidden" message began to sink in as I reflected on my very immature spiritual attitude, one of the thousand or so times that He tried to help me see it.

And God said, "Grow up, Davie Boy, and grow up quick! Understand that all this, this finding lost people and calling them to Myself, is not about you. This is not about your work and your service and your effort and your obsessive determination to prove to Me that you're worthy of My love.

"This is about being safe and secure in my Grace and Mercy. I save, you don't. Davie, Little Boetie, you've got a long way to go; you've got a very long and painful road ahead of you, especially if you think you need to build the road by your own effort before you are worthy of

163

walking on it; or worse, **as** you're walking on it. Maybe someday you will have the privilege to hear and experience for yourself the sound of spit and Grace." (Love, Father)

* * *

Earshotting

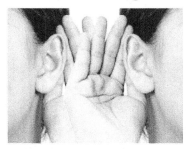

We were consumed with the desire and need to witness about Jesus wherever we went and whenever we went there. Every person who crossed our paths was a potential soul to be saved. Every regular or unexpected meeting or visit to the shop or school or on the train were all opportunities to speak for Jesus. *It's just the way it was—a way of life*. It was an expected, privileged and joyful norm of behavior. We believed God orchestrated and ordained meetings with people for the express purpose of them meeting Him through the words we shared and the prayers we prayed.

We were always trying to come up with new and different ways to make contact and tell our stories or to pique interest. For me, personally, as I have said before, it was also about me notching up marks on my Gospel sword handle—the more people you tell (keeping score), the more people will be saved—and the more God is pleased. Of course, He would be!

Pauline and Debbie used to ride on the train to and from school or from home to Cape Town almost daily. The trains were usually full, people sitting and standing, at the times they rode. They began to use a technique for witnessing that makes me smile even today. I called the technique, then and now, *"Earshotting,"*—defined as speaking within *earshot* of others so they can hear what you're saying and setting up any hearers with a series of questions and answers that made (scored) particular listening points.

One of them would be the *witnesser* and the other the *witnessee.* The witnessee might start the conversation with, "You know what you were telling me the other day about Jesus and how it's not enough for me to just go to church or read my Bible sometimes or be a good person? But that I need to make a personal choice to ask Him into my heart—that I must do it myself and cannot have a secondhand faith? I'm not sure I know what it means, and I'm also a little scared I might not do it right. Can you tell me more please? I think I really want to have what you have."

Then the witnesser would give the perfectly scripted answer to which the witnessee would say, "Wow! That makes so much sense! You're saying that He loves everyone—EVERYONE—the same and that He came to earth to show us His love and then died on the cross for our sins, MY sins?!"

Or the witnessee would argue a point, and the witnesser would give the perfect answer, which the other person would acknowledge as being insightful, helpful, and right. You get the idea.

The conversation would go back and forth like that for a while with the right questions, the perfect answers, and the right level of honesty and sincerity—all while others **within earshot** overheard. On the next trip, they would change cars and swap roles. There's a hint of manipulation and deception about it, I know. But reaching others, using any means possible, was our calling and life's drumbeat.

CHAPTER TWENTY-SEVEN

If You Don't Learn to Pray,
I ... Will ... Shut ... You ... Up
The Rees Howells Principle

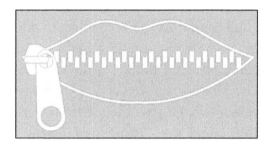

IN THE 1ST GRADE, back in my hometown of Trumansburg, New York, the teacher would put topics into a hat. We would draw one out and then speak on the subject spontaneously for two minutes without stopping. This was standard, and we got used to doing this. For me, I was like a piglet in mud. When I was in the 3rd grade (8 years old), I was in a high school play, and guess what?! Surprise, surprise! *I loved it!*

When I was a student at University of Cape Town (1973), though, I was very challenged about learning how to pray better, deeper, and more meaningfully with more authenticity—in secret and out of the limelight. How and why it became *the thing* in my life, I can't remember. This much I knew; I knew I needed to grow up and discover that prayer was less about giving God a shopping list and more about being available and opening my heart up, being vulnerable and learning from Him in the quiet place. I loved the noise and public things. Applause, not prayer, was my battery charger. ***Quiet and solitude was not my bag at all!***

There were people within the church who I respected greatly, and I suspected were people of "real" prayer. But to be honest, it sounded an awful lot like hard work to be really praying for so long and so deeply, whatever that might mean.

I, along with other young men and women from the young adult group, would attend the all-night prayer meetings from time to time, which was more about clocking in and being seen than really praying— whatever *really* praying meant. To be totally honest, and in ***my opinion only***, those prayer meetings were as often as not an attempt by the hyper spiritual folks to show off their ability to pray very, very long-winded theological prayers—on their knees, nonetheless—or endlessly speaking in tongues.

"Heck sister, He heard you the first time! Besides, He knew what you were going to ask or say before you said it ... 10 times! Sheesh!"

So, when I began this new phase of prayer discovery, in my own foolish, impetuous way, I prayed this prayer:

"Lord, teach me how to pray—I mean, you know, like, really pray."

At that moment, the angels who overheard me, elbowed each other in the ribs and said to each other, smiling and chuckling, "Oh wow, watch this; this'll be fun!"

* * *

Now, I kid you not—really, really, I kid you not—this thought came into my head as I prayed that prayer: *Read Ezekiel 47*. I can't say it was a voice; I can't say it was a secret word. All I know is that Ezekiel 47 came to mind, and that I had no idea what was in Ezekiel 47. Thank God for the table of contents!

I looked up Ezekiel 47. The prophet describes a vision of a rising stream in the midst of the desert. Different stages and levels and depths are described there in good detail. It is a very, very colorful story. My quick interpretation was that it is a story of going deeper with God, resulting in the beginning of new life and a reborn and transformed world.

I read and reread, mused, and meditated. I dissected it for hidden meaning, but thankfully, never looked at a Bible commentary. Plain truth is, it nailed me between the eyes of my heart and reminded me very quickly, very easily, that I really knew nothing—nada—about the depths of prayer.

> *The man brought me back to the entrance to the temple, and I saw water coming out from under the threshold of the temple toward the east (for the temple faced east). The water was coming down from under the south side of the temple, south of the altar. He then brought me out through the north gate and led me around the outside to the outer gate facing east, and the water was trickling from the south side.*
>
> *As the man went eastward with a measuring line in his hand, he measured off a thousand cubits and then led me through water that was ankle-deep. He measured off another thousand cubits and led me through water that was knee-deep. He measured off another thousand and led me through water that was up to the waist. He measured off another thousand, but now it was a river that I could not cross, because the water had risen and was deep enough to swim in —a river that no one could cross.*
>
> *He asked me, "Son of man, do you see this?" (Ezek. 47:1–6)*
>
> *"Davie, read good, look good—do you see this?!"*

* * *

About the same time as this was going on, someone gave me a book. It was called *Reese Howells: Intercessor* by Norman Grubb (son-in-law to CT Studd). In the book, there is a principle, one important secret of prayer, that this well-known and highly respected man of God discovered for his own life.

Put simply and impolitely paraphrased by me: ***Don't pray for something, anything, unless you're prepared to get off your proverbial knees and butt and be an answer to your own prayer—at least be willing to try.***

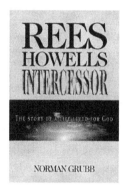

For example, don't pray for the peace of Israel if you're not prepared to go to Israel and help bring that peace.

Don't pray for someone who's sick; don't pray for someone who has a need for money; don't pray for somebody who's troubled or sad or having a difficult time, if you're not prepared to go and be part of the answer to that prayer.

* * *

Let me be blunt. That profound book ***nearly crippled me spiritually.*** I found that I was praying on one knee, as it were. When I put only one toe in the water, I felt like I was drowning. Why?

The message inside my head went something like this, *Davie, don't you even dare open your mouth for one moment, for one utterance, offer one prayer for others, or ask for anything if you aren't sincerely willing to be part of the answer to the prayer. Don't even think it.*

It wasn't about the content of the prayer. It was about sincere intent and true heart willingness. At first it seemed simple enough.

Don't say it or pray for it if you don't mean it.

The question that began to plague me was, if the heart of man is deceitful above all things and desperately wicked (Jer. 17:9), and I am a redeemed, but still, a fallen guy, is it even possible for anyone, much less me, to have a completely pure and sincere heart before God when I pray?

* * *

But Rees Howells took it to a whole new, painful level—don't say it if you don't mean it, and if you mean it, then do something about it. It wasn't about, "God helps those who help themselves, etc., etc." It was about, in a spiritual but practical sense, "Put your money where your prayer mouth is."

As a result, in my quest to learn to pray more and better and deeper, the reverse actually happened to me. I found that I couldn't pray—pretty much not at all! I struggled before I opened my mouth when I was kneeling before God, driving in my car, and even sitting in church.

My self-examination became extremely critical of my intent, reason, and motive, and all this became a blockage. To some extent, it was also a practical thing—if I prayed for my friend back in the US, or for so-and-so I met last week, do I need to jump on a plane or board a train to carry my part of God's answer to them? Because I was and am a performance-driven person with a tendency to measure success by whether I had reached the finish line in a certain way only, I struggled to know if I had arrived at that mystical place of better prayer. If ever I could ...

If this head-scratching, circular commentary is giving you a headache—welcome to my world!

* * *

All that said, what was going on was also a good thing, a healthy thing, spiritually. It felt like I was making progress, but I didn't really or totally understand what it meant or what was happening in me or what to do about it. I only knew that God had initiated this period and that I had begun to take steps in the right direction. I wanted to go with the "Ezekiel 47 Flow."

But I confess, it was also a painful process. I was a person of words —preferably public words—and lots of them. This wasn't going to be easy by any stretch.

Shortly after this, at the Breaking of Bread service, there was a visitor, a lady (Estelle F.). She was there for a couple of weeks and had a reputation for being something of a prophetess (public messages, not private predictions). I know this sounds weird to twenty-first century ears, but when she did give a public prophecy or an interpretation to someone's tongue, it was really good, in my opinion. It was very profound, very insightful, and very helpful. It wasn't so weird, wild, or woolly that you couldn't tune into the *heart of the theme* and apply it. What she shared was memorable and not easily—if ever—forgotten.

There was never a sense that she was making it up or had ever spoken it before, and it was always, well, a fresh blessing. To be a little negative for a moment, we were so used to vague, King James English-laden imagery about windy beaches and soaring eagles that she was a true inspirational breath of fresh air. Clearly, the leaders really respected her and welcomed her!

171

I sought her out privately in the pastor's house late one afternoon after church and asked for a private meeting.

She agreed, and when I sat with her later in the week, I told her about my Ezekiel 47 experience. I told her about the challenges going on in my life. I told her about my desire to serve God and honor God and to not only speak for Him but to also learn to pray better, more deeply, more sincerely, more powerfully. I didn't need to explain myself much. *She got me.* She listened to my heart and didn't give cheap formulaic answers. It was really cool.

I was about to tell her about my newest struggle (the Rees Howells Prayer Principle) when she stopped me and looked me straight in the eye.

"David, this is wonderful what God is calling you to do. It's not easy; it's very hard. It's a very difficult road to go down because it means brokenness and vulnerability. It means time alone, away from people. It means solitude. It means crossing a line from self to others. It means self-emptying. It may mean being misunderstood."

I was very much digging her! Well, sort of …

I mean, I was nodding my head like I knew what she meant, but at the same time, she was scaring me half to death because I loved the limelight. I loved standing up and teaching, sharing, and preaching. But I knew, really, I was not even ankle-deep in Ezekiel's water when it came to serious prayer. I had barely dipped my toe in the stream.

She continued, "David, as much as God is doing this for you right now, and I am thrilled for you, I also want to warn you and caution you very sincerely. Whatever you do, do not, I repeat, do NOT read the book *Rees Howells: Intercessor.* It will cripple you. You're not ready for it. Don't read that book."

As she said that, my heart sank, and I thought, *Oh God, I'm in trouble now. What have I done?!*

I didn't tell her that I was already reading the book; instead, I prayed with her, thanked her, and left ... shaken from heart down to my newly and sort of calloused knees and my only slightly wet toes.

* * *

In the days ahead and leading up to the following weekend when we had a youth retreat for a couple of nights at a camping site not far from Fish Hoek, Cape, I tried to avoid the subject with God.

As a poor student, I couldn't afford to pay to go to the whole retreat. I could be there during the day, and I could even stick around at night, but if I wanted to participate fully, I had to sleep in my car and bum food from others. My 1960 VW Beetle had a comfy reclining front seat, and I borrowed a sleeping bag; it doesn't get much better than that!

We did the usual events and fun stuff on Friday night, and then all-day Saturday there were a lot of activities, plus sharing, caring, and eating too much donated food (fortunately). I was quite good at, so it seems, walking around with a *I'm-a-poor-student-and-I-feel-led-that-you-should-give-me-some-of-your-food* look.

On Saturday evening, we had a time of open ministry; anyone could share, preach, encourage, or testify. I had prepared a short message, and at the appropriate time, I stood up to do my thing. My best friend, Vernon L., was there as well, and I noticed during my sharing that he was taking notes. For me to inspire Vern to take notes meant a lot to me. His level of intelligence and knowledge of the Bible blew anything I had to offer out of the water.

I felt good about what I shared. Added to this, it was kind of a build up to the next day because I had been asked by the pastor to share a short message specially on Sunday morning in a kind of keynote speaker slot—one of several others. I loved it!

Vernon came to me later that first evening during coffee and before I headed to my car to sleep. He had his notepad out, and as we sat alone in the corner, he opened it and proceeded to point out that I had:

1. Used a particular phrase 27 times ("… too repetitive … you should watch that in future …").

2. Misquoted several Bible passages.

3. Made my final, all-important concluding point quite poorly.

"Dave, did you pray about what you were going to share tonight?"

Ouch. "Yes, of course I did!" (Not.) I spiritually, and near literally, crawled back to my car.

Still stinging from what Vern had shared with me, I prayed, "Lord, please bless the word that I'm going to share tomorrow. Please bless the important study that I'm going to give."

But in the unspoken, secret place in my heart what I was really thinking was, *Please bless me as an amazing, outstanding, budding, public speaker who's going to wow the 100 or so teenagers and young adults who will be there. Help me be even more amazing than normal, Lord!*

Then that quiet, gentle voice—that still, small but very pointed voice—that I had begun to learn to hear a little bit better, whispered,

"Davie, if you don't learn to pray, I will shut you up."

Huh, what? Who said that?! Why would you say that?!

Now I was scared. I'd been avoiding this subject with God for days. I didn't sleep a wink. I didn't know what it completely meant, but I could guess, *and none of it was good*. I was completely befuddled and panicky about what the consequences of my speaking (or not) the next day might be.

If I had known what He actually had in mind, I would have

driven home then and there.

I arrived at the service the next morning, not sure what to do except keep my commitment to share with the group, as it was going to be one of three spiritual hors d'oeuvres of the morning. It was a real honor to be asked.

When I stood up and read the relevant portion from the Bible, I saw the excitement, interest, and enthusiasm on the face of the audience waiting to hear what I was going to share about that particular chunk of Scripture.

I'm psyched now!

But as I continued to speak, words began to stick in my throat ... Try again, repeat, clear throat, slight cough, clear! Try again ... nope, stuck.

Anyone in the room who understood, heard, or spoke Afrikaans knew that some letters had unusual, throaty sounds, especially to non-South African ears. Every time I tried to say a word that had a *g* or a *ch* in it, I got stuck and a guttural sound came out (imagine the noise you make before you clear your throat to spit. Sorry.). Nothing would follow. If I tried to complete the word, it broke into two pieces—throat mucus and a syllable.

It wasn't a stutter—no, it was throat clearing mucus "upping" followed by the rest of the word. We guys used to talk about this pre-spit action that we called *hoyking*, as in, to "hoyk up" phlegm. (I thought you'd like that! You're welcome.)

This happened with ANY English word with a *g* or *ch* sound—good, Gospel, God, church, glad, evangggggelism. You gggget the idea.

The more I tried to speak, the more embarrassing it became. I simply could not string sentences, phrases, or even a few words, together coherently.

Of course, by now I was getting a mental block (*Think before you speak, Davie; don't use words with "g"*). With my eyes and brow screwed up, I must have really been weird to watch and listen to.

Finally, after a very, very short time, I ended the talk and apologized, "I'm sorry. I'm havinggg some trouble; Gggggod bless you."

I sat down shamefaced. I wished the gggggground would open up and swallow me.

The whole rest of that day, when people wanted to have conversations with me, my *G*s and *CH*s would get stuck. When they talked to me about anything, including sports or baseball, it didn't matter, the *G*s and *CH*s would get stuck. Thank gggggoodness they didn't ask me about Paul's letter to the Ggggalations, the book of Ggggenesis, or the Gggreek translation of the Gggospel.

But if they had asked me about the time Jesus spat on the ground to make some clay to put on the blind man's eyes, I was very ready to, well, contribute.

Sunday night at the Gospel service back at the church, people talked with me, but I couldn't talk to them. I could only be silent, move my head appropriately, mumble mmmm-hmmm, and listen.

The next day at university, *G*s and *CH*s were still stuck. Come Tuesday, nothing had changed. I couldn't speak, I couldn't preach, I couldn't share, I couldn't witness. The only thing I could do was listen to that still small voice and to be quiet.

"Davie, if you don't learn to pray, I'm going to shut you up."

You're waiting for me to tell you what happened after that, aren't you? Right? How Dave Lutes disappeared into the wilderness to pray and then reemerged after several years with a mighty healing ministry, right?

You'll need to read the rest of this book and the follow-on sequel and companion volume (*Guidance, Goofs and More Grace*) to find out, and even then, you will see that it took me the better part of 15 more years to begin even a little bit to get the hang of the Rees Howells Principle.

CHAPTER TWENTY-EIGHT

The Hunger for Miracles – Part 1

OTHER THAN WHAT GOD HAD DONE IN MY OWN LIFE in touching my pitching arm with healing, I didn't really know what His miraculous intervention would or should look like. I was perpetually curious as to how I should, or could, expect to see a real, dinkum miracle.

Good Lord, how I wanted to see and be part of the real thing!

Depending on who was preaching or who you asked, coming up with a definition for a real miracle (method and result) was akin to trying to nail Jell-O (*South Africa/UK – "jelly"*) to a tree.

The most common miracle theme tune during those days and weeks of our lives were moments transformed by amazing timing and good feelings, and we loved listening to it. We created and re-created the miracle tune itself by learning to trust Him, falling flat on our faces, and getting up and trusting Him again, hymning as we went.

"Guidance, Goofs, and Grace" were the Top Three Tunes on our Hit Parade.

For me anyway, secretly, I had to be content with this substandard form of leading and guidance-type miracles. This deep, restless hunger to see God do stuff was no substitute for loving and enjoying the Word of God that was taking root in me. But I was so discontented about this miracle thing that it was really quite worrying.

The AOG leadership used to say, *"The Bible says it, I believe it, and that settles it!"* We said we believed in miracles, but in my mind, since they never happened, it was far from a settled truth.

That said, knowing that a train runs better on rails, I'm sure the AOG leaders saw a need for a dose of law as essential for helping the new Jesus people trains become the best trains we could be. We didn't need any more excitement and sensational moments in our lives. Control was needed, and I can see it was good and right—to a point.

Don't get me wrong, Brother Bond, Noel Cromhout, Jessop Sutton, Faans Klopper, Dave Valentine (all quoted in this book), and so many other leaders at the time loved, taught, sacrificed, discipled, and served us so faithfully in the Lord and laid such a sure foundation in our lives that it will certainly stand the eternal test of time.

> *But, I wish someone in leadership would have said—just once — "I don't know; I don't really know what that verse means."*
>
> *Or, "We don't really know how to be used by the Holy Spirit in the Gifts in order to see people healed and set free as part of the whole Gospel salvation package."*

* * *

Thank God for their open and honest hearts, open doors, and open Bibles! Regardless of where I have arrived at now theologically or in terms of my churchmanship preferences, I know I would be nowhere today as a Christian if it hadn't been for the AOG leaders and the foundation they laid in those early days of my own walk. It was a delicate and tricky time for us, as well as for those leading us as we sought to discover the difference, or the balance, between a new heart pulse and the cadence of a more regimented, marching, church drumbeat—*a kind of legalism with heart.*

* * *

I remember with some amusement once, when Pastor "Brother" Bond was about ready to preach at a Sunday evening Gospel service, and the place was filling up with regulars (plus the Hippies that mantilla-ed Sister What's-Her-Name in 1968 had prayed would be saved). As was quite normal for most churches, the first couple of pews at the very front were still relatively empty.

Brother Bond stepped behind the pulpit, welcomed everyone, said the opening prayer, and was about to give a short encouraging, introductory word, when a small group of hippie-type folk walked down the aisle to the front row pew. This all took place just before our small Men's Gospel group was going to sing a really boring, traditional rendition from the Bill Gaither Trio song collection.

Scruffy, long-haired, sandaled—kind of groovy and uncaring—they walked—no, glided and swayed to their seats. There was one girl, not more than 20–21 years old, wearing tight, navel-displaying, hip-hugger jeans, a cloth belt, beads in her braided hair, and lots of makeup—she was cute ... *very cute!* In addition, she wore a light purple chiffon, very see-through, fluttery blouse. (Remember, I was sitting on the platform, and I was single at the time and still learning how to look and appreciate God's beautiful creation without ... well, you know ...)

Oh, and did I mention ... she was very braless?!

Anyway, she plonked herself right down in the first row, right below the platform pulpit, and stared up and smiled, waiting expectantly for whatever message from God was to come. The epitome of AOG conservatism, Brother Bond stopped, dead tongue-tied midsentence, looking down, looking up, looking away, looking down again, looking at one of the Elders. I couldn't see his blushing, sheepish face, but I could feel it.

Brother Bond recovered deftly and moved on very spiritually to the task at hand. But the Men's Gospel group didn't. I'm sure I repented somewhere along the way, somewhere in the middle of the 3rd verse of "Where She—I mean, He—Leads Me I Will Follow." But I think we all sort of secretly wished she might need prayer and laying on of hands after the altar call, you know, to help her break out of her shy, ultraconservative shell—for the Lord, of course.

CHAPTER TWENTY-NINE

It Was Not All Rosy with the AOG

IN THOSE DAYS, when Anglican Bishop Bill Burnett and former St John's, Wynberg Rector, Bruce Evans (later Bishop in Port Elizabeth), came out of the spiritual closet and admitted to being Charismatic and to speaking in tongues, it caused quite a stir around town. While the news was met generally with cautious optimism, I think it threw the AOG leadership into a bit of a tizzy that baby-baptizers could get filled with the Holy Spirit (skeptically, à la Acts 10). I've probably done the leaders a disservice in saying that, since I wasn't anywhere close to being in the real know.

That said, it was slightly strange to me that Brother Bond and the Elders seemed to be basically, vocally, and publicly suspicious of the Charismatic Movement; there was already raised eyebrow frowning about raised hands and handclapping during worship (and having long hair while you did so). "Was it really authentic Acts 2, 10, and 19 tongues that the Catholics and Anglicans (and even some Methodists) were speaking … Hmmm?! And we notice that no Baptists are experiencing this Charismatic thing … Hmmm … Why's that? Is it because they don't baptize babies?!"

Don't say it.

At times, it seemed like we AOG-ites practiced a kind of controlled exuberance or, as one friend put it once, "Pent-up-costalism."

* * *

As for myself, while I favored a logical and reasoned approach, combined with a passionate love for the Bible, I earnestly, secretly, and seriously craved the adventure, energy, and certainty about God's power and presence that The Headquarters crowd and *Jesus Revolution* folks demonstrated!

I was convinced, Biblically and logically, that supernatural guidance and miracles were legit and meant for today, and therefore, could and should be genuinely and proactively sought after. The idea of leaving things to Him, and not cooperating with and being used by Him directly, and taking no responsibility for the consequences of my choices and actions, was unacceptable. On top of that, the church expecting only a handful of gifted spiritual superstars to be the only ones blessed with supernatural gifting, didn't sit well with me.

Still, I knew I needed to learn how to put my brain on hold and run out of my own ability and run into His, to learn how to be led by Him— whatever that was. If the Full Gospel equaled salvation, healing, and deliverance, then where was it happening, and how would I get there?! Could anyone teach or train me in this stuff?!

But I was unable to cross over into what I believed was a necessary abandonment of logic into a more sensitive feelings-based faith that I thought was needed to unlock the Holy Spirit from the prison of my reasoning and AOG traditionalism. I just didn't know how to get there. Later, a few of us experienced what we thought was the real dinkum deal in terms of the Gifts of the Spirit, which was very educational, troubling, and amazing all at the same time. It was the start I was looking for, but it also got us into a lot of hot water with AOG leadership (more on that in a later chapter).

* * *

You'll Always Remember Your First Time – My First Word of Knowledge

Oddly, at that time, even though I had no idea—**none!** —how the Word of Knowledge worked (the AOG barely had a theoretical explanation for it), I experienced it for the first time in a way that still makes me smile even today—at least I think it was a Word of Knowledge.

It was the single, future, young adult, and budding pastor guys' frequent habit to be invited to Pastor Noel and Merle Cromhout's house next door to the church building for lunch. Looking back, I have no idea how they could afford to feed so many of us on their meager salary!

Anyway, I was standing in the kitchen while Noel and Merle were having an unusually heated disagreement about their car. The keys had gone missing—"Who had them last? I'm going to be late. Whose fault is it?! I've looked everywhere!"

An idea popped into my head, and I blurted it out loud without thinking, "Have you looked in here?" I walked straight into the pantry (having never been in there before) and found the keys three shelves up halfway into the small room. (No, I did NOT see them lying there!) I grabbed them and handed them to a gob-smacked Noel. (Who knows, maybe I saved their marriage, too!)

So that's how a Word of Knowledge works?! If so ... Cool!

* * *

Like I Started to Say, It Was Not All Rosy with the AOG...

How I desperately longed to learn how to abandon myself and be used powerfully by God! But if I'm honest, I simply wanted more of that— whatever that was. I did not want to just swallow and follow. I questioned so many things. For example, when we were told not to associate with Christ Church (Anglican) around the corner in Kenilworth because they taught infant baptism *("... a doctrine that has deceived and sent more people to hell than any other ...")*, it made me all the more determined to find out for myself what all the fuss was about, as I'd heard the teaching was pretty sound there.

My confession these 50+ years later is that I secretly went to Christ Church for six straight weeks of Tuesday night Bible studies on Colossians. The teaching by the then Rector, David Prior, was so powerful and fed me so well, that I still have and use his notes today! Amazingly, he kept the singing, prayers, and sermon sandwich to one hour max. Very impressive!

I wanted to change the world but *not by doing so* in the theoretically awesome (but predictable, confined, restrained, and lukewarm) power of the Holy Spirit we talked about in the AOG. Whatever it might look like, however you can discover it, I wanted it, but I had no idea how to arrive at wherever I needed to be and whatever I needed to know. To be nonlogical and unpredictable was not in my DNA, but I was willing to change and try.

We talked a good game, in the AOG or other meetings, about the Full Gospel and the manifestation of *all* the Gifts as if we really knew what they were or how they actually worked. Myths and ecclesio-urban legends abounded as to how one would actually know that one had a Word of Knowledge or how you would use, or be used, in a Gift of Healing.

Was it a gift God gave to pass on through one person's hands to someone needing healing? Or a gift to the person needing healing, and the other person just happened to be there to encourage them? Or did they need to say or do something to release the gift given to them or in someone else? If they didn't do whatever it was that they were supposed to do, then would the gift still happen'? Could not using it right somehow thwart God's working?

Leaders were quick to recount the amazing, legendary acts of Nicholas Bhengu ("The Black Billy Graham"), or the AOG founders, the Mullan brothers, but we saw nothing of that level of manifestation in normal AOG or The Headquarters life. Actually, we never did see many, if any, miracles in all the time I attended my eight meetings per week over three years.

We seemed, as a group, as a church, and as individuals, to be locked into pretty much only tongues, interpretation, and prophecy and then mostly vague and poetic imagery—"Yea, even the Lord would sayeth unto thee, yea, to thee He would sayeth, 'Yea, walk on the water, and yea, remove flotsam and jetsam from thy life.' Yea, even He would say to thee, 'Breathe and don't drown …'" (my paraphrased version).

* * *

Oh, how I loved the process of learning how to share and preach in those days! Pastor Noel Cromhout was so loving and helpful, so encouraging and supportive, both to inform and comment on my preaching content and steer me toward my own style and also to give me constructive feedback afterward when I didn't do so well.

If I'm any good at preaching and teaching these days at all, I credit Noel as one of my mentors. I'll never forget how he shoved me to the front of the crowd outside the Claremont CNA (Central News Agency) during a Saturday morning outreach, and I preached in public for the first time—so scared, so clumsy, so blessed.

Thank you, brother!

* * *

Personal Opinion Note: It was an interesting learning time for me when it came to understanding preaching and teaching styles and the business of God anointing a message. Noel Cromhout and others, including Reg Berowsky, used to preach at the Sunday evening Gospel service. Noel was a teacher, and funny, systematic, and clear. I loved listening to him!

Reg—how should I put it? —*was not.*

He lumped verses together, breaking every hermeneutical rule, interjected emotional, heart-tugging stories, and tended to ramble. When Noel (not always, but quite often in my memory) finally made an altar call, in my heart I was saying, *Yes! Yes! That message nailed it; it was so clearly a call from God to repentance, so perfect for this congregation—spot on!*

Maybe three people would come forward, and then, only for rededication.

When Reg reached his conclusion (*Finally, thank God!*) and was making the altar call, in my heart I was saying, *I love Reg and his enthusiasm and his amazingly good heart to bits, I really do; but that sermon was simply awful! Unclear, off topic, confusing, and certainly not sound Bible!* as I bowed and shook my head, praying for sinners to (unlikely) come forward in spite of the really quite awful message. Amazingly, 12–15 (and often more!) would not just raise their hands but would get up and virtually sprint down the aisle for prayer and to give their lives to the Lord!

Since those days, I have personally discovered that what I consider my best sermons have had the least (obvious, visible) impact. I can't begin to count the number of times people have come to me or contacted me to share about something I preached or taught (often years before) that touched their lives, which were, in my mind, inconsequential things.

* * *

All that said, in AOG services, I remember harboring a secret, dry-mouthed, insane, rapid, heartbeat fear that if I finally plucked up the courage to speak in tongues in a meeting (all the while trying to differentiate between nervous hyperventilation symptoms and a true anointing). I was worried that the message would be followed by a long, awful, pregnant silence with no interpretation. Then, I would hear an Elder or Pastor Noel or Brother Bond utter those loving but faith-squashing words, "We thank our brother for that utterance of praise, but we won't wait for an interpretation." Then, everyone would mumble a confirmatory, "Amen," Hallelujah," or "Praise the Lord," which would roll like a quiet grateful wave across the congregation with a hint of *"Whew, that was close!"* mixed in.

It didn't help that there was an old, somewhat odd, but lovely brother (whose name escapes me now) who the younger kids nicknamed the "Kiddi Kiddi Man" because his tongues language was basically *"kiddi, kiddi, kilihari, kiddi, kilihari, etc."* His public messages almost always produced an Elder's response, "We thank our brother for the uninterpretable utterance" or, "We thank our brother for that expression of praise—we won't wait for …!"

Nobody, including me, wanted to be on the receiving end of **that quasi-rebukey** baptism of cold water.

CHAPTER THIRTY

Other Things Going on in the Cape –
Testimonies from Others

THE FOLLOWING IS AN EXCERPT from Dave Valentine:

Many new churches were sprung up after "Give God a Chance," one of them being Meadowridge, which became Peoples Church in Constantia.

The Upper Room became a popular venue for young people in Meadowridge as more and more gave their hearts to the Lord and were baptised in water and the Holy Spirit, which led to a revival in all the schools in the area to which Brian and his team were invited to speak. The revival spilled over to the parents who were influenced by their children's faith and enthusiasm.

Some of the Anglican churches became disturbed by the teaching on the baptism of the Holy Spirit. Then Archbishop Bill Burnett from Grahamstown was filled with the Spirit while worshipping in his quiet time; he was thrust forward on his knees and started praying in tongues. He phoned Noel Cromhout, who was then the local Assemblies of God minister, who confirmed that he had been spontaneously filled with the Holy Spirit. Soon afterward, Bill was elected as the Archbishop of Cape Town where he began to take his ministers on retreats to be filled with the Holy Spirit, which led to the Charismatic revival that swept Cape Town and South Africa.

– Dave Valentine, 1985

* * *

Excerpt from a Discussion with Brian Helsby – Youth for Christ (YFC):

Dave Lutes, through Sanet Stander, asked me recently, "What were those days (early seventies) like?"

As far as I'm concerned, there is no other way to describe it: exciting, radical, revolutionary, no fear whatsoever. It was an amazing time.

We were on fire. I was working almost exclusively with young people 14 years old and upward. There used to be preaching on Greenmarket Square in Cape Town every day. People were preaching on trains. It wasn't just a Hippie Revival; younger people, older people were being touched, and other religious groups were also impacted.

Recollections:

During the holidays, we would take a group of approximately 20 young people (around 14+ years old) to Green Point Common. We would spend our time praying, handing out tracts, and testifying on Sea Point promenade.

We hosted coffee bars at Wynberg Baptist on Friday nights. We'd have youth until 10:00 p.m., and after that, the young adults would stay behind, clean up, and set up the coffee bar. There was a cinema around the corner from the main church, so as the last show would finish, we would invite people into the coffee bar. It grew from 6 to 50 people. Sunday evening services gathered around 100 people—90% of those in the area—who were saved through coffee bars.

YFC had a monthly rally in Cape Town—the Koffiehuis—on a Saturday night that was amazing.

I also remember a nightclub in Wynberg. The owner had a very bad reputation. They were only open on weekends, and we decided to hire it out from Monday through Thursday for youth meetings and gatherings. We were definitely not shy, and it was quite radical. Dave Lutes attended and spoke a few times at the coffee bar as the "Christian American Baseball Player."

Initially our paths crossed where he gave his testimony at Koffiehuis, and then I did an interview with him for *IN Magazine*. Having an American sharing his testimony was positive, special. He was very committed—on fire.

I remember a young man that was saved at that time. He had many challenges and troubles in his life. He decided that since he was saved, the church would be a good place to die! A suicide attempt followed. Thankfully, we were able to intervene and took him to hospital.

I met Jerome outside a nightclub while he was high. I spoke to him, sharing the Gospel, and led him in the sinner's prayer. (At the time, I was driving a VW Beetle covered in Snoopy/Charlie Brown pictures). I wanted to follow up and see how he was doing. He had given me the wrong address when we met so I had trouble finding him. Eventually, I got his correct address from school.

I knocked on the door, his mom opened it, and he ran out the back. I tried again, and the same thing happened. The third time, his mom told me where he was, and I quietly entered their home. That was the start of a three-year relationship. Interestingly, the more interested he became in Christ, the more his participation in crime increased. On his 3rd offense (18/19 years old), he landed in jail.

I went to visit him (at the time, his girlfriend, who later became his wife, was also pregnant), and he told me that he became a Christian. When his court case came up, I was his only defense. I told the judge how we met and Jerome's story as I knew it. The judge had pity (probably on me!), and Jerome ended up getting a suspended sentence.

From those days onward, I was a staff member of YFC for a total of 31 years. Working with young people at that time was different—it was a time of revival. At YFC, we tried to minister while in the culture of the day, and at that time, people were memorizing Scripture—a fire that caught. Everyone was witnessing and on fire for Christ.

I have no, absolutely no, regrets or disappointments about that time.

Anything Else Going On at That Time?

Besides the hippie church, there were also other churches involved in the Jesus Revolution. At Wynberg Baptist, I had free rein (at age 19) to lead a youth service once a month. This was in 1969! We would also be the first church to eventually introduce drums into church worship. We took a group of young people to the rallies that were held. There were also non-Christians in attendance. They were 15-20 years old—too young for the hippie culture, but God's timing was so right for them, too.

Any Challenges at the Time?

I felt no real difficulties or challenges, except maybe finding enough time in the week! But I can imagine that it could've been challenging for the young people in school to be Christian if they were among non-Christian classmates. Also at the time, there was no music, worship, or contemporary services for them.

About those days, I can only describe it like this: I touched the fire myself. I became passionate, reckless. It set the foundation for a life of youth and young people ministry. 50 years with YFC. 55 years face-to-face with Him and those He wanted to reach. The Jesus Revolution planted in me the DNA for a life of serving Christ and youth.

– Brian Helsby, 2020

* * *

Some Testimonies from Then

Noel Sanderson:

I was introduced to Jesus at the Upper Room, [by] a schoolmate. We played in the same rugby team at Bergvliet High where I had a remarkably unsuccessful career. It was through his persistent witnessing, and his bringing me to the weekend meetings in the Upper Room, that I encountered Him in January 1972 after quite a struggle with the Holy Spirit. My first steps as a Christian began there and across the road in the just planted Meadowridge AOG with Faans Klopper as my first minister. Little did I know it then, but those were revival times.

February, 2012

* * *

Moira:

Those Upper Room days were such an amazing experience for me. I was just a kid, and I listened in awe as Johnny Weber, Mark Starbuck, and others gave their testimonies. Secretly, I wished I could have lived such an exciting life as these hippie guys. Little did I know just how blessed I was to be saved so young. My husband and I went into the ministry from Constantia AOG, and today we are living in the USA—still in ministry. Our neighbours are Noel and Merle Cromhout. They were a huge influence in my life as a teenager.

March, 2012

* * *

Eric "Tom" Sawyer:

I only really got into the second wave of the Hippie Revolution pipe dream in 1974-75. When I was 14, Johnny Weber shared his testimony at our school. When I was 16, I witnessed the conversion of Mark Starbuck at Teen Centre (Rondebosch), and though I wanted to be a Christian, but my heart was not yet ready. I went along to the tent campaign and watched Kim Glynn singing about Jesus with a cool band. I was invited to the Upper Room in Bergvliet, but though I saw strange stuff, I was prevented from seeing Jesus. Though I was open to and interested in strange spirits, and had been from a very early age, and as a result, I was prevented from coming to Christ until I was 18 when God opened the floodgates of Heaven and blew my cotton socks right off my feet.

My O.C. Lieutenant Commander 'Colin' Chambers, who was a member of the Harfield Road Assemblies of God, had told the youth about this person (me) whose life was on the brink. He had no idea how far gone I really was; at the time he visited me, I had decided to buy a gun and kill myself (my body) so that my spirit might fly free to Abraxas (my god). He visited me at teatime on the 7 July 1976, and though he did not say much, just "How are you doing?", I abruptly said, "Excuse me, sir? I need to do something." I immediately dropped to my knees on the cold cement floor and lifted my hands up and asked Jesus to come into my heart—my whole being.

A week later, I was invited to attend a retreat at Apostle's Battery, near Llandudno Beach, and while I was praying with Colin on the mountain, I was knocked clean out of my socks by the baptism with the Holy Spirit, and I spoke in tongues as the Spirit afforded me the freedom to do so. I have not, then, or since, experienced anything that equaled the experience I had that day. Though I have fallen down many times, and been a terribly bad example at times, I have been carried through each valley by the Grace of God in Jesus Christ. Praise the Lord God Almighty!

December, 2012

CHAPTER THIRTY-ONE

The World Needs a Revival Like This Again!

WE ASKED JOHN ATKINSON to reflect back on the Jesus Revolution days and those events and aspects that still stand out in his mind to this day. John and Dave had both made the transition to full-time Anglican ministry later in that decade. The following are excerpts from a Zoom meeting with Sanet Stander and Dave Lutes—transcribed and slightly edited.

* * *

I can remember being arrested (I think with Jack Hartland) in 1972 on the steps of St. George's Cathedral—made the front page of *The Argus* (newspaper) for protesting for equal education in the country. I was really young to be arrested at a demonstration, and other things that I was involved in that were very much a part of the time, dagga (marijuana), etc. It was a very intense time, not just because I was a teenager, but the environment was very intense. I think I was very distrustful of authorities and what I've been fed over the years as so-called truth.

I wandered into The Hippie Market and hung out there because that was where young people hung out at that stage and got into a discussion with Brian O'Donnell about truth. While he wasn't very articulate, in my opinion, I noticed something about him and his sense of security that I didn't have. That's really what woke me up to the possibilities of a commitment to Christ.

I gave my life to the Lord on my own—quietly—the way I kind of do things.

* * *

The spiritual climate of that time—we were in a revival. We didn't know it, but we were in the middle of a revival! **And it would be great to be in that sort of environment again—the world needs it.**

We used to meet in a warehouse that later became an AOG—with Mike Coleman, Chrisman Stander, Brian O'Donnell, Jack Hartland. We used to go out in the evenings in pairs to share the Gospel with people on the streets, and people would come to repentance and kneel and pray a commitment prayer on the pavement in front of everybody.

If you tried to do that today, I can't imagine it would happen! But that's how different the atmosphere was back then. I cannot remember an evening of going there when we didn't pray with somebody to give their life to the Lord. **It was amazing.**

* * *

Lots of events stand out. The rallies, the marches, the street preaching, everything was extremely powerful. One has to give credit to the AOG who provided a place for people who did not fit the AOG mould. John Bond was reprimanded by some Elders to speak to the hippies regarding their dress when they entered church. He in turn said the Lord will take care of that, not them (the Elders). You could see the Grace of God at work, not just in the conversions, but also the established church (Pentecostal) spilling over into the Anglican Church and Catholic Church through the Renewal Movement, and that's how Dave and I end up making a move from the AOG to the Anglican Church later.

* * *

I must say, I went through similar things like you, Dave [going through an AOG ban and connecting with Anglicans – see Chapter 49], being told that I must "come out from among them and be separate"; "returning like a dog to its vomit," and all sorts of nasty things. But Faans Klopper (AOG Meadowridge) supported me the whole way through. I'm still in contact with him. He is one of the unsung heroes of that time.

[*NOTE:* See end of Chapter 39 and comments about Faans Klopper who passed away in December 2020. John and Dave both attended his memorial service.]

* * *

Something else is the Upper Room coffee bar in Meadowridge —I led the coffee bar. The way that it worked was that we had a group of Elders from AOG (Richard Holt), Presbyterian Church (Le

Matré), the Pimms, and one or two others who were like parents to this youth movement. That was really where I cut my teeth in terms of learning about ministry and learning about Bible teaching and open ministry in AOG (which no longer exists; they control everything now).

Open ministry was after the Breaking of Bread service. You got between 5–10 minutes to stand up and share something from the Scriptures, and if you got it completely wrong, one of the Elders would come to you afterward and tell you that you completely misunderstood the passage but would then say, "Well done for standing up."

Ministry was encouraged in those days. I think when they stopped open ministry, they started failing as a denomination—really quite sad. It's very human to try and control what God is doing.

The AOG back then was out of the box on the one hand, but on the other, it wasn't. All we (society) knew was Catholic, Anglican, Presbyterian, Baptist, Methodist, and along came this group who were thoroughly orthodox really—Bible-based, conservative. There was nothing about them that was radical in that sense. They weren't like every new church that pops up today that's got some gimmick—nothing like that.

In fact, you would say that they were the least likely people that would have converted hippies, and the people who were trying to be trendy (the Anglican Church) were completely ignored. Very interesting. And you can see, there's the contradiction. On the one level, yes, this is radical, but on another level, it isn't radical at all.

And that's why, I think, it makes it a move of God. Nothing in the human sense would've attracted that.

Asked about Dave back in those days:

Quiet chap—he seemed quite organised. Very surprised to see you in an Anglican context [later – 1979]. Dave was neat; we hippies were scruffy and dirty. He was always neat. I always associated him with baseball, and he was always well turned out.

I identified with him; I could see us coming out of the same mould basically. Not in appearance but certainly theologically.

> *It would be great to be in that sort of revival environment again.*
>
> *The world needs it.*

– John Atkinson, July, 2020

CHAPTER THIRTY-TWO

I Believe in This Cup of Coffee

THIS ACCOUNT WILL BE SHORT, sweet, maybe a little shocking, and for sure, utterly embarrassing for me. There is a small bit at the end where, probably for some readers, I am going to use offensive imagery or suggestive content. By today's standards, it's nothing, but still, *I just want to alert you.*

When I used to drive or ride to and from Somerset West for home group Bible study or to support an outreach coffee bar that we had set up there, I would often see a hippie (my impression and word) walking along the N2 motorway. Let's call him "John." He had the long flowing hair, beard, floral headband, long white cassock-type garment, bare feet, and denim shoulder bag—actually, he had the fashionable quasi-Jesus look working for him quite well.

He never seemed to be in a hurry, and he never stuck out his hitchhiker hand or thumb to flag a lift. Occasionally, I noticed he wore shoes or sandals and even a coat a few times, especially when the weather got cooler, but I got the distinct impression that he didn't dress like that for show or image or to make a statement. He gave off the air of someone who was quite comfortable in his own skin. Then again, I was usually whizzing by him at 120 km/hr., so my impressions are not based on many facts.

I never offered to give him a lift.

I'm quite ashamed to admit it, but I judged him. In my 120 km/hr. opinion, John was lost and a loser, or at the very least, seeking something or someone but was unable to find it or them. Probably a drug addict, I thought more than once. I had many hippie friends who were part of the Jesus Revolution and The Market on Loop Street in Cape Town, but interestingly, looking back, I never ever, *not once*, sat down with anyone and actually had a conversation about their previous lives or personal journeys—drugs involved or otherwise—leading up to being found by the Lord.

Salvation stories about responding to altar calls were fine, but discussion about prior beliefs or current possible addiction struggles and moral, ethical, or social conflicts or dilemmas as part of their transition to their new life in Christ, never happened. I was very good at self-isolating. Other than knowing now what a hippie might look or talk like, my understanding of their other or previous life hadn't evolved much beyond my conservative, small village perception.

You see, I was beginning to be programmed to have a slick, sharp, pointed, rapid-fire, and accurate Bible-only vocabulary. Caring, understanding, or "come alongside" caring was not in the training plan. Empathy in any shape or form, didn't really exist in me in those days.

It was simple. As a young Christian now, I tended to believe, that God said plainly and simply, *"What I allowed before in your life, I don't allow any more. Stop it or be outside my Grace and Mercy."*

Adding in some of the spiritual laws that the church stressed under the guise of Grace was a subtle, but real, trap to fall into. (More on that later.)

I didn't really take the time to hear anyone's spiritual growing pains. I certainly had a pretty good idea that my casual friend Hippie John on the road to and from Somerset West needed to get sorted out or be lost forever.

I mean, look at him! Scruffy, unkempt, probably high, obviously aimless (and shoeless), and strolling on his way to hell.

That said, I did manage to fling a quick prayer or two up to Heaven for him from time to time, that quite likely only reached the roof of the car.

Truth be told, he made me a little curious.

* * *

You can imagine my shock when I saw him walking on the UCT campus, strolling past me as I preached on Jameson Steps during one lunchtime (i.e., not stopping to listen).

Now, at least, I could see him a little closer up and in slower motion.

Oh yeah, clearly, he was lost; clearly, he was high; clearly, he needed me to speak to him and set him right and bring him to the Lord!

Oh yeah, man, you're on my Gospel radar! I've got you in my sights now!

John strolled along the pavement or down the road like he didn't have a care in the world, never speaking to anyone and always carrying the same denim bag over his shoulder—just groovin'. I wasn't even sure he was a student.

Over the next few weeks when I saw him, I would pray for him, asking the Lord to speak to him, convict him, reveal his sin to him, and help him see the error of his lost ways; all the while kind of hoping he would stop and listen to my amazing preaching!

In my secret place of prideful giftedness, it wasn't so much that John was ready to come to the Lord, but I believed *that I* was ready for him to come to me—to bring him to the Lord.

"Just bring him to me, Lord! I'll help You sort him out!"

* * *

One afternoon, after preaching on the steps, I was sitting by myself at a table in the cafeteria having some hot chocolate. I was pretty much alone. As I glanced around, there were maybe only five people in a place that could seat 150+. Essentially, the place was empty; near closing time. I was facing the main entrance, which was about 25-30 meters away.

Then, John glided in with a fixed, glazed look on his face. (I'm *sure* he was high—yeah, right, like I knew what that was like!)

Immediately, I began to pray for him. *Lord, bring him to me ... Lead him to sit with me ... Cause him to park **right here** and give me a shot at sharing You with him.*

I didn't smile at him or greet him, nor did he me; he just cruised past me as if I wasn't there. He went to the service counter behind me and bought a cup of coffee.

Imagine my shock when he came straight to my table and sat down opposite me. From the dozens of empty tables to choose from, he chose mine. We both said nothing. He looked bad, smelled bad, and was bad —the dirt under his fingernails was truly gross.

But here he was! Right here! I was totally gob-smacked. My pulse was racing. *Now what do you do, Davie, you **spiritual hotshot, you**?!*

Inside my mind I *umpfed* and *ermed*, not really sure what to say ... *where to begin?*

What I didn't say was, "Hey" or "Hi" or "I'm Dave. What's your name?" or "What are you studying?"

No, with my spiritual antenna vibrating and humming crazily, what I said was, "What do you believe in?"

Now I'm thinking to myself, *Good grief, Dave, that's it?! That's the best opening line you could come up with?! Wow, that'll really show him you're a switched-on spiritual guru and that you really mean business!*

He looked me straight in the eyes—I noticed they were clear and focused—and said, "**I believe in this cup of coffee.**"

My mind was racing so fast now that I could hardly keep up with myself ... but, but, but *I don't have a Bible verse for that! The answer to that is not in the Witnessing 101 Handbook!*

Before I could speak, or not, he said, nodding his head toward a girl sitting behind me at another table, "And I believe that girl is totally groovy and choice, and I would really like to do her good right here, right now, and then do her all night."

In one quick, final swig, he drank the rest of his coffee, nodded a sort of, "See ya," and turned and walked out of the cafeteria.

I was nonplussed, floored, and utterly stunned into silence— verbally, mentally, and prayerfully.

In case your slightly naughty mind is thinking it, *no*, I didn't turn to look at the girl he referred to.

What I *did* do was to never forget that moment and that day. Now 50+ years on, I'm still embarrassed, and it still bothers me for some egocentric and stupid reason that I didn't have a scripted witnessing answer. Even having *that* thought or regret now is really quite pathetic when you think about it! No notches on my sword handle that day!

What a pity. I was so off beam and out of line that it doesn't really warrant comment, analysis, or a verdict.

I ask myself now, and wish I had asked myself then: would empathy, compassion, caring about the whole person ever worm and wheedle its way into my narrow heart? You would think that when you look at my own salvation story of God's proactive Hound of Heaven tracking me down in the Piketberg Mountains nearly three years before, that I would have some appreciation for the tender Mercy and caring heart of God!

He didn't just save my soul; He saved the whole of me! He saved my life!

I never saw John again that year—or any other year for that matter —and I suspect he forgot about me the moment he walked out the door or maybe before he even reached it.

I know that I would have.

CHAPTER THIRTY-THREE

Memories of the Jesus Movement

THE FOLLOWING IS AN EXCERPT from Avril (Mills) Meeker:

The funniest story which I remember about the Jesus Movement is when we were asked by Brother Bond of the Assemblies to go and give our testimonies at a church in Retreat, Cape. We had already been to the church previously to give our testimonies, and they were such a fantastic community and were having a baptism service on the Sunday at Princess Vlei. We hadn't yet been baptised, so they invited us to join them and also get baptised, which we did. We duly arrived at Princess Vlei, and there were about thirty or so of us holding hands and all walked into the murky water and were gloriously baptised by the minister.

When Brother Bond asked us to go and give our testimonies at the same church, we were only too happy to go and see everyone again and arrived at Brother Bond's house in Plumstead dressed as we always were in jeans and T-shirts. He took my sister and me aside and asked us if we wouldn't mind going home and changing into a skirt or a dress as the church in Retreat would be offended to see women dressed in pants.

We were only too happy to oblige and went off home and came back dressed in our miniskirts and boots. The miniskirts barely covered anything, but we didn't want to offend anyone by wearing pants! Brother Bond later spoke at a conference and told the story to the gathered clergy as the turning point in his realisation that what people wore didn't matter to God; it was what was in their hearts, as he was more embarrassed about the miniskirts than the pants, which we had originally worn. The church, which had accepted us with open arms the first time we visited there, had never been offended to begin with. A real learning curve for the Assemblies.

* * *

Another story which springs to mind is the first time I met Johnny Weber. I had been saved for a few weeks and had heard about Johnny who was visiting from Jo'burg at the time but had never met him. We were all at Bishopsford School where we used to gather on the weekends and have informal fellowship. Johnny arrived late really excited about a wonderful group of people he had met at a beach where they were so close to God that they didn't even wear any clothes, and he had spent the afternoon with them. We all laughed as he had stumbled onto Sandy Bay, the nudist beach. In Johnny's mind, these people were very close to God, as they didn't even have to wear clothes.

We later visited Sandy Bay with the Harfield Assemblies for their annual picnic. When we were told where we were going, we went to the Pastor and told him it was a nudist beach, but his response was that there were no nudists beaches in Cape Town. I have some nice pictures of John Bond sitting on a rock with his walking stick. I thought he may have used it to rebuke the nudists. I remember him chasing the nudists to the other end of the beach—such good memories.

We all went along and spent a lovely day there and were just told to look away when the nudists came past. I don't know what the nudists thought of us!

My own experience of the Jesus Movement was when I went to Harfield Road to watch my brother Keith get baptised. I hadn't been to church in years and went along just to appease my mom who had been a Christian her whole life. At the meeting, we saw all the Jesus People who were also getting baptised— Brian O'Donnell, Marge Ballin—who we had known from the Jo'burg days and Loader Street days.

Marge invited us to The Headquarters coffee bar for a Monday night meeting the next day, and my sister Jenny got saved at this meeting. I wasn't too interested at this stage, as I was involved in other things and really thought that all the Christians were a bunch of idiots anyway.

The next week, I went along to the meeting and met with all the Jesus People. That night there was a woman speaking. She had been a prostitute and was nicknamed the "Vodka Queen of Cape Town." She spoke about the love of Jesus, and for the first time in my life, I heard about how much Jesus loved me, and coming from a very strict Pentecostal background, where all we heard about was the Judgement of God and how we were all going to hell, this was the first time that I heard someone speak about a loving relationship with Jesus. This really touched my heart, and I went forward for prayer and gave my heart to this wonderful person, Jesus, who loved me so much.

I suffered from panic attacks, which used to grip me in the night so that I couldn't go to sleep. I opened a Daily Light, which my mother had given one of us and read from the reading for that day, and the Word was, "Your God neither slumbers nor does He sleep, He will give His beloved perfect peace when she lays her head down to sleep" (Psalm 121:2–4). For the first time in years, I fell asleep with no panic attack and woke up in the early hours of the morning being bathed in His presence and love. It felt like I was being baptised in liquid love that seeped into every part of my being. Speak about being a new creature in Christ! I felt different, looked different, and was so in love with Jesus I finally understood what the Vodka Queen of Cape Town had been talking about.

– Avril (Mills) Meeker, 2005 & 2020

CHAPTER THIRTY-FOUR

You Didn't Go to Vietnam

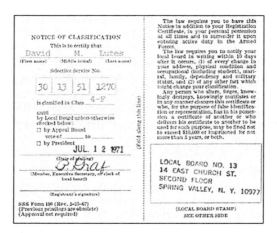

WHEN I RETURNED TO SOUTH AFRICA in August 1971, I worked for a company called the Old Mutual. It was an insurance company based in Pinelands, Western Cape. The baseball team had arranged for me to get a job there because others in the area who were involved in the baseball scene also worked there. They pulled some strings, to be honest, so I could at least have a token job that paid the bills (and have a visa).

What I knew about actuarial and insurance stuff generally was dangerous, but they tolerated me in my basic gopher (*go for,* as in "go fer this," "go fer that") admin role. The big thing was that it allowed me the flexibility to tour with the baseball team and to play baseball throughout the week or on weekends without any sense of obligation to the company.

It was a fix, I admit it. But it was also God's timing, and so, as wrong as that may sound, I'm still grateful. About the time of this account, I had moved into the Old Mutual staff hostel right next to the Old Mutual train station.

In Chapter 9, "I Insist That You Come to Dinner," I described how a circuit Methodist Pentecostal-type minister (Haughton B.) from Somerset West prayed for my girlfriend, K, and me to receive the baptism and release of the Holy Spirit. It was after that experience that he introduced me to "the only show in town," the Assemblies of God Church in Kenilworth (Southern Suburbs), and to the Jesus Revolution and Hippie Movement, as it was called then. He took me to The Headquarters (HQ) on Longmarket Street in Cape Town himself. It was basically, so he told me, a saved former drug den and nightclub. The sign above the door had a picture of a hippie, but it looked remarkably similar to some new, trendy pictures of Jesus; which was kind of ironic.

The Headquarters was very much connected with the Assemblies of God where I was beginning to attend. It was quite an emotional place, and a bit fanatical by my conservative, very small, US farming community standards. There was a lot of singing, a lot of clapping, a lot of speaking in tongues, a lot of loud music, and a lot of dramatic preaching—like nothing I had ever seen or experienced anywhere! I didn't know it at the time, but some of the theology was really off-the-wall odd or questionable, but there you go; just goes to show that God doesn't need our perfect theology to get His work done. It was the *happening place* in Cape Town as far as Christian things went.

As mentioned before, the Hippie Market on Loop Street was a business that sold lots of hippie items—everything from beads to hats to flower child type stuff—was not my world at all! The key leaders of The Market were a few guys, Brian O'Donnell, Dave Valentine (both

212

mentioned earlier), and Mike Coleman (although, I seem to remember Mike and Dave had other jobs, but I can't be sure).

Wonderful men, great leaders, inspirational, powerful, lovers of God and people—I'll say it again, they were ***truly great leaders.*** They were the first few guys I met in this weird and wonderful new world I found myself in.

Occasionally, The Headquarters would have guest speakers come in from outside. I don't know who was controlling the choice of speakers; all I know is that some of them were quite strange, at least to me. But everyone else seemed to get a great deal out of it, so I went along for the ride. I had no historical context anyway to assess any of this—pro or con.

* * *

On one particular evening, there was a guy preaching on and ministering physical healing. The place was absolutely chockablock full-full of people—I mean, dozens and dozens of people crammed into this small nightclub-type environment. He was rapid-fire preaching, preaching, preaching about healing, machine-gunning Bible verses like nobody's business, convincing and persuading and filling the room with belief that supported the idea that God does physical healing today. ***Tonight! Right here, right now … through him!***

Of course, I had heard something about it. I'd read some things, and the Assemblies of God taught about it and prayed for folk on Sunday mornings. That said, while I had experienced my own healing of my pitching arm (Chapter 13), I'd never seen someone get healed in a public environment. But I desperately wanted to.

So, here I was, fresh from work and from baseball, still wearing my suit and my glasses, with long blondish hair, really thinking I'm cool— and ***I wanted a front row seat to see God do stuff.***

* * *

After a short while, it suddenly dawned on me: I'm blind, legally blind in my left eye, as a result of being hit on the left side of my head with a baseball when I was fifteen years old. It tore a hole in my retina and officially, technically, I was classified as legally blind in that eye (20/300 vision). Because of that, I was given a permanent military deferment, even though my number had come up in the military draft lottery earlier that year. Instead of going into military service, I came to South Africa to play baseball and to discover what God had in store for my life.

As I came to this realization, something happened inside me, like a spiritual prick or twinge. For some reason, I felt like I owed it to God and to those around me to go forward to be healed, *to see for myself and to show others how it was done.*

Looking back, I see that I desperately wanted to be the guy who was the leader, the one who's got his act together, the one who's very spiritually wise, and a budding spiritual superstar. I was already a bit famous, as it were, for being a baseball player; now I wanted to also be in the limelight for being a great Christian sportsman on whom God had poured His obvious favor *by healing "special" me.*

To be honest, I really didn't have a clue how to live the Christian life at all—day-to-day. "Hit-and-miss discovery mode" best describes my experience and life. I still had some *fake-it* DNA working actively in my head and heart.

Long story short, the preacher made an appeal for people to come forward to be healed. I could feel others watching me going forward. This was my moment not to drop the true Christian living example ball, to show, no—*to persuade*—God that I had enough faith to receive healing from Him; to demonstrate to others how real faith worked in these moments.

* * *

Secretly, deep down in the recesses of my hidden, *I-haven't-got-a-clue-what-I'm-doing* heart room, I thought of healing faith like carrying a teaspoon of water across the room with your eyes closed. **IF** you could make it across the entire length of the room without spilling a drop (not even a drip), now *that* was real faith! **IF**, however, you spilled a drop, you had to go all the way back to the beginning and try again to prove you had what it takes to maintain faith all the way to the blessing's end.

AND, if you had only limited time to "action-believe" (show your faith with real, practical action), then you had to be REALLY good at holding that spoon steady—no trembling or nervousness or doubt allowed.

AND, in another deeper, darker place waaaaay down inside, I dreaded the day when, as I arrived with my faith-filled spoon and a smile on my over-achiever face, God would say "Nope, sorry Davie, you're using the wrong spoon or the wrong water or the wrong grip or the wrong walking pace or using the wrong hand —go back and start again, and this time, believe right!" (Do not pass "Go" and do not collect $200).

The preacher asked, "What's wrong with you?" and I said, "I'm blind in my left eye." He immediately laid his hands on the sides of my head; he shuddered and shook, breathed quickly and heavily in and out—and tried to push me over, speaking in tongues as he did so. He also whipped me up and challenged me to begin to speak in tongues myself —so, I did!

"In the name of Jesus, be healed!"

Things were getting louder and more emotional—I'm feeling it now!

Oh yeah God, I'm really feeling it!

Eyes closed, head looking toward heaven, I'm speaking in my own private worship language, and everybody in the room is being carried along with the excitement of this moment; worshipping around me saying, "Wow," "Hallelujah," and "Fantastic!"

"Dave Lutes is up there; He's unlocking the faith that he needs to believe and receive a miracle!"

I could see it on their faces; I could see them whispering to one another, "Dave Lutes is being prayed for to be healed. This is amazing, fantastic! God brought him all the way from America to be healed—oh bless him real good Lord!"

Flipping the final believing faith switch that I was sure would help God do His thing and act, I threw my hands in the air and shouted, **"Thank you, Lord, I'm healed!"**

The preacher said, "Hallelujah, you're healed!"

I took off my glasses, about to dash them against the wall (where there was a really weird psychedelic painting that the HQ leaders hadn't painted over yet).

But I didn't.

Instead, I panicked.

Absolute truth, I was afraid to close my right eye and look only with my left eye to confirm whether or not I had been healed. To test my left eye would be a real lack of faith, so I reasoned. I put my glasses in my jacket pocket and went back and sat down; people backslapping me, congratulating me, praising God with me—and I'm smiling and saying "Yeah, yeah, hallelujah, praise the Lord, I'm healed, I'm healed. Yes, isn't it wonderful? Praise the Lord, *blah, blah, blah … cliché, cliché, cliché …*"

I felt like such a fraud. *I wanted to have faith in my faith that I had the right kind of faith* to sustain me, to make it work, *to make Him work*. I was so scared I had let the others down—and even let God down; made Him look bad.

I know. Don't say it.

I refused to look with only my left eye to test things out. As I sat there, I was still holding onto that spoonful of water—shaking in my hand, quaking in my boots—*only a few more steps to go, and I'll make it … I think I can, I think I can … Oops; oh, damn!*

The *Little Spiritual Engine that Could …* didn't.

* * *

The meeting went on very late. I went to Cape Town Station, as normal, and just managed to catch the very last train back to Pinelands —about a 20-minute ride. I was the only one in the carriage. Sometime around the 10th minute, I fell asleep, completely dog-tired, dead asleep —and alone on the train.

It was about 12:15 in the morning when I woke up with a start as I heard the sound of the train screeching to a halt and the air pressure *whoosh* sound that told me the doors were opening. I sat up in my seat and looked out the window. I saw that we were next to my platform; I jumped up and ran to the door just as it closed—*ding, whoosh, thump*! I shoved my fingers into the soft molding in the middle of the doors but couldn't pry *(British Eng. – "pryse")* it open.

The train began to pull away. Without a moment's thought, I ran back to my seat, threw down the window, and jumped out of the moving train onto the platform.

OK, that's not completely true about not giving it a moment's thought. Actually, in a nanosecond I reminded myself that the next stop, Thornton, was a mile or more away along a notoriously dangerous road that ran along a more ominously risky *people-get-mugged-here* cemetery. And that I would need to walk through it … alone, in the dark … and, and …

Jump, Dave, jump!

So, I did.

I landed on the platform, and slightly shaken, I walked up the platform stairs, across the pedestrian walkway over the tracks, down the other side—then three or four hundred yards to the hostel where I was living. I went into my room, breathing heavily, heart thumping, happy-ish, and quite relieved.

Until I remembered my eye.

A sense of failure and weak-faith-guilt caught up with me then. Up to this point, I still hadn't dared to close my right eye and look with and test my left to see if I had been healed. My glasses were still inside my suit coat pocket. ***I gotta do this!***

But then I said to myself, *If I test my eye, then it's just saying I'm lacking in faith. If I don't look with my left eye, I'm saying I don't believe God. If I do look with my left eye, I'm believing, but then again, I'm showing unbelief at the same time.*

Rock and hard place ... sheesh! What a treadmill!

It was very confusing and a stupid, immature faith dilemma. I started shaking again, feeling another uncomfortable moment of truth fast approaching my heart.

I went into the bathroom down the hallway, closed the cubicle, sat down, and said, "Sorry I'm doubting you, Lord," and, in the same breath, "Yes, I believe you, Lord ..." Beginning to sweat, I hoped I wasn't about to get another flash of confusing insight.

I covered my right eye with my hand and looked through my left eye. *I wasn't healed.*

I started to cry.

"Lord, I'm sorry I didn't have enough faith. I did not have enough belief; I was not strong enough; I was not a good enough Christian! The people were counting on me to believe in you!"

Tearfully, but tinged with anger (at myself or God?), I said through trembling, gritted teeth:

"Lord, if I needed more faith tonight to be healed than what I had, then it will never happen. So, Lord, I don't know what's going on, but I will never, ever be healed because I can't have more faith than I had tonight. I can't give you more ... I can't show you more ... I can't. I simply cannot believe more than I did tonight!

"That's it, Father. I shot my faith bolt tonight. That was the maximum faith I could ever show at this stage of my walk, Father! I'm sorry, but I just can't do this anymore."

Then I explode-blurted out: *"What do You want from me?!"*

Then in His loving, caring, gentle Mercy—in the same way that He still-small-voice whispers into your heart, into your mind, into your spirit, into your soul *as only He can*—He said:

"You didn't go to Vietnam."

Stunned! The light blazed on full! Suddenly it all made sense: the Orchestrator of the Universe, the One who knows the end from the beginning, the One who laid His hand on me and called me to Himself by my name (*He knew my name!*) in the mountains near Piketberg; this same One, had a purpose and good reasons for me to be where I was, at this moment in time, empty teaspoon in hand, *an empty teaspoon of flawed trust and struggling faith …*

… and I am not in Vietnam right now!

* * *

To recap, in July '71, the American military draft lottery, was held on national TV. On that occasion, they were drawing 19-year-olds, surnames A–M. An official drew out 365 numbers and 365 birthdates from two large, previously spun, cylindrical containers—lottery drums. They matched up the birthdate with the number—28 June, surname letter "L"—number 52.

That was me.

According to the available data, and with my track record as a team captain, president of the school, honor student, etc., the chances of me going somewhere in the world for four years as an officer leading the troops into battle were pretty good. Vietnam was a likely destination. Actually, the data showed that lottery numbers 1–200 were not staying home for long and that there was a jungle or overseas location in their future.

My mom sat at home that day and watched the draft lottery live. When I came home from work, she was devastated having seen that my number was 52.

But because of my blind eye, which classified me as being legally blind and disabled, they wouldn't accept me and gave me a permanent medical deferment (category 4-F). I went back to South Africa. When I went back there, I was filled with the Holy Spirit. I got transformed. I got changed. I got called into the ministry. I began to serve Him. You know the story up to now …

* * *

That deferment resulted in 13 total years in South Africa discovering and serving Him. Using my human reasoning and not divine intervention logic, if I had gone to Vietnam or any other place for four years in the military, that might not have happened.

God reminded me that I didn't get healed so that I could have this moment to learn more about His purposes and to be grateful that He knows the end from the beginning—*my* end from the beginning.

Yes, but, but, but … So why couldn't He heal me then?

I realized later that, according to US Selective Service rules, if I had gone to the doctor, and it was confirmed that I could see after all (i.e., I had been healed), then I would no longer be a category 4-F, permanently disabled and deferred. According to the rules then, legally, I would need to officially inform the US Embassy, and as a result, I could be called back to the US and quite possibly go into the military as part of the draft program in those years.

Or, worse still, in my insecure teaspoon-dripping-huge-drops-of-water state, I might feel cornered and feel the need to lie about God **not** *healing me or at the very least not proactively, willingly, gladly, powerfully, and publicly declare that My God had healed me.*

That was a nonstarter! (But it did cross my mind if I'm honest.)

I was spared huge wet drips and drops from my unstable teaspoon. *I was spared for a reason*, and I began to feel a growing sense of purpose because I didn't go to Vietnam, because I wasn't healed, because He wanted to make sure I remembered that this was all by Grace, that it was all by Mercy alone and that …

He's calling the shots for my life, and that my teaspoonful faith, full or empty, didn't turn on or off His love for me. A pretty cool lesson.

There's more. It gets even better.

Things came very powerfully home even more to me when I went to get on to the train and go back to Cape Town the next day. As I stood on the platform and looked over to the other side of the tracks, I realized that the door that I could not open and the window that I jumped out of were about three yards short of the overarching bridge; the stone pedestrian bridge that went over the tracks. If I had waited one more second, maybe two, I would have jumped out of the window straight into the pedestrian bridge wall and quite likely would have bounced off it and fallen under onto the tracks under the train—ouch!

> **"By the way, Davie Lutes, you didn't go to Vietnam. I'm in control."**
>
> *He also added, "I don't need your 'perfectly expressed faith' to overcome my unwillingness to bless and heal you, to somehow force me and pry my fingers loose from the blessing I have for you. I love you unconditionally, no strings attached. I do what I do, in my time and in my way. I have a purpose for you."*

* * *

Author's Note: I am doing the final edit on this chapter on February 18, 2023, while watching *The Chosen*, Season 3, Episode 6, "Intensity in Tent City." In the show, Barnaby brings his 10 yrs.-blind friend, Shula, to Jesus to be healed. Jesus softly, no drama, places His hands over her eyes and prays a silent prayer. When He is finished, she cries but won't look up into Jesus' face. Shula says, "I am afraid to look." Jesus tells her, "It's time, Shula." She looks up and can see.

> *"I am afraid to look." Oh, how I can relate to that!*

The joy that follows (when Barnaby is also healed) is so natural, so human, yet so divine— and dance-worthy—that I began to weep with amazement and joy. Jesus was also moved by the Father's love for these two people—Himself smiling, laughing, and crying.

Now I know the way the event is portrayed on screen is not in the Bible. But there was something about the compassion of Jesus in the midst of her fear and uncertainty that reminded me again of how His purposes and ways are not ours. Regardless of our desired outcome, He still loves us with an undying and unconditional, total love. He loves and takes joy in showing us His love.

CHAPTER THIRTY-FIVE

Prayer Boxing IS a Christian Sport!

MARCH(-ISH) 1972 – I WAS 19 YEARS OLD, and I was playing baseball for the Varsity Old Boys, doing, attending, and supporting dozens of Christian activities in and around Cape Town, and steam cleaning carpets for Steam Valet Carpet Cleaners in Observatory, Cape. As you know, prior to this, I was working for and living at the Old Mutual insurance company in Pinelands, Cape.

Both of my bosses were committed Christians. Roy was a Methodist and strongly Evangelical. Denys, who also played baseball for the Sea Point Cardinals, was a Presbyterian, an ex-alcoholic, and an excellent batter (at 53 years!) who was extremely difficult to strike out.

I had one young guy reporting to and assisting me with carpet cleaning—Willie—a so-called "Colored" guy who was with the

Apostolic Faith Mission Church (hyper-Pentecostal) in Athlone, Cape. Donovan—also a so-called "Colored" guy— helped out on another side of the business and was with the Plymouth Brethren Church (ultraconservative, Evangelical). We prayed every morning as a team and often shared about the Lord with each other and with customers and clients as and when the opportunity presented itself. We had a number of lovingly heated theological and doctrinal discussions from time to time—actually, too often—but they were more healthy than not.

Backtrack for a Moment

Priority-wise, I was on a very fast track in learning about life's delicate balance between wants and needs, between having things now (or as we said in South Africa, "now-now" or "immediately") and building brick upon brick for the future. I was a jumble of "I-must-prove-myself" pride, evolving values, newly discovered and evolving emotions, "beliefs" fierceness, and added to the mix, a collection of erratic hormones. I had no one really to talk with about it.

Oh, and I was, by nature, a risk-taker.

Oh, and I had an impatient and sometimes volcanic opinion, temper, and decision-making tendency.

At this stage, the sum total of my knowledge was, "Once I was blind but now, I can see … And this is how it happened to me when I wasn't looking for it or asking about it. And in fact, I knew literally nothing about Christian things and, quite honestly, had never cared to, etc." I mention this to underscore the fact that I was very much a guy who was out to prove something—by myself. As the smallest kid in school for many years, I had to run the fastest—both in terms of actual physical running *and* in the way I used my wisecracking mouth while I did so. Everything was a competition. Every moment in life had a winner or a loser. I had failed before (getting my girlfriend pregnant), I was not going to fail again … ***and I'll prove it to you***! Some have said about me that I was *focused* and *determined*. You better believe it!

Back to the Story

My boss' brother, Peter, was also Plymouth Brethren. Hard-core. He was not just pro-King James Bible as THE authoritative Word of God and only true translation, but also hyper-pro-Brethren doctrine. And not just pro-Plymouth Brethren but also equally rabidly and aggressively anti-Pentecostal and Assemblies of God. Let's put it this way—his Gospel sword was a thousand times more sharply honed with years of use than mine. He was a walking, talking Bible quote, and while I got the impression that he was pretty inflexible, he did celebrate with me the fact that the Lord had laid His hand on my life the previous year and that I was trying to live for Him.

It also seemed, though, that he derived some form of satisfaction and pleasure from scoring points with young converts like me. Perhaps he felt it was his duty to put me straight about the false doctrine I was being exposed to. I'm not sure. Actually, I have a far more pleasant memory of him as another brother and man of God than anything negative.

However, because my assistant Willie and I had begun to share with Donovan about the Holy Spirit, the Gifts of the Spirit—e.g., speaking in tongues, etc.—Peter decided that it was time to put us straight. Day after day, we had lengthy discussions on the subject. He quoted verses at us, at me especially, that I didn't even know existed. What I knew, really, was dangerous, in that I couldn't really argue the case to save my life. He could and made case after point, proving that the Gifts of the Holy Spirit were no longer needed, that they died out after the perfect had come— i.e., the Bible was canonized (I think that's what he meant. See 1 Corinthians 13:10).

He got a bit heated sometimes. I just kept falling back on my own simple, true story and experience and tried to leave it at that.

That is, until he sort of hinted that I may have been influenced by something evil—even demonic.

I prayed about it. Interestingly, not to be right, but to make sure Willie and Donovan didn't turn negative and the disagreement upset our working together. That said, in my competitive heart I said, "Let the contest begin!"

I said to Peter, "I'll tell you what. You pray for Donovan, **in the name of Jesus,** that he will NOT be filled with the Holy Spirit and speak in tongues. And I will pray for him **in the name of Jesus** that he WILL be filled and speak in tongues. Agreed?"

Surprisingly, Peter cautiously said, "Agreed."

I also said I would not lay my hands on Donovan, or personally pray with him, but would leave him to go before the Lord and ask Him, himself, alone as and when he chose to—if he chose to. Peter agreed to whatever the opposite of not laying on hands was.

While I think we were both uncomfortable (Peter more than I), entering into what, by then, was beginning to seem like a Spiritual Power Boxing Match, we also agreed not to talk about it again or put a time limit on when or whether Donovan prayed or didn't pray. We didn't tell Donovan what we were doing or not doing.

Looking back, I mean…seriously?!

We were going to try to prove whose use of the name of Jesus was more powerful or more listened to?! I can't believe my sort of Elijah and the Prophets of Baal mentality, à la 1 Kings 18:24: "You prophets of Baal, pray to your god, and I will pray to the LORD. The god who answers by setting fire to this wood is the true God" (NIV)!

To be honest, I'm not sure actually how Donovan would have felt about being a spiritual soccer ball without his knowledge, but we left things like that. The ball, so to speak, was really in Donovan's court, and I couldn't honestly assess his level or degree of "want it"—his hunger and thirst for something more in his Christian life.

Since Willie was closer to Donovan, it was harder to hold him back; his spiritual, bubbling intensity made me look like a warm, calming bath —but I think he managed to hold off pushing too hard and controlled his spiritual laying on of hands urges.

I know (now more than then) that beliefs and doctrine should not be built on a foundation of experience (i.e., my experience of the Holy Spirit and tongues). But such was the absoluteness of my belief in what I had personally experienced in my own life and what I was being taught, that I entered into the fray and boxing ring with Peter. Oh, and by the way, I was taught and firmly believed that speaking in a tongue was THE sign that someone had been baptized in/by and filled with the Holy Spirit—the ultimate "no-no" to the Plymouth Brethren.

What began to bother me more was this idea that I really, really wanted to be able to get into Peter's Plymouth Brethren space and say, "I told you so" after Donovan got totally zonked by the Holy Spirit.

* * *

The thing that I was not aware of at the time was that it was highly likely that if Donovan admitted to anyone in leadership in the Plymouth Brethren Church that he had been "baptized in the Spirit and spoke in tongues," or even that he was considering it, he would bekicked out of the church. The price attached to Donovan even sort of going down this path must have weighed very heavily on his heart and mind.

* * *

About three weeks went by, and to be honest, I had a lot of other things going on, so I didn't really register when Donovan came into

228

work beaming brightly, grinning from ear to ear, and sheepishly but excitedly said, *"It happened! Willie prayed with me, and it happened!"*

Was I delighted? ***Absolutely!***

Did I feel vindicated? ***Absolutely not!***

Did I discuss it with Peter later? ***Not a chance!***

Did Donovan get pushed out of the Plymouth Brethren? ***No, he left voluntarily and joined a Pentecostal church.***

Did the Lord have a word with me about all this? ***Yes, then—and for about 25 years afterwards.***

"Davie, Little Boetie ... Welcome to the world of Church Point Scoring —Right or Wrong, Black or White, In or Out, and Attack or Defend. I would heartily recommend that, sometime soon, you learn to say, 'I don't know.' Don't encourage competition, as much as you love it; don't feed it; but most of all, don't let your brother or sister ever stay wounded or crippled because you used your 'sword' (in your opinion) very well.

If anything, learn to 'take a sword or take a blow' **for him or her.** *Heal and mend—actively, proactively. Nobody 'wins' when you don't. Oh, and by the way, if you ever think about putting my Name up against my Name in prayer with another brother again, I'll shut you up!"* (See Chapter 27 - "If You Don't Learn to Pray, I ... Will ... Shut ... You ... Up.")

The Hippie Market Committee: Andre Olivier, Johnny Weber, Jacq Krige, Brian O'Donnell, Dave Valentine and Marge Ramsden

Western Province Team - 1972

YOB

Rondebosch Boys High School – mid-1971

USA

YOB

TIMES SPORT

Dave the destroyer!

By JIM KIDMAN

JESUS REAL PE...

Preaching my 1st sermon. Cayuga Lake, Taughannock Falls State Park, United Methodist Church, July '71 (19 yrs. old)

Jong Yank Hier in Standerd Elf, Verlief op S.A.

Fetzer invites man to Detroit

By JIM KIDMAN

V.O.B. Finalist South Ent League Champions 1971-1972 Season

231

CHAPTER THIRTY-SIX

Sharing and Praying with People – Growing AOG Resistance

DURING THOSE HEADY "SOARING IN THE SPIRIT" days, there was no situation, no circumstance, no location, or person where and when and who we weren't willing to pray for—in public, on the street, on the train, or on a stage or in a church or in a car or in a back alley.

We believed God was real, powerful, present, and willing to touch lives—all the time! We only needed to be willing and available.

There was no formality to it; almost no one I knew had any formal training on **how** to pray, only which version of the Bible to quote to help us *thee* and *thou* the person into blessing while laying on hands or whatever else was needed.

Of course, over time the hippies and I also became more entrenched or came under the influence of the AOG dogma, and we were increasingly under pressure about how to dress, speak, study, follow, and pray properly, which included using the only true version of the Bible, the King James. As for me, I had no spiritual or church experience or reference points whatsoever, so I pretty much watched and tried to learn (and conform).

While I was most definitely not hung up on experience to justify Bible teaching (my logical brain was too complicated for that), I did look for what worked. That said, I was very silently and passively against gimmicks, techniques, and traditional tried-and-trusted methods. Deep down inside, I think, I was searching for my own perspective, hoping it would lead me to find His purpose for my life. Swallow and follow really rubbed me the wrong way,

Sure, we all learned the "ABC Sinner's Prayer Formula" when praying for someone to lead them to Christ and be saved and to cement and make the commitment real that someone made.

A CCEPT—that you are a sinner; that God is right, and you are wrong; that your sin has separated you from Him; that you can't save or rescue yourself and that you need Him to save you and do this for you—and redirect your path away from eternal death and hell.

B ELIEVE—that He sent His son Jesus to do for you what you can't do for yourself; that Jesus has bridged the gap between you and God and that He loves you with an eternal, no-strings-attached love; that He did this personally, for you. Believing means to trust Him, to give your life to Him, and surrender to His Lordship over your whole life. Believing means handing over the keys of your heart and life to Him.

C ONFESS—to someone (tell someone) what you have done because if you believe in your heart that Jesus died and rose again from the dead for you, and *confess with your mouth* that Jesus Christ is your Lord, you will be saved!

* * *

To be totally upfront, emotionally passionate and completely biased about all this, I could not and cannot think of a greater privilege and honor than to share Christ and the Gospel with someone (either through preaching, public testimony or one-to-one witnessing and sharing) and then to be able to pray with them to give their lives to Him.

Because of my public profile as a Christian American sportsman, I was often the messenger who helped people respond to the message and then watched as others prayed with people to make their personal commitment. Hand on heart, for me, it was never about the numbers (well, maybe sometimes); it was about the thrill of people beginning their eternal journey with Christ.

Admittedly, I confess that I was a tad jealous to see Johnny Weber or Brian O'Donnell, and so many others from the Jesus Revolution days, kneeling down on the street, at the stadium, holding someone's hand on the train, publicly, openly, weeping and linking arms with those who had responded to the Gospel message. I had opportunities to do so as well, often on the back of preaching and speaking, and it remains my highest and greatest honor, privilege and joy to this day.

What was so cool and goose-bumpy amazing, *even now*, is that this was a normal part of life in those days that followed close on the heels of just expecting God to be moving, working, wooing, and winning people to Himself *daily.*

We didn't know how to counsel, not a bit, not really—just the A, B, Cs mentioned before. The Bible was our counseling manual; and whether in context or out of context, a collection of verses was at our disposal as the tool, the sword, to cut deep, reveal intent, expose and heal hearts, to offer His love and help open up a soul for Jesus to enter and begin to take control. Jesus, through His Spirit; this was the key to unlock it all.

We believed in this utterly and completely.

"If you open your heart, turn your back on your sin and past, and say 'Yes' to Him, then He will forgive you, come into your life, and change you forever. He did it for me. He can do the same for you. It is that simple."

* * *

Praying for People to Receive the Holy Spirit – Things Began to Get Awkward

The AOG taught that the baptism *in, of, with, into* or *by* the Holy Spirit was a separate and distinct experience from accepting Christ into your heart and being saved, which by and large should be a moment-in-time experience in its own right. Salvation should be a time and place event when you said "yes" to Him and accepted Him as Lord. Being baptized in the Holy Spirit should also be a 'calendar event', so to speak.

AOG and other Pentecostal doctrine taught that the really, truly blessed person gave their life to Christ, got baptized as new believer by full emersion in water and received the Holy Spirit along with the gift of speaking in tongues as a sign they had received, preferably in that order.

Looking back, I can recognize the theological gymnastics and doctrinal pretzel twisting we needed to do to justify the steps and stages one went through when the Holy Spirit connected the Gospel dots in us and began the process of change in our lives.

- Yes, Jesus comes into your heart when you accept or receive Him. But how? And how completely?

- Yes, by His Atonement, the Holy Spirit breaks the power of sin in your life and is working to spiritually bury the old man and raise up a new one—the New Creation—when you are baptized in water (but it must be by full immersion for it to work, of course).
- But then, there is the need to be empowered, to receive a special (but not really special, as it should be the norm) infusing and receiving of power to be His witnesses.
- When He, the Holy Spirit, does this, He will confirm it has happened in you by enabling you to speak in tongues—a language you have not learned, a spiritual prayer and praise language. This will be *the sign* that you have been baptized in, by, and with (that you have received) the Holy Spirit for witnessing and service.
- If you haven't spoken in tongues, then *it didn't happen yet*, but He's inside you, and if you try and speak, then the language can come out, and this is the proof that you have *received the Spirit* properly … but only then—

AAAAAAAGGGGGGHHHHH! STOP!

Or was it *"by"* the Holy Spirit?

Or was it *"with"* the Holy Spirit?

Or was it *"of"* the Holy Spirit?

Or was it *"into"* the Holy Spirit?

Or was it when the Holy Spirit *"came upon on"* you?

Or was it *"empowered"* by the Holy Spirit?

Or were you *"in-filled"* with the Holy Spirit?

Or did you *"overflow"* (like a river) with the Holy Spirit?

Or did you *"release"* the Holy Spirit (already in you)?

Or did the Holy Spirt *"release you"* to witness with power?

Or did you receive *"the second blessing"* of the Holy Spirit?

You get the idea? You see the problem?

Usually, because enthusiasm and quite noisy urging was the best way to keep up spiritual momentum and to reduce doubt and increase somewhat blind acceptance, often little time was given to explaining what was really going on. The AOG had a bit of a problem (no, obsession) with controlling how and when He did His thing. Predictability was a necessity. Everything must be done "decently and in order" (1 Cor. 14:40 KJV).

> *"Don't think! Just let Jesus and the Holy Spirit do Their/His thing!"*
>
> *"The Bible (and I) says it, I believe it (and so should you), and that settles it! Trust me!"*

On a personal note, I, of all people, could have built my baptism in the Holy Spirit and speaking in tongues "theology" on personal experience! But I tried not to, as hard as that was.

* * *

Since the birth of the Pentecostal Movement, typically considered to be around 1905 at Azusa Street, California, more than 25,000 Pentecostal, Charismatic, or "Other-costal," or "Other-Asthmatic" denominations or movements have sprung up.

What is interesting, *and sad*, is that the differences between them far too often hinges or depends on *two things* to make their point and establish their credibility in the Kingdom where acceptance in more mainstream Christianity was becoming increasingly essential:

1. One very small Greek word "ev" (ἐν) translated multiple ways in 1 Corinthians 12:13. "For we were all baptized [by, with, in, into] one Spirit so as to form one body...."

2. A strong, charismatic (as in compelling, vibrant, and gifted) personality who made his or her point about the Holy Spirit better than the next person, while claiming some special insight or revelation that sees and knows the truth more completely than "them" down the Christian Road.

* * *

Liberating and Threatening – Squashing and Quenching

These issues were really beginning to emerge and have an impact during the early seventies, and it was both liberating and threatening at the same time. God had invaded our worlds and had broken into our histories with unbelievable power and loving force. We unchurched younger folk were crying out for purpose, meaning, direction, and transformation and were willing to go with, and dive into, whatever spiritual river was flowing without much concern about some of the possible *doctrinal and personality nasties* that might be lurking in that water.

On the other hand, the established Pentecostal church, like the AOG —including and especially Harfield Road, Kenilworth—saw a problem of *containment and conformity*, but at the same time didn't want to squash or quench what God was clearly doing. Pastor John Bond prayed, "Send in the lost ... including the hippies," and *He wonderfully did!* To Pastor Bond's and some of the leaders' credit, they did an admirable job of not letting the boat get rocked too badly by the new wave of enthusiasm and life the Jesus Movement brought with it.

It wasn't easy, as theological intolerance and inflexibility tended to dominate, or at the very least, to rear its historically correct head, in those days. As I have said elsewhere in this book, knowing that a train runs better on rails, I'm sure the Assembly leaders saw a need for a dose of law as essential for helping the new "Jesus People trains" become the best trains we could be. It was needed and was right. I get it.

This is only my opinion, but I also believe that, at a time when spiritual things were headline news, the AOG was trying to establish its legitimacy as a "kosher" and respectable denomination. Very few of the AOG pastors had theological degrees (or any degrees for that matter), and this created image problems when, for example, active pastors leading sizable congregations couldn't obtain a state license to marry people because they hadn't attended an accredited theological college or received a degree of some kind. In addition, I knew of some degreed guys who were tipped for AOG ministry who left to become part of other movements.

The AOG had real problems accommodating, trusting, or even believing the authenticity of the Charismatic Movement in the Anglican, Catholic, or other mainstream churches. This was especially an issue as they baptized babies, which "… [had] misled and given false salvation assurance to millions over the centuries and sent more people to hell by doing so than any other doctrine or movement."

The AOG taught four baptisms, which I won't bother to support or explain with Scripture here:

1. Salvation by personal acceptance of Jesus as Lord and Savior was **baptism into the Body of Christ,** the universal correctly saved and born again believing church but not (probably not) baby-baptizing institutions (e.g., Catholics).

2. **Baptism in water or into Christ** (**only** by full immersion as an adult believer).

3. *Baptism in, by, or with the Holy Spirit* (*only* with speaking in tongues as a confirmation sign).

4. *Baptism in or into Suffering* (which was not highly sought after and seldom fully explained; of course. Why would you want to?).

* * *

Then, There Were Formulae, Tricks, and Techniques (Sanctified, of Course!)

When it came to receiving or having an experience of the Holy Spirit, I considered myself very fortunate. Not only did I *not* have any denominational hang-ups, baggage, or barriers, but I had no expectations about how things were supposed to happen (i.e., doctrinal or preference containment) because in my youth, I'd never even heard of it (Him)!

On the flip side, I think the Lord knew my logical, twist-and-turn, need-to-figure-it-all-out pretzel brain would get in the way of Him doing His thing. So, when I got baptized in water as a believer and knelt and prayed afterward, by merciful design, He filled me, overwhelmed me, overflowed in and out of me, and gifted me a new prayer and worship language—tongues—essentially when I was minding my own business.

Historically, mentally, or experientially, I knew absolutely nothing about the Holy Spirit and His workings. In addition, because I knew my heart at the time, which was full of absolute trust and surrender to the One who had already invaded my life and changed and turned it upside down, I accepted and embraced it all as, well, simply normal.

I can really relate to some of the believers in Ephesus.

"While Apollos was at Corinth, Paul took the road through the interior and arrived at Ephesus. There he found some disciples and asked them, 'Did you receive the Holy Spirit when you believed?' They answered, '**No, we have not even heard that there is a Holy Spirit.**'

"So, Paul asked, 'Then what baptism did you receive?' 'John's baptism,' they replied. Paul said, 'John's baptism was a baptism of repentance. He told the people to believe in the one coming after him, that is, in Jesus.'

"On hearing this, they were baptized in the name of the Lord Jesus. When Paul placed his hands on them, the Holy Spirit came on them, and they spoke in tongues and prophesied. There were about twelve men in all." (Acts 19:1–7)

* * *

The AOG had basically two approaches when praying with people to receive the Holy Spirit or to experience His infilling and releasing or overflowing—*whatever it was called. It often depended on who you asked or who was doing the laying on of hands!*

There were men and women in the AOG movement who, as rumor had it, had "special gifting" when praying for people to receive the baptism of the Holy Spirit. Many people from those days will tell you about Paul Lange, one of the early founders and establishers of the AOG in the Cape Town area. They will testify that he had the gift of praying for the baptism in the Holy Spirit. By that they meant, for some special reason when Paul Lange prayed for people, whatever mental, emotional, or spiritual barriers or resistance that existed that might block or prevent the Holy Spirit's working, were overcome and folk received.

For most of the rest of us, we had to use some technique or other sanctified method to help overcome concerns, wrong expectations, fear, uncertainty, worry about being embarrassed, etc. After all, praying for someone to receive was a true *"Miracle Moment" in our minds and hearts.* God was going to do something to and in someone that defied logic; it was not a hoax or mental trick—it was a *dinkum miracle!* To prove it, *He was going to give you a new prayer and praise language you had never learned* (or ever could learn). Speaking in Tongues defies logic.

The problem, however, was often simply mental or spiritual blockages, so we had a range of methods to help remove or reduce them. I really do know that the following list and description will raise doctrinal and churchmanship hackles in some people. Don't judge too harshly, please. I'm just telling it like it was back then.

1. *Instruction*—sharing a few relevant verses of Scripture if they had not already been shared in the pre-prayer teaching session.

2. *Getting Things Straight and Right with God*—encouraging a time of confession and repentance, not as a matter or question of being perfect or deserving, but as a Grace gift that you could not earn or be good enough for.

3. *You Need To Ask*—demonstrating to God that you really wanted power, to not only witness with words, but also to *be* a witness for Him with your life—in power.

4. *Don't Be Shy*—being willing to be a fool for Christ (if you can't be a fool in a safe place like here, with us, then how can you be "bold for Him on your own out there"?).

5. *Keeping It Light*—encouraging openness and explaining what to expect (the procedure).

6. *Laying on Hands*—praying for them when they've finished praying for themselves.

7. *Asking for the Right Thing—Asking Him* to give them the Holy Spirit more fully and completely (*not* tongues!).

The result: you will speak in tongues—don't be shocked. Breathe in —deeply. Expect Him to do things inside you; you may feel Him stirring and moving you. Speak out! **Don't be shy!**

Humorous Aside

We used to talk about getting folks to "suck and breathe": breathe the Holy Spirit in and out more and more—faster and faster. Then, when they began to feel His presence working in them, as they were breathing out, we got them to *wiggle their tongue!*

Don't laugh! It "worked!"

Then the big connection moment came—the laying on of hands (on their shoulders or head). I often shook and shuddered, sucking, and breathing myself and massaging their scalp (-ish)—*oohing* and *aahing* and being moved powerfully, and speaking in tongues myself (to help them feel less inhibited or shocked).

Now I need to be honest here. Let's face it, when you breathe in and out too much, too quickly, you begin to hyperventilate (i.e., you get the balance between carbon dioxide out and oxygen in, out of kilter). Of the typical seven symptoms of hyperventilation, three of them are:

1. Dizziness (or even a brief feeling of euphoria).

2. Fast, pounding, or skipping heartbeat.

3. Numbness or tingling around the mouth and in the fingers.

"Now, breathe in, breathe out, and wiggle your tongue! Wiggle and mumble ... anything! Do you feel it, my brother/sister?! Now try to copy me ... copy my tongue, copy my language!"

If they didn't or couldn't do this because of, say, a mental block, we might say with a hint of challenge or rebuke, "You have asked Him for power to witness for Christ, to be a fool for Christ! Right?! Yes?! Are you willing and ready to be a fool for Him?!"

"Oh, yes, yes, I am! Yes, I am!"

"OK, then breathe in and breathe out some more—deeper! Keep it up! More! When you feel His presence touching your tongue, your body, your heart! Now be a fool for Him and say these words: 'Here she comes on a Honda.'"

"What?! You're kidding!"

"I thought you wanted to be a fool for Christ—try it!"

"OK. Here she comes on a Honda."

"Come on, with some spiritual enthusiasm and emotion! Again, faster—with some feeling!"

"Hereshe comeson ahonda!"

"Again, faster… Hallelujah, brother/sister! Breathe Him in! Breathe Him out!"

"Hereshecomesonahonda! Hereshecomesonahonda! Hereshecomesonahonda!"

And that's how you do it! You're welcome.

* * *

Optional Sanctified Gimmicks:

- Say, "She sells seashells by the seashore," then, "Shesells seashellsby theseashore," then, "Shesellsseashellsbytheseashore" … faster!

- Say, "Humdellyicous" three times without hesitation.

- Say, "Kiddi killy kitty kiddi kiliharri" (made famous by Ol' Brother What's-His-Name—The Kiddi Kiddi Man—at Harfield Road AOG 1970-74).

- Say, "Supercalifragilisticexpialidocious" with passion and meaning, *backward* (which would be "Suoicodilaipxecitsiligarfilacrepus."

(You're welcome, again!)

CHAPTER THIRTY-SEVEN

When Your Spiritual Ego Hits a Speed Bump

IT HAD BEEN ABOUT SIX MONTHS since I had returned to Cape Town because, as I would share in my public testimony, "I signed a baseball contract with the Varsity Old Boys baseball team, fell in love with a local girl, and gave my life to Jesus—my whole world had changed, and I was headed in a new, good, and eternal direction."

Something like that.

I was playing a lot of ball, cleaning carpets for a steam cleaning carpet company in Observatory, Cape, off-the-charts active in church and other Christian activities and events, and I drove a company kombi. The kombi was greatly used and blessed—always full of young people it seemed—and used to transport youth from all over the Cape to and from events, meetings, camps, and outreaches.

My girlfriend, K, was a boarder at Wynberg Girls' High School, and I was sharing a house in nearby Claremont with a friend from church. We had a pool. It was a fairly classy neighborhood; it was convenient, the rent was low, *AND* my friend had a second car, a 1960 red—and loud—Austin-Healey *convertible.*

In the words of Ferris Bueller, *"It was so choice."*

As you know, I was not a hippie by any stretch of the imagination. Really, I was just a conservative kid from a very small hyper conservative farming village in New York State with longish hair and a bit of a high-profile, sportsman's reputation. I also had truly terrible taste in cool, with it, or groovy clothes.

Actually, I had no taste whatsoever, and anytime I wanted to make a hip fashion statement, I needed to borrow from friends. But even then, it never really seemed to work for me.

An old friend of mine from those days, Cedric Cross, recently (2020) wrote these words about me, and I am so pleased to humbly and smugly re-quote him here.

"Dave arrived at the pinnacle of the Jesus Revolution period. I would refer to him as Tom Cruise in contemporary form. He had the looks, the walk, the talk ... the girls went gaga!"

Cedric was always so perceptive and insightful! Check out the photo again at the beginning of this chapter. You've got to admit, the resemblance to Tom is striking.

Now, as this story goes, I played the dedicated boyfriend card really very well and enthusiastically. I used to come to the boarding hostel every weekend to pick K up for church—faithfully, devotedly, predictably. K told the other girls about her American guy who had returned to South Africa to play baseball—and for her. ("Oh, and he plays for Western Province, too; did I mention that? He, he, he ...")

K very, very much liked to show me off, either with the stories she told about us or, as on this occasion, to literally point and say, "There's MY American boyfriend!"

* * *

The school was having a music concert one evening. K let me know that the event started at 7:00 p.m. and that the boarding house girls would be processing from the hostel to the auditorium at precisely 6:45 p.m. She instructed me to arrive and slowly drive up the driveway toward the auditorium at exactly the same time as the girls would be walking by.

She also wanted me to wear a floral shirt with a huge collar (which I had to borrow), a soft, brown leather vest with tassels and beads (also borrowed), sunglasses (borrowed), my long blondish hair, a big smile, AND I must arrive in my friend's Austin-Healey convertible—the ultimate cool statement, and image.

At precisely the right time, I turned into the school campus driveway and slowly, ever so slowly, top down, my right arm resting on the top of the door, glided toward the girls who were emerging from the hostel.

I revved the engine—*oh yeah!*

Revved it again—oh yeah! Work it, Dave, work it!

When revved, the convertible gave a kind of mini-roar, *like a red lion stalking its prey*, as though I had the power to turn her loose—or tame her wild side.

I could see K in the near distance. There was pointing; her classmates were either giggling or had their hands over their mouths in wonder and awe (my interpretation). K had a grin from ear to ear.

On the final bit of driveway before I turned into the parking lot, there was a speed bump. Without a second thought, I slowly ooched up onto the bump, as my engine revved *just right*.

See me! Look at me! Look at me!

K was saying at that precise moment, "Look at my boyfriend! Look at my boyfriend!"

Then it happened.

I got stuck, rocking like a teeter-totter on top of the speed bump. I tried to lean and rock forward so the front tires touched down. But it was a rear-wheel drive car, so all that happened was my rear tires spun wildly while my engine noise drew attention to the fact that I was stupidly stuck.

I pushed myself back into my seat, *hard*, to try to get the rear tires to gain some traction. *Yes!* For about two seconds. The car lurched forward, the sound of grinding chassis and other parts of the undercarriage making the most horrible, screeching, fingernails dragging down the blackboard sound. I hit the brakes, and the car rocked forward onto the front tires. I was totally hung up—the proverbial seesaw effect was on full display.

All heads turned to look. *Of course, they did.*

I opened the door, put my right foot out (British side steering wheel), tried to rock the car until the rear tires took on the asphalt and hoped I'd gain enough umpf to get the car over the hump. I lost my footing and twisted my ankle as my left foot slipped off the clutch. The car lurched and stalled, *still on top of the bump.*

At least the engine wasn't growling now for the world to hear, "Look at me, look at uncool, non-groovy, stupid me!"

I was running out of cool man credit very rapidly. You would think, **wouldn't you**, that I would put the car in reverse, back up, grind the undercarriage a bit, turn around, drive slowly out of the gate with my embarrassed tail between my rear tires, and park on the street.

But nooooo, not me. It never entered my head.

Instead, I started the engine, shifted into gear—undercarriage, twin exhaust pipes, and chassis **be damned!** —and I tore over the bump in the ugliest, uncoolest, gut- and metal-wrenching way imaginable and carved a trench in the top of the speed bump while I did so.

Now my face and the car were color coordinated!

As I entered the parking area, the laughter of the girls was turning to a murmur as they disappeared around the corner to go into the auditorium. My armpit sweat glands were a nightmare for me in those days, and my cool, borrowed, floral shirt was drenched.

As I painfully limped slowly toward the auditorium, for some reason I remembered the Old Testament story of Jacob wrestling with the angel in Genesis 32:22–30 (sarcastically mistranslated and paraphrased below).

"So, Jacob was left alone, and a man [an angel] wrestled with him till daybreak. When the man saw that he could not overpower him, he touched the socket of Jacob's hip so that his hip was wrenched as he wrestled with the man … [the angel] blessed him there. So, Jacob called the place Peniel [today it's called Austin-Healey-Peniel]. The sun rose above him as he passed Peniel, and he was limping because of his hip." (Hebrew. Lit. "ankle").

I think I was trying to spiritualize my experience by justifying my ego-stupidity and finding some way to put the responsibility on *Jehovah*

Broke-Timex, The God of Imperfect Timing for putting the speed bump in my path at that particular time.

And the Deep Spiritual Lesson is ...

... it's exceptionally hard to learn something of deep and meaningful value, spiritually, when you are not cool in the slightest, and you're driving a very cool, red convertible sports car, and you're really dumb, and you twist your ankle while being especially stupid ...

CHAPTER THIRTY-EIGHT

But I Saw You at Cape Town Station!

SOMETIME IN 1973, I hadn't quite completed a year of study at the University of Cape Town but had decided that it wasn't right for me to continue; so, I found a job operating a computer for a large pharmaceutical company and returned to work. At the time of this story, K was staying with a friend (L) from school who lived with her mother in Plumstead, close to where I also lived.

In those days, as described in other chapters, I was also extremely active speaking for parachurch organizations, churches themselves, or church youth groups. On this occasion, I was scheduled to do a very important session with YFC at a youth meeting in Durbanville (Northern Suburbs), and it was particularly important that I arrive by

7:00 p.m. to prepare. The meeting would begin at 7:30 p.m. It was a Sunday night. The schedule was tight, and it was a school night.

K and L had gone to spend the weekend with K's family in Paarl and were returning by train early Sunday evening. I'm not sure, these many years later, why I decided that I would detour to Cape Town Train Station to meet them when they arrived from Paarl, but that's what I did. The trains were normally on time, but I knew they would only have a few minutes to change train lines and get on the Southern Suburbs train headed to Plumstead. I knew it was going to be tight and that I needed say a quick "hello," give a quick kiss, and say a quicker "goodbye" before getting in my car and driving to the YFC event.

There was some conflict in my heart and mind about this because I knew that if I was completely honest with myself, I was compromising my values, and I was putting a girlfriend ahead of my commitment to share with teenagers about Jesus. I knew the timing was going to be critical, but hopefully God would manage the time for me.

Don't say it.

I checked the arrivals board in the station. The train from Paarl would be arriving at about 6:30 p.m., just enough time for a quick hi-hug-kiss-bye before driving about 20–25 minutes to the youth event (probably over the speed limit). If I was lucky and blessed by the Lord for being both a good boyfriend AND a faithful sharer of the Gospel, I'd make it.

Yeah, sure, right, Dave.

The train arrived at the platform on time, and I saw K and L get off the train and begin to walk along the platform down to the main hall where they would then need to double-check the departure timetable for the trains headed south. I was probably 50 meters away, and I saw what they were wearing, saw the overnight bag each was carrying, and I saw that they were laughing and joking.

They hadn't seen me yet. K wouldn't be expecting me to be there. She'd be totally surprised. This'll be fun!

For fun, I stepped behind a section of wall that also had a glass front where advertisers displayed products and the like. I planned to wait, say 5–10 seconds and then jump out and … *"Surprise!"*

As I began to hide, I noticed a copy of a music album cover on display. It was Santana's latest album, *Abraxas*. I can't tell you why or how, but that cover grabbed my attention, and I felt a sense of foreboding. It really creeped me out. Maybe it was the image of a naked demon with angel wings—I don't know. I'm not saying the cover was evil, and I may be overblowing the significance of it, but I will certainly never forget that cover. There was just something spooky about it.

I shook off the strange, creepy feeling and jumped out from behind the wall.

"Ha! Surprise!"

They weren't there. Gone. I moved toward the platform and looked left and right, up, and down.

Gone.

Oh, I get it—they must have seen me and decided to hide behind one of the large square pillars. Laughing, I looked behind the nearest one expecting to see their smiling, joking faces. Nope.

Ah, the bathroom! (They must have had to pee really badly to get there that quickly!) I ran down to the restroom section of the terminal, and I shouted the girls' names. No answer.

I went into the main terminal area and looked around the kiosks; I looked and called out in other parts of the main hall. No answer.

No girls.

Truly troubled by all this, I looked at my watch and realized that I was now *very* late for the YFC meeting. I drove way too fast while trying to prepare my talk in my head and still struggling with my misguided values but even more with the disappearance of the girls.

The YFC leader, Brian Helsby, was a dear friend but was very upset with me for being extraordinarily late. He was very worried that I might not even be coming at all. This was pre-mobile phone days. He thought he would need to cancel or alter the program. There were a lot of people there! They came to hear me.

I had been feeling so guilty and so troubled while I was driving, and I was still feeling this way as I tried to calm myself down and reassure Brian with my inspirational presence that all would be good. Brian said nothing, which wasn't a good sign. He was skilled at the withering stare.

Instead, God's still, small voice was saying to me, "Davie, you're trying to be a teacher and messenger of right priorities, about putting me first, honoring me with your time, with your talent, with your heart, with your life. Do you hear yourself? Do you see yourself now?"

I was going to stand before a large group of teens and young people who were expecting me to deliver a life-changing, eternal message that could dramatically and wonderfully affect and change their lives, including the direction of their futures, for good, forever. Instead, I had put my own selfish, personal interests first, especially my misdirected focus on a girlfriend. I was heartsick.

As I opened the session in prayer, and as I stood before this group of expectant, spiritually hungry, and searching young people, the Lord really broke me and humbled me and challenged me yet again. In the unspoken quietness of that prayer, I pledged at that moment that I would not let this happen again.

The group heard the call of God. They responded to the message that He was sending into their hearts, not because I was talented, not because I was obedient, and not because I had finally honored Him with my time—or that I had finally put Him first.

They responded simply because He is faithful to do His work and because He will keep His promises, do His thing, and change lives, even if His Word is delivered by a faulty, flawed, stupid, young guy like me. For someone who likes to talk, I didn't have a whole lot to say in the end.

I don't remember what more I shared with that group. I don't remember or can talk much of what transpired after I left that evening. I only know that, despite me, many young people gave their lives to Christ and that in terms of lessons learned, I was living on borrowed time and extended Grace credit.

I drove back to my apartment in Plumstead—about an hour's drive. By now, it was very late and the girls had school the next day. But I could not resist going to L's apartment where K was also. I knocked on the door, and they both came to the door with shocked looks on their faces when they opened it. I told them what had happened and chided them a little angrily about why they'd hidden from me and didn't answer my calling out for them at Cape Town Station.

"Where did you go?! Why didn't you say something? I was frantic with worry!"

They laughed out loud. "What are you talking about?! We never came to Cape Town Station! We got off the train at the Salt River Junction. We didn't need to go all the way into Cape Town. You know that."

"No, no, no way! I saw you both when you got off the train in Cape Town. **I SAW you at Cape Town Station!**"

Some more incredulous laughing. They looked at each other, smiling and grinning, then back at me. "Oh, really?! OK, if you saw us then, what were we wearing?"

257

I described to them their jeans, their sweaters, L's long tan-colored trench coat, their handbags, the bag over K's shoulder, their small hand luggage, and even their shoes to a T.

I've used the word *gob-smacked* a lot in these stories, but this is really the best occasion where it is totally appropriate. Shocked and openmouthed, they confirmed I was exactly right.

OK, maybe this can be explained away. Maybe I saw them wearing these clothes before. Maybe it was a lucky guess. Maybe God used Santana's album cover to pull off a weird mental stunt or something (OK, I didn't mean that!).

All I know is, that night, my focus, my priorities, my commitment to live for Him and live His message out loud were seriously challenged, and God said very specifically, *"I saw YOU, Davie, at Cape Town Station."*

CHAPTER THIRTY-NINE

Do These Two Things,
and God Will Change Your Life

SOMETIME IN 1972, THE ASSEMBLIES OF GOD held its annual conference in Bloemfontein. I remember it well because the Varsity Old Boys baseball club was going on tour to Southwest Africa at the same time. I made the hard decision not to tour with the team and chose rather to attend the conference. I've often recalled the conversation I had with 'Buzz' C. about my decision. Buzz was the first player to follow me out from the USA to play ball in Cape Town. He called me at work and kind of castigated me for my decision.

I told him, "I've prayed about it, and I believe God wants me to go to the conference."

He replied, *"I'm a Christian, and I'm not going to pray about it. We have a duty to go on tour with the team; they brought us here from the States to play!"*

He was right actually, but for me, in those days, being right and righteous were more important than being caring or loving. Point scoring was a close 2nd, even if the shot should never have been taken in the first place. This was all part of my Christian modus operandi at that time.

Anyway, I went to the conference—my first one. Some of us went as semi-freeloaders, as we were broke and couldn't come close to fully paying our way. As I had shared a ride with friends, as had others, no one really knew about my situation. I had a place to sleep, but otherwise wandered around and looked hungry until someone felt led to offer me some food. Sound familiar?

I was really pumped up about attending because all the big AOG names were going to be there. The legendary, miracle working Mullan brothers (James and Fred), John "Brother" Bond (of course), Paul Lange, John Stegmann, Paul Watney, Noel Scheepers, Jessop Sutton, Noel Cromhout, and some others who I really, greatly enjoyed hearing minister, especially "Brother" (Faans) Klopper.

I had my cassette tape recorder and four blank 90-minute tapes ready to catch every word of every talk, because rumor had it, that the focus would be on a better understanding of the Gifts of the Holy Spirit. I was particularly keen to hear and learn more about this, not least because I was feeling a little spiritually miffed—no, disappointed—that we only had a steady diet of tongues, interpretation, and prophecy. (Then, pretty much the same people using the Gifts had quite repetitive messages.) You've read about my "miftness" before.

And why were there never any sports-related prophetic messages?!

Personally, I was very much challenged to use the public Gift of Tongues, and more often than not, felt that what I expressed in spiritual/tongues words came from deep within me. Yet, the interpretation didn't seem to capture that aspect—the heart sense.

One thing I did come to know and experience, sometime later, was that *kinds* of tongues (1 Cor. 12:10) was not only a reference to different languages but also to what the tongue was used for (e.g., praise, intercession, rebuking, a message, etc.). The kind of tongue was dictated by the need, as it were. Maybe I was being a little critical because the only kind of tongue expected in a meeting context would be the message type. I accept that my thinking on this was on very thin ice theologically, but no one was explaining it to me so I went with the flow as I understood it and was experiencing it.

Anyway, I wanted to broaden my knowledge and understanding and hoped the conference would help. I was also really curious about how the Lord did or didn't do miracle things, ever since He had wonderfully healed my arm and **not healed** my blind eye the year before.

* * *

These 50+ years later, I can only remember two teaching sessions from that conference, which is surprising (as in, "You're kidding! You can remember back *that* far?!").

As I write, I am reminding myself that nearly my entire Christian and biblical foundation was AOG. I seldom actually questioned what was taught but had tons of questions burning inside me.

I hated the unspoken expectation that we needed to swallow and follow and keep a set of new spiritual laws [e.g., no drinking, smoking, rock music, bioskoop *(Afrikaans – "movies")*, sex, along with regular quiet times, witnessing, meeting attendance, etc.]. As I have said before, I don't ever recall, *ever*, an AOG teacher of any repute (except Brother Klopper) saying, "I don't know what this verse of the Bible really

261

means," or admitting that there were equally valid, differing views on a portion of Scripture.

Throw into the mix the tried and trusted *"How to Be a Good Christian"* formula—**Facts + Faith + feelings** (with small *f*) = **Good Bible Believing** and "God said it, I believe it, so that settles it!"

This pretty much summed up my hesitation to ask questions or to challenge, well, pretty much anything.

That said, and I repeat, the teaching, pastoral care, and support I received in those early years from Brother Bond, Noel Cromhout, and other leaders and Elders at Harfield Road AOG in Kenilworth, Cape, (especially Brother Klopper) holds *eternal worth in my life that cannot be overstated.*

I owed my life to these men of God, yet I was so desperate to discover the "real" Dave Lutes' life—the authentic me who knew God's power in his life. I was on doctrinally solid ground, yet my walk was shaky and wobbly because I didn't own the theological shoes I was walking in. The AOG leaders owned them, and I was scared to try to walk in some other pair or style, much less tell them that the shoes didn't fit so well or to question why the shoes pinched sometimes.

* * *

The first session that I remember from the conference was on the Gift of Faith. Several guys shared a range of, what I would have called even back then, Bible-based but "theory-logical speculation." I was recording it all, but as it dragged on and on and really didn't go anywhere, I finally turned off the recorder. They clearly had no actual experience of that particular gift.

What really surprised me, however, was when one of the Mullan brothers stood up, and in the least kind way I had yet heard or seen up to that time in the AOG, basically said that the previous speakers were talking nonsense. My ears perked up, and I was now on the edge of my seat with my finger poised over the "Record" button.

He gave a short summary of what he believed the Scriptures said, cited a couple of examples of outstanding acts of faith and healing in the Bible and then transitioned to, in my mind, *the crucial points*:

- What is a Gift of Faith? *Whose* is it?
- Is it something that I, as the user, received and then gave to someone else in the form of a miracle, or is it something someone else, or something I'm praying about or for, receives?
- How do you know you have it (or need to give it to someone else), and how do you exercise it—practically?
- Are you in control of your thoughts and feelings, choices, and actions when the gift comes?
- Is it more about faith miracles with things (e.g., water into wine), events (e.g., stepping out of the boat and walking on water), the natural elements (e.g., parting the sea), people's healing (e.g., go wash the spittle-mud out of your eyes and you will see again), or death to life (e.g., the raising of Jairus' daughter)?

As Brother Mullan paused to make what I sensed was going to be a profound and powerful point, I fumbled with my recorder to make sure I caught it on tape.

I did.

Essentially, he said this (and these many years later, I so wish I had kept the recording):

> *"When I lay my hands on a corpse and pray, I don't take my hands away until I feel that corpse tingling with life. That's the Gift of Faith."*

> *Mouth wide open, at first, I said in an awe-filled whisper,*

"WOW!"

Then I caught my breath, stilled my heart, and mused, "That's it?!"

Yep, that was it.

I sat there absolutely stunned into disbelief mixed with something inside me saying:

That's presumption on an epic scale!

It was either that, or God, who was watching over the corpse alongside Brother Mullan, felt cornered into doing something because His reputation was at stake if He didn't pull it off as per Brother Mullan's word. Or He would ignore him, **and** the corpse, and let Brother Mullan sweat (while Brother Mullan came up with a plausible explanation about why his prayer of faith didn't work.)

The big question that loomed before me was this: If Brother Mullan didn't know that raising a dead person up was in God's plan for that person, at that moment in time, then he (Mullan) could be standing there for a very long time?! Does God only PUT A MIRACLE INTO HIS PLAN when He sees someone exercising faith like that?!

My head and heart began to spin out of control with questions.

Then another worrying thought crossed my mind: *This view and approach to miracles was a breeding ground for High-Profile Gurus and Faux Spiritual Superstars!*

Is that where this was headed?! Is this what we really wanted?!

But because it was one of the Mullan brothers, we all loudly said, "Amen! Praise the Lord!" … and went to have coffee.

* * *

I went to a friend's cabin in a state of frustration and confusion. This may sound unappreciative, naïve, arrogant, or just plain dumb, but I felt cheated by such an offhanded, kind of cheap faith one-liner.

Not that I deserved special revelation or help, but what Brother Mullan had said just didn't help me at all!

I mulled it over, paced the room, and decided I needed to go and see the one man, an Elder at Harfield Road in the AOG, whom I truly, truly respected, and completely trusted in deep heart-to-heart moments. His teaching was never loud, pompous, opinionated, or lacking in humility, and he was always patient and tolerant of my millions of questions— Faans "Brother" Klopper.

I found his cabin, knocked on his door, and was invited inside where I found him sitting at a table with his Bible open. I apologized for barging in on him and told him I needed to ask him something important. I noticed immediately, however, that something was different, not wrong, just (now don't accuse me of exaggeration) mystical, like the room was charged with Holy Spirit energy: with His presence. I don't know how else to describe it. God was just very *there*.

This was a new one for me.

As I began to speak, he placed his hand on his Bible and kind of stroked it with reverence and had a faraway look in his eyes that even my youthful "I-need-all-the-answers-and-I-want-it-all-and-I-want-it-now" impatience could recognize as something very powerful and special happening within or to Brother Klopper.

Now was NOT the time to bother him.

He was in a special place and moment with God, and I needed to butt out. *Even I* could sense it.

I stopped talking, made a mumbling apology, and excused myself and went straight to get my tape recorder. I just knew that Brother

Klopper was going to be sharing with the group when we returned to the session—and whatever it was, *I knew it would change my life.*

I just knew it.

It was one of those young Christian life, beginning to "know in my knower" moments. It didn't happen often, and I was still learning to know when something special was going on; this was one of those times.

I prepared my recorder, put in the Gift of Faith Mullan tape to record over it, made sure my batteries were fresh, got to the room early, found a seat right in the front row, and waited for Brother Klopper to share.

* * *

I'll say it now and repeat it again at the end of this chapter: *what he shared DID change my life.* I have never forgotten it; it has become a cornerstone in my Christian life and ministry. As I write about it these many years later—with grateful tears—I would guess that I have preached on the same message in various forms at least a hundred times.

Many people from all over the world have shared with me that that message was profound and eternally foundational for their lives.

I fully accept that it may have been a God's-perfect-timing thing for me and that what he shared was specially right only for me at that stage in my life. For someone else, it may not have been relevant or may even have prompted them to ask, "What's the big deal?"

I'll try to do justice to what Brother Klopper said and taught.

* * *

In essence, he shared the many places in Paul's letters where he consistently, faithfully, and lovingly did (or said) two things for and to those who received his letters.

1. ***He gave thanks to God for them*** and that the Lord had broken into their personal histories with His love through the Gospel, especially when they, as Gentiles, had no historical context that included a living, powerfully creative, history-invading, life-changing and nation-shaping God— unlike what Israel had.

2. ***He prayed for his readers*** that they might discover, see, experience, taste, and enjoy the multifaceted, pure, white light spectrum prism-ness of God (my words) —that they wouldn't just look with their eyes but would see with their hearts; they wouldn't just take a sip of water, but they would drink fully, completely, deeply and overflow with His love and power to the world.

* * *

In short, he thanked God for them and prayed for them to be filled with the fullness of God (Eph. 3:19).

Brother Klopper believed that it was these two foundational truths (and best practice) that enabled Paul to be able to say to the Romans:

*"**I know that when I come to you, I will come in the full measure of the blessing of Christ**" (Rom. 15:29).*

You do this for others, and God will do it for and in you.

Oh man! Wow!

* * *

Give thanks to Him for others.

Pray for others.

He stressed that it was almost like a sanctified spiritual formula or recipe. If you did these two things faithfully, consistently, humbly, and with a sincere heart, then you, yourself, would be filled with the fullness of God.

> *"Do you want to live and walk in the Light and in the fullness of the Spirit and be a blessing to others and transform the world? Do you want to bring with you, have as part of your life, the full measure of the blessing of Christ? Then, spend a lot more time focused on Him and others and a lot less time on yourself. Throw away your prayer shopping list mentality and change yours and others' worlds by beginning to do those two things."*

Brother Klopper cited other references in Paul's letters, which emphasized that it was **what** *he prayed that was so important* and *not* just the fact **that** Paul prayed for those reading his message. He stressed that it isn't a question of using the words of Paul's prayers verbatim, like some kind of mantra or liturgy, but to capture the essence and meaning and to **want it** (for them) and **mean it** (for them) from the deepest part of your heart.

* * *

Note: Please understand, I'm not trying to give you (readers) a Bible study here, but I do urge you to pray-read the following verses in their entirety. While you do so, picture or focus on one or two people in your life and as you read, reach out and give. **Want** the truth in those verses for them; **grab them** spiritually in your hands and arms and imagine embracing those people with the eternal, hope-filled, life-changing meaning of the words.

* * *

Ephesians 1:15–19

*"For this reason, ever since I heard about your faith in the Lord Jesus and your love for all God's people, **I have not stopped giving thanks for you, remembering you in my prayers.** I keep asking that the God of our Lord Jesus Christ, the glorious Father, may give you the Spirit of wisdom and revelation, so that you may know Him better. I pray that the eyes of your heart may be enlightened in order that you may know the hope to which he has called you, the riches of his glorious inheritance in his holy people, and his incomparably great power for us who believe."*

Colossians 1:9–12

*"For this reason, since the day we heard about you, **we have not stopped praying for you.** We continually ask God to fill you with the knowledge of his will through all the wisdom and understanding that the Spirit gives, so that you may live a life worthy of the Lord and please Him in every way: bearing fruit in every good work, growing in the knowledge of God, being strengthened with all power according to his glorious might so that you may have great endurance and patience, and giving joyful thanks to the Father, who has qualified you to share in the inheritance of his holy people in the kingdom of light."*

Philippians 1:7–11

*"It is right for me to feel this way about all of you, since I have you in my heart and, whether I am in chains or defending and confirming the gospel, all of you share in God's grace with me. God can testify how I long for all of you with the affection of Christ Jesus. **And this is my prayer:** that your love may abound more and more in knowledge and depth of insight, so that you may be able to discern what is best and may be pure and blameless for the day of Christ, filled with the fruit of righteousness that comes through Jesus Christ—to the glory*

and praise of God."

2 Thessalonians 1:11–12

*"With this in mind, **we constantly pray for you**, that our God may make you worthy of his calling, and that by his power he may bring to fruition your every desire for goodness and your every deed prompted by faith. We pray this so that the name of our Lord Jesus may be glorified in you, and you in Him, according to the grace of our God and the Lord Jesus Christ."*

* * *

Brother Klopper concluded his time of sharing with this portion from Ephesians 3.

Ephesians 3:14–19

*"... for this reason, **I bow my knees before the Father**, from whom every family in heaven and on earth derives its name. I ask that out of the riches of His glory He may strengthen you with power through His Spirit in your inner being, so that Christ may dwell in your hearts through faith. Then you, being rooted and grounded in love, will have power, together with all the saints, to comprehend the length and width and height and depth of the love of Christ, and to know this love that surpasses knowledge, **that you may be filled with all the fullness of God."***

The implications for my own self-centered, performance-driven, egocentric, love of the platform and the applause? My Christian life took a serious bless-ed knock that day.

That spiritual kick in the pants changed my life.

* * *

Author's Note and P.S.: Some years later, maybe as many as five, I bumped into Brother Klopper at a coffee shop in Cape Town. I don't remember the context or why we were in the same place at the same time, but I know how my heart leapt for joy when I saw him. In the years since he'd shared at the conference, I'd like to believe I had learned some things—albeit usually painfully.

But two things I definitely knew were:

1. I'm a better person, pastor and leader because I focus more on others in prayer and worship and in my giving of thanks for and appreciating others.

2. It is hard, and sometimes depressing, when you've faithfully shared from your heart—in a sermon or otherwise—and you get the impression that the hearers didn't appreciate, didn't understand, or didn't benefit from it. In short, it's nice when your stuff is remembered and appreciated sometimes.

When we sat to chat, I reached across the table and took his hands in mine, and with tears in my eyes, I told him what his conference message meant to me and that every time I think of him, I think of his faithfulness to us young guys at Harfield Road AOG and how he always shared from his heart and from a place of deep humility.

But it was still ***that message*** at the conference that had changed my life.

He was so shocked and so shaken emotionally that he could barely speak.

In a hushed tone of genuine and profound surprise, all he could say was, "Really?" Then, "Thank you for telling me. You have no idea what it means to me."

I didn't yet, but that didn't stop us as we cried together.

* * *

Tribute Footnote: This week, as I write (4th week of December 2020), I received a message from Brother Klopper's daughter, Margie, that he had passed away on December 24, 2020—ten days short of his 96th birthday. I had only that week added some of the final touches to this chapter, and the news of his death touched me deeply.

Isn't it profoundly amazing how eternally sown seeds, planted in love and in His name, by faithful men and women of God, can produce eternal fruit all over the world?!

We will never know until that Day when all is revealed just how wonderfully Brother Klopper touched many thousands of lives. As I reflected on the news and gave raucous, but humble, thanks for Brother Klopper's life, I found myself wanting to say to him, "I've got a song on my cassette tape player now—save a worship dance for me, Brother Klopper!"

CHAPTER FORTY

Now WHAT IS Your Problem, Mr. Lutes?

I WAS A CO-LEADER IN THE YOUNG ADULT GROUP at the AOG church in Kenilworth, I was absorbing and memorizing the Bible (KJV, of course) at a rate of knots, and I was attending as many meetings as I could go to in a week—at the church, someone's home, or in Cape Town central—while at the same time studying or working a job, playing baseball nine months out of the year, and further exhausting myself with frequent Youth for Christ events where I often spoke as a Christian sportsman. You already know all this.

I was armed with a spiritual sword that was finely and beautifully honed through being able to tell anyone who asked me, on any given day, "What did you get in your quiet time today, brother?" In addition, I had accumulated an impressive number of notches in the sword handle by lopping off witnessees ears with well-struck verses from Romans (à la Peter in the Garden of Gethsemane).

What's odd, is that even though the church would teach us, again and again, on the deep, amazing truths about God's Grace embodied in justification by faith and substitutionary atonement, *I didn't, for some reason, get it.* They, of course, taught that there's nothing we could do to earn our way into Heaven and that our sin and even our own good works only led to spiritual death—that the very best we could offer through our own effort was merely filthy rags in His sight when compared to His holiness and perfection ("… all our righteous acts are like filthy rags …" Isaiah 64:6b). But, like I said, I didn't grasp the deeper truth of this in my heart.

They stressed, rightly, that our sins—past, present, and future—were forgiven and forgotten, that He had broken the power of sin in our lives, and that, through the power of the indwelling Holy Spirit, we could live righteous, victorious, and holy lives. We were reminded that He promised to come into our lives by His Spirit and transform us from the inside out.

Amen to all of that! What Mercy and Grace! Hallelujah!

But it didn't matter; I still needed to prove my acceptability. I was all about achievement—a dance that must be performed to a fanatical and energetic tune and drum-heartbeat.

We were taught that the blood of Jesus was enough to cleanse and was enough to give us access into God's presence. We didn't need to, indeed could not, come to God any other way or on any other basis. All we needed to do was repent, turn our back on our sin, call upon Him to forgive us and to wash our sins away, indwell us by His Spirit (enabling us to walk in the Light) … and we would be saved and transformed. He would give us power to overcome sin and live for Him.

It might not be easy all the time (indeed, the Bible promised us it could be exceedingly difficult!) but keeping short accounts (repentance and confession on the run), having a mindset of walking in a state of continuous cleansing, walking in the light—*yeah, that's the ticket!*

"... if we walk in the light, as he is in the light, we have fellowship with one another, and the blood of Jesus, his Son, purifies us from all sin." (1 John 1:7)

It was all by Grace and Mercy, not by effort. Whether we passed or failed, did good or bad, achieved some goal, or fell flat on our faces; whether we did hundreds of righteous acts, or messed up daily, the only basis for entry into His presence *was the blood of His Son.* The price He paid through His sacrifice was sufficient.

* * *

Note: At the precise moment that I was editing the above sentence, the following quotation was posted on Facebook. "Christianity isn't about the sacrifices we make but in the sacrifice we trust."

Preach it, brother!

* * *

While I was really wow-digging these truths and really trying to understand and live them (and I could certainly preach about it with power and vigor), I was still a young man who was not only a baseball player, not only something of a local sports celebrity, not only a leader in the church, but also a normal guy with testosterone kept reasonably well in check by good church spiritual laws.

My girlfriend at this time (K) had by now transferred to the Southern Suburbs of Cape Town to attend and become a boarder at a girls' high school. In other words, she stayed in the boarding house most of time and got out on weekends and came to church or other events with the permission of her parents and the school—or she would sometimes go home on the weekends to her family. Sometimes I went with her. You know this from earlier chapters.

As was our custom, on a Saturday or Sunday night, I would pick her up and we would attend church together. We would attend the service, maybe stay briefly for any after-service thing that was going on, and then I would take her back to the boarding house—before a certain time —only a couple of miles away.

On one particular occasion, the Saturday outreach service ended a little bit early, and while I'm driving K to the boarding house, as was our custom, we stopped and parked somewhere private. I had a company kombi, and we would usually sit and kiss a bit, do a little cuddling (nothing too serious), and we would pray together.

Certainly, by today's standards we did absolutely nothing wrong at all—no touching, no aggressive pressing of our bodies, or other "misbehaving." We had never crossed that line, never had sex, and had not even wanted to—nor had we, to use a quaint South African phrase, *gronched* or "groped."

As I said, we always prayed.

But about that teenage guy hormone problem … For some reason, on this occasion when we stopped, we had a little extra time, and so there was a little longer time not praying and a little bit longer time kissing. The breathing got a bit heavier and romantically aggressive— not by mutual consent, I might add. To say we got carried away would be overstating things considerably; it was absolutely innocent, comparatively speaking.

Still, we crossed a line that neither of us wanted to cross because we believed to do so would be to dishonor God. I even worryingly suspected one of the church Elders would supernaturally know the minute we came back to church and give me the *anointed, all-knowing, withering stare.*

The idea of having sexual intercourse never entered our minds, and we never did during the entire time that we were together as boyfriend and girlfriend (nearly 3 years). Nevertheless, we both felt guilty that we had become a little bit too passionate (me for pushing it; she for allowing me to). As soon as I dropped her off, I raced home to my apartment full of the deepest remorse and guilt I had ever known. A sleepless night followed; the pain of guilt only worse in the morning as I prepared to go to church.

Time for church … time to perform … time to be: "Hey bro, yeah, I'm great, praise the Lord! Amen, brother! Thanks, I'm great, just great!"

I could not pray. I could not speak. I had no Bible verse to share. I couldn't testify to an amazing quiet time. I couldn't even think of doing anything publicly (the usual measuring stick: pray out loud, testify, share a word, give a message in tongues, etc.). I was fully expecting one of the Elders at the end of the service to this time ask me, "Were you even in neighborhood this morning, brother?"

I was so full of guilt and so remorseful and so utterly broken that I had failed God and failed my girlfriend and failed myself and failed the church, I could barely breathe. Such was the mental and spiritual beating I gave myself. I was borderline crippled emotionally—utterly numb with regret—which is quite startling considering I carried with me to South Africa back in 1970, before I became a Christian, the awful guilt of my girlfriend's pregnancy and abortion.

I skipped the normal lunch after church with the pastor's family and other aspiring young ministry guns and went back to the apartment barely able to think. I cried, and I sobbed heart wrenchingly for ages.

I was a prisoner of remorse-filled guilt.

Without belaboring the point, I repented, and I confessed before God that I had failed Him … over and over again. As I began to feel some spiritual relief, yet another wave of failed performance, I let the side down, "What-a-terrible-person-I-am" guilt racked my body and soul. It was a truly terrible, terrible time. I'd never known such remorse for something that I had done (or not done) that I felt was so utterly wrong and bad. *Unworthy.*

Promises and vows of atonement and deal-making poured out of me as I tried anything to make things right. I wondered, *In the light of this dismal failure of the night before, could I ever again be good enough for Him?*

What was bothering me more? *Could I trust myself to ever be truly faithful to God and the promises I had made? I felt I had failed Him so easily. What if a real temptation ever came my way in future?!*

After some time, I got out pen and paper, and I wrote a letter to K apologizing, telling her how sorry I was, how badly I felt, how wrong it was, and that it would never, ever happen again. As I was writing, the tears welled up and dripped onto the letter; the inked words on the paper now stained and smudged.

But I had to finish it—*I must!* I got the letter finished finally but still could not shake the guilt; still could not get free; still could not find forgiveness and peace.

"That's OK, I didn't deserve His peace anyway, you scum of a Christian! You loser!"

I sealed up the letter, put it in an envelope, and was going to find a way to get it to K, perhaps that evening somehow when she came to the Gospel service. Maybe I would drop it off at the boarding house.

But I didn't see her. She didn't come. She couldn't come. Maybe she didn't want to come, and I couldn't call her. I didn't drop the letter off at school. Instead, my heart slowly, but surely, dropped through the floor.

I numbed my way through the Gospel service that evening and was even less engaged than in the morning. A verse we sang from the hymn,

"The Love of God"—"The guilty pair bowed down with care ..."—didn't really help much. It was crippling in the extreme.

People, of course, asked me what was wrong, and I said, "Nothing, no, nothing, I'm great, just great ... Praise the Lord!" and I had all kinds of Christian slang and jargon quick to hand so everybody still knew that I was on top of my game and that I was still the same strong, amazing Christian that I had hoped everybody had come to believe I was.

I went home that evening, cried some more, repented some more—it didn't help. I couldn't sleep that night at all and woke up an absolute wreck. I had to go to work and get through the day somehow.

* * *

Both of my bosses were Christians, so of course, they noticed something was wrong. They probed with concern, and I kind of sidestepped it with, "No, it's OK; nothing is wrong. I'm not feeling so good, blah, blah, blah ..."

* * *

I got through my day somehow and was in my kombi, driving back along the main artery of the Southern peninsula to my apartment in Plumstead. As I was driving, I was crying, and as I was crying-driving, remorse, regret, and self-doubt crush-grabbed my soul again.

I had failed!

Quit fighting it, Lutes. Deal with it—you're a "failure kid" (my nickname back home). *Forget being the new Davie; you've fallen short, again, just like before ... Get used to it.*

I agreed with the inner demon voice. Despair joined me in the kombi. This was the end of me. I guess I always knew it would happen ... that I would fail like this eventually.

* * *

Then, in the middle of the soul-dying remorse, came that still small voice; that unique whisper in your spirit; that calm but firm word that finds its way into your soul. A glimmer of light began to break through, to peek through the jail cell window. I can't say it was a real voice. All I know is that it happened inside my head and deep inside my heart and was as clear and loving as anything I've felt and known before or since.

I knew in my "knower" that the voice had purpose, and it was purposed on me.

"Now, WHAT IS your problem, Mr. Lutes?"

Yep, it was God.

My words quickly machine-gunned out of my mouth: "Lord, you know, you know, you know what happened! I did this and this, and then I did that and that, and I crossed the line with K, and it was oh so bad, and I feel so bad, and it was terrible, and I'm so sorry. I'm so sorry!"

He said, "You know, wow, that's really bad. What did you do about it?"

Barely able to choke out the words, "You know, Lord, I repented. I said, 'I'm sorry,' I confessed; I asked you to wash it away, to break its power, to forgive me … to give me a chance to start again!"

He *hmmm'd* and then said, "You know, I remember that, but it's funny, I don't remember what it is that you did. What was it again?"

In anguish, I near inaudibly whispered, "But Lord, you *know* what I did!"

Like a litany of guilt, I retold, redescribed, relisted, and recounted all of the bad stuff that was part of my sinful behavior. On top of that, *I managed to drag stuff that I had done in my teenage years before into the mix while I was at it.*

He said with so much love, so much arm-around-my-shoulder understanding, *"Wow, that's really bad. What did you do about it?"*

Now with a tear-drenched scream I cried out, "Lord, you know what I did! Why do you want me to keep telling you?! OK, OK … I know I deserve it!"

I was barely able to see the road because of the tears.

At about mid-Claremont, now I was not just crying; I was wailing, and I was pleading with Him: "Lord, you know I said I'm sorry. I confessed; I told you that it wouldn't happen again. I asked for your forgiveness to wash it away, and … and …"

Not sounding at all exasperated, He interrupted, "You know, I remember that, but I can't remember what you did."

The light came on, and the penny dropped.

* * *

You know that moment of exhilarating awareness, the feeling you have when you first fall in love, that sense of awe when you look at the ocean or snowcapped mountains for the first time; when you are mesmerized by a young baby's smile, or when the brilliance of a long-concealed mystery breaks through to your heart and mind?!

"My son, my child, my boy, my delight, the one whom I love enough, so much, that I sent my own Son to die for you—my Davie, listen to me—it is enough! It is enough. He is enough."

The blinding realization overpowered me: that if we confess our sins, He will forgive us our sins and cleanse from us all that's wrong.

He would take our sins and throw them as far as the East is from the West, and He would remember them no more.

He would *choose,* out of love and Mercy, and because it's His nature and His promise, to forget our sins.

In a flash of light-filled revelation wrapped in sheer joy, He reminded me that no matter what wrong we did, if we would but turn our back on it and call upon Him, He would not remember our sin. It was gone, forgiven, and forgotten, cleansed—a new beginning. He cannot lie and He cannot, by choice, remember our sins!

He chooses not to remember our sin! He chooses not to remember MY sin!

Oh, my word!

As the light came on, and as those words and that truth became washing-over-and-through-my-soul real to me, I began to float-drive. I began to sing, in English, and then in the Spirit! I began to worship, and I hoped a cop was not following me because I was definitely breaking the speed limit as I worship-cruised (but really, I cared very little). I don't even remember driving the next half dozen miles home.

I was so eye-popping aware of the extraordinary fact that my God was bigger than my sin, and that my personal God, my Friend, my King, my Dad, my Abba, my Papa, the One had taken up residence inside me and had decided to be partners with me—my Leader—in my new life.

He had given and was giving me the freedom to walk in light and to walk in love and to walk in peace and to walk in forgiveness—as well as giving me the power to change things, to make a difference in the world, to not be crippled by guilt—or by my past or by my regrets. He had erased and set me free from all the burdens I had kept over the years that had told me, as I had told myself, that I was unacceptable. He accepted and loved me unconditionally and totally—***wow!***

"So, what is YOUR problem, Mr. Lutes?"

"Dear God, I have no problem ... Well, yes, I do, but sort of ... My only problem is me. Mr. Lutes can't learn to forgive himself. But I'm working on it; please show me how to do it."

* * *

Author's Footnote: I have probably spoken about, shared privately, or preached about this story at least 40–50 times in the last 50+ years. It's been truly humbling that so many, many people have come to me or contacted me, often years later, to tell me how the message of this story touched or changed their lives. Even now, while writing it this time, yet again, I was moved to goose bumps, grateful tears, and deep soul appreciation for God's Patience, Mercy, and Grace—and His unconditional love and forgiveness. I hope some part of the account touches you as well.

CHAPTER FORTY-ONE

Huge Changes and the Pastor Nipper Miracle Show

THE FIRST SIX MONTHS OF 1974 WERE A BLUR. I was living with a family from the church but knew I only had a few more months before I had to move out. Looking for a new place was a time challenge as I couldn't fill any more hours and days with Christian activities of various kinds.

But while that time was a blur, one thing I knew was that there was a deep, deep longing inside me for God to be more evident, more obviously powerful, and more supernatural in both my inner life, and in terms of how I wanted to live and work for Him. I really believed He was in the business of miracles—the whole package—soul, body, spirit, mind; salvation, healing, and deliverance; relationships, society; restoration of the whole person—the whole of life.

Looking back, I can truly and honestly say that it was not the sensational that I was seeking; I wanted Him to be powerfully real and for me to be part of Him offering the Full Gospel package to everyone that I came into contact with. The world needed to be put back together, and I wanted to be part of it.

Then hormones got in the way, or rather, decided to disrupt my focus. I was on my way to being seriously derailed if I wasn't careful and didn't get my priorities right. The mix of conflicting obsessions really began to take its toll. Gratefully, He stepped in and brought me to my senses, but it wasn't easy or painless.

Actually, I was becoming way too intense about everything I did. I wanted the miraculous, but I also wanted it to be done decently and in order with a logical, predictable format that was found in the *How to Do Miracles Handbook,*—which had yet to be written.

That said, I was reading and listening to everything I could get my hands on about the miraculous, especially material being put out by Derek Prince, Don Basham, Bob Mumford, Ern Baxter, etc. (the Fort Lauderdale crowd). They weren't gimmicky or about the big name and show from the platform. They talked more about the how-to aspects. I was lapping it up. I wasn't sure how I felt about their statement, "At least 75% of all born-again Christians have at least one demon," but they seemed to cite real-time, practical evidence, so I tried to remain open to the idea.

In the process, I not only lost my spiritual rhythm, but I decided to force my rather strong hormone-driven will on K. It didn't work or happen—instead, rightly, on a cold winter's day in mid-1974, she broke up with me. Worse (or better, depending on how you look at it), she told me she was in love with one of my best friends, F. I was devastated and really quite crippled emotionally and spiritually. It wasn't until sometime later that I began to realize how unhealthily dependent I had become on K for spiritual sanity and balance.

That said, I couldn't bear to be around their budding romance, so with the caring understanding and blessing of Pastor Noel, I left the AOG in Kenilworth and offered to help out at the newish fellowship in Pinelands. It was predominantly a late teen, young adult crowd that met in the Municipal Library Hall. The pastor, Paul W., was on long-term sick leave, so the roles of leading fell to Johnny Weber, Vernon Light, and me (each of us working full-time jobs) with some support from a few married couples who provided the necessary "parental" oversight and stability.

As it was midwinter, there would be no baseball until at least mid-September, so I got stuck into whatever God had in mind for me, taking it with both hands and arms and a full heart, diving in headfirst, and throwing every bit of time and energy I had into discovering the serving power of God. I still didn't have a clue what it meant or how to do miracle stuff, but at least I felt like I was on the road to recovery—and discovery. Johnny and Vernon were at least as hungry as I was for this as well. It was almost all we talked about. Preaching, teaching, laying on hands, bold witnessing, exhorting, prophesying (in AOG tradition), and stepping out of the boat with as much faith as we could muster, became our lifestyle.

Fortunately, none of us was romantically encumbered ... for the time being.

* * *

In August 1974, I was keener than ever to know more about miracles, and suddenly, at the same time, to know more about Pauline (a very good friend from the young adult group) who was now a potential girlfriend. Isn't it strange how you can know someone for a long time and then suddenly see them with entirely new eyes?

We spent one evening together, in fading light, with a weak briquette fire in the fireplace, drinking lukewarm hot chocolate and listening to Derek Prince tapes on the Gifts of the Holy Spirit. It doesn't get much more romantic and intimate than that!

On our first official public date, I took her to "A Night of Miracles" at Claremont Civic Centre, hosted by Pastor J. M. Nipper, "Worker of Miracles." I mean, you gotta admit, I really knew how to show a girl a good time!

Concerned that the place would be packed, we entered the hall a good 30 minutes before things got going. We received a sing-along sheet at the door and went down the sloping aisle to sit in the very front row below the stage—right where all the action might be. I did this for several reasons:

1. I didn't want to miss a thing.

2. I didn't want to miss a thing.

3. I didn't want to miss a thing.

I was aware that people were looking at us, sort of. I gathered so because by this time I was fairly well known as the "Christian Sportsman" and youth speaker and because many of those in the hall were from the same AOG church from just around the corner in Kenilworth. I admit it felt good to be known, but oddly, I also felt a degree of responsibility to be a good listener, an attentive observer and participator, and an "experiencer" of any miracle-ly stuff that might happen that evening.

It may sound arrogant, but I felt like *my* behavior and *my* reactions to what might go on there that evening would be some kind of litmus test of authenticity, if I can put it that way. I knew I really wanted anything special that happened to **not** be a so-called *miracle*, something good that sort of happened or an "I accept the miracle by faith even though nothing really happened" event.

I was looking for the real deal ("dinkum"), and I wanted to be up close and personal with anything "real" that might take place.

While we sat waiting for the place to fill up, we noticed a couple of men placing a stack of towels on the edge of both ends of the stage; for what reason, I didn't know. Water balloon fight later, maybe?

There was also an empty chair next to the towel stack. Next to the chair was another stack of tithes and offerings collection plates. A piano was on the hall floor at the far end of the stage. Bill Gather Trio music was playing in the background.

The entire front row, maybe 50 seats, other than the ones Pauline and I were in, was empty.

A skinny, odd looking, elderly, mustachioed guy in a long gray trench coat was frenetically moving from place to place, table to table, sound speaker to sound speaker, and from the chair to some box in the corner. He was adjusting the volume, checking the tape recorder, arranging a stack of printed material—moving, moving, moving. He was a bundle of nervous energy.

He reminded me of a hungry experimental mouse in a laboratory maze or a human pinball machine. No, wait, I know! *The Energizer Bunny!*

The place was filling up; maybe 200-250 people had arrived and settled in. The front row was still empty, except for us. I didn't realize who the guy on stage was until he somewhat dramatically took off his trench coat. It was Pastor Nipper himself (though he looked much younger on his advertising flyers … *hmm*, curious).

He **WAS**, himself, the entire setup, sound, media, staging, and organizing crew. When fully unveiled, I did a double-take because he was wearing a maroon jacket, a navy-blue shirt and pants, a white tie, a white belt, navy-blue handkerchief in the jacket pocket, and white shoes —and a *very* gold watch. His lapel mic had a long, long, long cord that, while connected to the sound system, still kind of wriggled and followed him as he walked to center stage to begin the meeting.

A very pretty, utterly conservative, well-kept young girl began to play the piano, and we sang "Oh, How I Love Jesus," building up to a loud rendition of "How Firm a Foundation." Then, after being exhorted to look around and see how everyone was "standing up for Jesus!" (of course, we were: Pastor Nipper had told us to!), we crescendoed with "Standing in the Need of Prayer," which, as Pastor Nipper neatly segued to and reminded us, was the reason why we were—and especially why *he* was—very there.

I won't go into too much detail about the sermon except to make two unrelated points.

First, Pastor Nipper spoke dramatically, walking all over the stage, his mic snake cord following him, and he gave the impression he was talking to a huge football stadium filled with tens of thousands of people. Second, at some point, he compared salvation through Jesus with the flushing of a toilet.

I guess the toilet imagery works and is relevant on some level or other, but it says something that 50+ years later, I still remember it with "flushed" queasiness. (Get it?) (You're welcome!)

He preached for a good 50–60 loud, dramatic, sweaty minutes— often theatrically whipping out his navy-blue handkerchief to mop his brow. He periodically went over to adjust something on the tape recorder, and by doing so, each time he caught his second, third, and fourth sermon wind and would dramatically let rip again!

Now the healing part was to begin. I sat up straighter and more expectantly in my seat.

Pastor Nipper gave another 20-minute healing-focused sermon, citing numerous amazing moments in his long healing ministry career when Heaven came down in power and did stuff that still amazes the world today! He was building up now to the moment when he was going to pray for folks; yes, he personally was "going to lay hands on people in this place tonight!" and pray for the "*Glooory* to come down and touch us!"

I think at this point, I noticeably slunk down further into my front row seat somewhat regretting that we had sat there.

That said, I didn't want to be influenced or have my faith-opinion shaped by anyone else's experience (or lack of it). As I mentioned, there were people in the meeting who knew me, and like at The Headquarters, they may have attached some degree of credibility to me as someone legitimate who was in the limelight sometimes. I wanted to be able to attest to the Lord's healing power and learn the ropes, as it were, in terms of how to minister to people, while I was at it.

I decided that I would be first in line when he called for people to come forward for prayer.

I also decided that I would not tell him about my blind left eye or my painful ingrown toenail, for that matter. All that said, I was feeling a tad guilty for using Pastor Nipper to simply show me how the healing thing was done. After all, God had *not* healed my left eye already—and for good reason.

He invited people up for prayer. First to jump up, I walked to the stage and looked straight up at Pastor Nipper who was looking straight down at me as he leaned over the edge of the stage in his chair.

As I stood there, four usher-type men gathered around me to pray with Pastor Nipper for me, I assumed. Nipper didn't ask me anything and didn't just gently lay his hands on my head. Instead, he put his left hand behind my head and neck, slapped his right hand quite aggressively against my forehead and shouted loudly, "In Jesus' name be healed!"

He tried to push me over. *Hey! You tried very hard to push me over!*

He pushed hard enough for me to stumble backward, and the ushers grabbed me under my arms and dragged me to the floor, leaving me lying on my back.

The place went nuts with "Hallelujahs!"

Pastor Nipper said a few more faith-encouraging words as he slid his chair to the left. People began to rush down the aisles. The ushers also moved along the stage front to wait for the next person.

I stayed on the floor.

* * *

Now, as I was lying there, what I was *not* thinking to myself was, *Wow! That was a powerful touch from God!*

No, instead I was thinking, *He pushed me! He … **pushed** … me … over!*

Good grief. I'm on my first date. I really like this girl. She's looking at me lying here; I can feel it. Maybe I should speak in tongues or do something spiritual, something that at least looks like I've been specially touched and blessed and that I'm worthy of this mighty blessing. Just lying here like a dummy is … well, just dumb.

I got up and went back to my seat. Others were queueing up at the stage edge. People were falling over like single dominoes. Now I understood what the towels were for! When ladies wearing skirts (as every conservative woman in the hall was, along with a hat or a mantilla) fell backward under the so-called "power" of the Spirit onto the floor, the ushers—very well-practiced, it seemed—quickly and tastefully laid a towel over the woman's knees and legs. It was well-rehearsed and definitely prepared for.

This went on for 15–20 minutes. Slick, quick, systematic, efficient.

Miracle Handbook (**pg. 12**) – **Mandatory:** Chair, lean, stare mystically, speak in tongues, hands, grip neck, smack forehead, shout, push, pull/drag (or let fall), catch, lay on floor, float towel (if needed).

Recipient (Optional): Shake and shudder, fall down, get up, and praise God!

Except for the pianist.

She was "touched" soon after me but continued lying on the floor near the piano the entire time with her towel-covered legs exposing only her carefully crossed ankles, her hands angelically folded over her bosom, and her longish hair laid out gracefully around her head. She hadn't moved and didn't move.

Having "chaired" his way up and down the length of the stage a couple of times, when the last of us had been prayed for, Pastor Nipper mopped his brow, adjusted the sound on the tape recorder, and began to wrap things up.

Now it was *Come to Jesus!* altar call time to give people an opportunity to come forward and accept Christ for the first time. The offering (collection), we were told, would follow shortly after.

Pastor Nipper reminded us that God's power had been present, that Jesus is alive, and that people needed Him—the usual and quite typically safe, pre-altar call Gospel message. He began to ramp things up, challenging people to make a commitment. He went to the tape machine and adjusted the volume up again and called upon any unsaved people to, first of all, raise their hands to show Jesus they were coming to Him.

"Come on, raise 'em up! Raise 'em up!"

Now, I knew a fair number of the 200 or so people in the hall as committed believers from the area. But after one or two people put up their hands, Pastor Nipper began to shout enthusiastically:

"Thank you, I see that hand! Thank you, I see those hands! Oh, yes, praise the Lord, I see your hands all over this place! Those of you listening to this message all over the world, there are dozens of people, no, hundreds of people, raising their hands in this place tonight! All over this huge auditorium people are giving their lives to Jesus!"

He mopped his brow and checked the tape recorder. All good ... keep going!

The pianist on the floor still hadn't budged.

He then exhorted those "hundreds" to stand to their feet: "You folks around the world listening to this message right now, people, hundreds of people, are standing in this place for Jesus! Hallelujah!"

I almost didn't dare look back and around the hall. But I did. I counted maybe 20 people standing, and I would have guessed, as I said, knowing some of them, that they were recommitting or were standing for some other reason other than to get saved for the first time.

When that tidal wave of salvation blessing subsided, Pastor Nipper reminded people to see one of the ushers immediately after the meeting so they could pray with them, etc. He concluded this section with a loud, *"Amen!"*

We *"Amen"-ed* back at him.

Now it was time to cough up into the collection plates. As the ushers moved forward to grab a plate and take up their stations at the end of the rows of seats, some guys at the back actually closed and guarded the doors. We were then reminded that tape recorders and sound equipment in the Kingdom of God cost **A LOT!** Distributing meeting tapes all over the world after evenings like this one cost **A LOT!**

A guilt-laden appeal after manipulative urging followed. Pastor Nipper even put an actual price tag on how much was needed that evening "to make the trip worth it."

Oh, and did I mention, the pianist was still lying motionless on the floor?

He then went for the spiritual-financial jugular. Pointing to the pianist, "You see that lovely, blessed, young girl lying there still under the powerful blessing of the Holy Ghost?!"

(As he mentioned her, I swear I saw her eyelashes flutter with an accompanying, slight Mona Lisa smile.)

"She's being blessed so mightily right now because she gave $300 (R600) to this ministry this evening *before* the meeting even began, so much did she want God's touch tonight. It's time to give, people! Amen!"

I almost didn't want to look at Pauline. I assumed the relationship was, by now, on shaky ground at best. If she liked the evening and was blessed by it, and I criticized it, then I was an insensitive, unspiritual jerk.

If I said (i.e., lied) that the evening was a blessing to me, and she was thinking it was a circus, then I was potentially a weird fanatic in her eyes.

If I said nothing, then the obvious question would be, "Were you even in the meeting this evening, brother?!"

When we got to the car, I tiptoed into the subject garden diplomatically and asked, "So, what did you think?"

"It was … um, different, that's for sure."

I said, nervous-lightheartedly with a chuckle, "So, for our first date you weren't really **swept**, I mean **shoved**, off your feet then? Ha, ha, ha!"

"No, but you were. I can't believe you did that! What on earth were you thinking?! But I won't tell anyone else about this, I promise... Oh, and yes, I'd love for you to take me to dinner on Friday."

CHAPTER FORTY-TWO

Talk About a New Dawn!

TRUE, IN THE HEAT OF THE JESUS REVOLUTION and the incredible life-transforming waves of the Holy Spirit in the early seventies, we had come to expect God to be real, present, and proactively guiding all aspects of our lives.

That was just how it was.

There were few questions about His closeness or His commitment to us, His children. We were partners with Him to change the world.

It was a given. It was our new normal.

Of course, there were always sermon warning bells going off all the time cautioning (rightly) against, and finding the balance between, being led, stepping out in faith, and presumption. Added to this, unfortunately, was the early birthing of the idea that only unique, especially anointed men and women of God could be used in a special or miraculous way.

No one could actually tell me or show me how to use or be used by the Lord—assuming He might want to equip and use me in the first place!

Maybe it seems a bit over-enthusiastic and even naïve, but I was beginning to formulate the thinking and belief that if God is proactive, stalking, wooing, calling, touching, and offering full salvation to people, then why isn't the fullness of salvation—body, mind, spirit—more evident? More than that, shouldn't it (whole Gospel salvation) be total, daily, and done through anyone who offers themselves to Him to be available as a tool, instrument, or vehicle to do His thing—anywhere, anytime?

If the family, the Church, is to BE that place (a people) of wholeness, then surely, we need to offer more than services, home groups, Bible studies, and all-night prayer meetings, etc.? Those activities fed the social fellowship needs—and brought a sense of belonging and of being part of something bigger and important. But I so wanted the gifts of restoration and healing and recovery to be discovered and unleashed within the normal life of the family of God. We shouldn't need to go to a spiritual guru specialist at a high-profile event.

* * *

It was about this time that I was praying alone one evening, asking God where He wanted me to go or to learn whatever it was—in response to a tugging in my heart. I felt in my "feeler," knew in my "knower," that I was on the brink of learning something profound and eternally relevant and practically life changing. It didn't enter my head that it also meant learning somewhere else … geographically.

297

I had no desire to escape my situation. It was more of a desperate hunger to know more, to discover His real-time, real life, 'today power'; to walk with Him in a new way, to hear His voice, to know His presence. My heart was so much wanting Him to be with me, and work through me, to others, with power, in the here and now! Not as occasional spectacular supernatural events—but as a lifestyle—as part of what we do and who we are as the Church.

Then, He whispered one word in my heart-head-ear:

"Chard."

"Huh?! What?! Really?!" I asked, not because I'd never heard the word (name) before, but because it scared me half to death. It was also combined with the hope of a life and learning experience that I never thought myself worthy of.

∗ ∗ ∗

There was a couple in the AOG who were anything but typical AOG-ites—Dr. Prof. Frank Bowey and his wife, Hazel. They were both smart, sophisticated, authentic, bighearted, oozing God's love, and not afraid to ask the tough theological questions—as well as being willing to step out of the boat with Jesus with no life jacket or strings attached. I wasn't sure how they got away with it in terms of AOG Elder oversight, but they hosted a weekly interdenominational home group that oft welcomed speakers or ministry from all over the show—experientially and denominationally.

Some speakers came from Chard periodically, more specifically South Chard Full Gospel Church in Somerset, England, and shared with the groups that met in the Bowey's home. I had never heard either of the two guys, Ian Andrews and Andrew Jordan, speak before, but the way the Boweys talked about them, about the authentic and real-time sharing about the Gifts, miracles, etc., made me so, so eager to be part of it.

It never happened. I never even got to meet them, much less hear them, anywhere in South Africa.

Frank and Hazel used to retell South Chard stories that seemed to be borderline myths and legends—that made my jaw drop. For example, to simplify it (and hopefully not freak you out while I do so), if someone stood up to say or preach something during open ministry at South Chard on a Sunday morning and were not *in the Spirit,* God would shut them up—literally—, so intensely and jealously did He guard what the place was about and what He was doing there.

South Chard was a global, spiritually refreshing, airport lounge for those who had been serving in other parts of the world and needed to fly in, kick back, and do nothing but be immersed in the healing atmosphere of the community.

Frank and Hazel told many more hair-and-heart-raising stories, not in an attempt to paint the place as a spiritual haven or paradise, or even as some kind of miracle shopping center, but simply to help me to know that God was real and powerful—daily and personally—there.

I was in awe.

When I went to Frank and Hazel to tell them that I believed that God had told me that He wanted me to go to Chard to learn something important, they were truly shocked.

"Dave, do you have any idea what you're saying God said to you?! Do you have any idea what that might mean?!"

They then proceeded to repeat to me some of the awesome and quite astonishing stories about what kind of spiritual "school" I might be attending.

By the end of the conversation, they had given me the name of the pastor (Uncle Syd) and the address so I could write and ask if it was OK to visit them—*and why.*

I wrote and waited while my spiritual hunger and curiosity grew.

* * *

By the time spring began to show herself in late September, apart from the baseball season beginning again, and had experienced Pastor Nipper, Pauline came well and truly into my life (at least into my consciousness in a *"Hmmm, could she be the one?"* sort of way). Even though we had known each other ever since I came to the AOG a few years before, and I had considered her a good friend and sometimes spiritual confidant, I never thought of her as more than my new girlfriend (-ish). Besides, Vernon and I had begun to think and talk about going to Bible school together somewhere. Down the road, I even shared the idea with Nicholas Bhengu!

So much for my big ideas. ("Oh, Davie, Davie … about you and your big ideas and plans," God said, shaking His head again.)

* * *

It wouldn't help to go into all the things that began to happen at that time, and unfortunately, listing them reads like a nonstop personal diary entry. But I do need to say that it was one of the most interesting and intense few months of my life up to that time. Not that I deserved it or even grumbled about not seeing enough miracle action, but God chose, it seems, to show me how utterly committed He was to me, even when going on dates, by doing a few mini miracles.

Date No. 1: As you know, Pauline and I spent an evening together in front of very lukewarm, waning fireplace embers listening to Derek Prince talk about the Gifts of the Holy Spirit. Other than kissing each

300

other goodnight with a "Wow,-now-that-was-not-what-I-expected!" kiss, the evening sparked something akin to a spiritual awakening in me. There was a sense that He was doing something special and unique, and I was (we were) going to be part of His work, not just maybe part of each other's lives.

Date No. 2: See Chapter 41, "Huge Changes and the Pastor Nipper Miracle Show." If you've read it, I know you smiled. Soon after this, Pauline started to attend the Pinelands AOG fellowship group as well.

Date No. 3: I met Pauline's parents and was invited to stay for dinner. While helping wash up dishes afterward, we heard a horrific scream coming from the street. We ran outside and found a neighbor holding onto his near-completely severed arm, bleeding profusely. I ran back inside, found some dish towels, soaked them in water, ran back out, and wrapped them tightly around his severed arm and squeezed hard to try to stop some of the bleeding. Pauline called the ambulance.

We stayed and prayed with him until the ambulance came. He had been cutting something with a power grinder in his garage, and the grinding wheel broke free of its machine and sailed through the air and hit his arm. He lived, and many days later came to thank us for our help in saving his life. I'm not so sure about that, but I also remember the incident because I was wearing a cream-colored safari suit (with uncool long pants; Google it, if you're bored and want a good chuckle), and there was not a speck of blood on it! It's weird what we remember sometimes.

Date No. 4: I had to work late one night soon after the events of date number three, doing a special invoice run on the monster IBM I operated. Pauline took a bus to where I worked and sat with me in the computer room for a few hours. We talked and connected, and I was smitten to the core. I proposed. She said, "Yes." We decided to get married in less than three months. She was almost 20, and I was 22.

Go on—I know—you can say it.

* * *

Miracle No. 1: Soon after this, we realized we would need a newish car before we got married. I had a 1960 VW Beetle that was in rough shape. We prayed about it but not a casual, hopeful wish list-type prayer punctuated quickly at the end with, *"Nevertheless Lord, thy will be done ... Whatever you decide ..."*—hope, wish, hope.

No, believing that if our hearts were right and sincere under His Lordship, and we truly wanted what He wants for our lives (daily), then our chances of asking for something that was in His will were much better. We were beginning to transition into our pray-specifically phase.

Our theory-logic went something like this: *God is for us, not against us. If we walk in the light, delight ourselves in Him, and want Him and only His best (Psalm 37:4), then He will sneak His desires into our hearts, we will want what He wants; and we will pray and ask according to His will ... more often.*

With that approach, it was hard to go wrong—*so we reasoned.*

With that somewhat tricky and presumptuous belief system in mind, we asked (why, I don't know), very specifically, for a 1968 VW Variant semi-station wagon with no more than 75,000 km on the clock, good tires, and selling for no more than R725 ($675).

"Oh, and uh, Lord, we'd like it to be beige, please."

We read the newspaper want ads expectantly. Just to be sure we weren't in the realm of pipedreams, I checked with a local VW used car dealer and he told me that VW didn't make a beige Variant in 1968.

Bummer. But I tried not to let it get to me. After all, our new prayer formula had not been tested yet and was hardly proven.

A few days later, Pauline excitedly called me at work saying, "I found it! I found it! Exactly R725 and, guess what, it's beige! I called them and told them we would come and look at it tomorrow!" Before I could ask if it had an engine, she hung up.

It did have an engine, and it was an amazing buy, and it was ours the very next day. Very cool.

* * *

Miracle No. 2: As the day of the wedding approached on December 21st, things got quite intense—in a good way—at the Pinelands AOG fellowship. Interest, need, questions, and hunger for God among the group began to take on a new fervor and enthusiasm. I was preaching nearly every week at some venue or other, and by this time, the numbers were growing considerably. I remember teaching on the Gifts of the Holy Spirit (à la Derek Prince) for 1½ hours, and no one seemed to notice the time.

Except Pauline.

By our prearrangement, she would surreptitiously tug on her right earlobe to let me know that I had reached the normally acceptable 30–40-minute mark. It's *a miracle* her ear wasn't bleeding profusely!

I also mention this because this was the first time in my budding ministry (if you could call it a ministry) that I felt truly led and, in the flow, or in sync, with the Holy Spirit. It wasn't just about being able to find the right words or remember a Scripture reference; it was a sense that I was picking up on or tuning into needs in the hearts and minds of those listening, as if my spiritual radar had truly been activated for the first time.

I could see, sense, feel, and detect what people were thinking, feeling, were worried about, or needing—or questions they were asking in their hearts and minds. Then I would shift gear, change emphasis, find an illustration that seemed to click with people—if the tears and worshipful expressions and joyful faces were anything to go by.

Along with Pauline's ear that didn't bleed, no one fell asleep, which was also a good sign. Maybe Miracle No. 3?

It was at this time that I began to sense a new dawn. A different direction and godly momentum were building; going where and for what purpose, I didn't know. Chard was still hovering in the back of my heart and mind, but I still hadn't heard anything from Pastor (Uncle) Syd in South Chard. I had not told Pauline about Chard to this point.

* * *

I quit my job at the pharmaceutical company and accepted a position at a large corporation in Pinelands. Pauline, who was working in the Cape Town City Town Planning Department, got an equivalent job at the Pinelands Municipality. Now all we needed was a place to live in Pinelands.

Miracle No. 3: No need to go into all the details here, but suffice it to say, we found a place advertised (semidetached cottage) near both of our new jobs and near where the fellowship met. The owner agreed to let us come and look, but she mentioned on the phone that there had been a lot of interest and that the rent was, for a young couple, probably too much for our budget.

As we drove down the street to have a look, including at the neighborhood, we decided to drive past the place and park around the corner. Not as specifically as I would have liked, but *we prayed again* that the Lord would "Give it to us … maybe, please." A kind of confirmation bell went off in both our hearts, but we were too inexperienced with this new leading of the Holy Spirit thing to know for sure that God was giving it to us. We just kind of felt that He was.

The landlady showed us the place. It was perfect. She reiterated what she had said before—lots of interest, higher than average rental price, pending deadline, etc. It was then that I opened my mouth without actually deciding to open my mouth, much less deciding what words to say—and certainly not checking with my future boss/partner and better half first.

I spoke without any arrogance or pushiness, or even boldness, but with a calm, albeit shy, matter-of-factness. "Mrs. N, we really like it, very much … and we believe God thinks you should rent it to us." A little taken aback with a nervous laugh and smile, she said she would let us know. Pauline looked at me with, well … you know, that future wife "You've **GOT** to be kidding me" look?

Two evenings later, at Pauline's parents' place, we were washing dishes and listening to a Christian program on the radio (no TV in those days). The announcer simply quoted this verse, "Seek ye first the kingdom of God and all these things will be added unto you" (Matt. 6:33 KJV).

We turned to look at each another and said at precisely the same moment, "That's it. The apartment is ours!"

I kid you not—really, truly, absolutely true, with no exaggeration— five seconds later, the phone rang (no caller ID in those days). Again, we both said at the same time, "That's it!"

It was the landlady confirming that the cottage was ours and for a reduced rent and not even a hint of a suggestion that she had been struck by lightning.

* * *

We were married on December 21, 1974, and went on honeymoon in our beige 1968 Variant station wagon to my spiritual father's (Noel) protea farm in the mountains near Stellenbosch. We came back to Cape Town on Boxing Day at the insistence of the baseball team leaders to play against the Goodwood Demons (Pauline's first-ever game).

We won. I pitched and struck out 12.

Miracle No. 4: I hit a homerun.

Now, how's that for a heavenly sign?!

CHAPTER FORTY-THREE

Done! – Part One, Miracle No. 5

AS YOU KNOW, BETWEEN 1971 AND 1974, the hunger and desire to go into full-time ministry was sleep disrupting and all-consuming. It bothered me immensely that whenever leaders and others at church discussed ministry, when we talked in terms of going full-time someday (and I was fairly often mentioned in the conversation), someone would preach about the fact that Jesus was thirty before he began His public ministry, and David didn't become king until he was thirty, yada, yada. Then someone would always, wisely, mention Moses and Abraham's ages … sheesh!

Talk about crushing blows to enthusiasm and momentum!

I yearned to know what it would take to be recognized as being ready for a pastoral and/or teaching role. I mean, how hard could it be?! I was chomping at the bit, psyched, pumped, and ready! I didn't like the idea of waiting until I was thirty. True, I was self-confident at best and arrogant at worst, on one side of the coin; but on the other side, I was obsessively compelled and passionate with a profound and urgent sense of calling to get to work for Him—whatever form that took—as soon as possible.

But also, I was only 22. Don't say it.

Many times, after I had shared in the young adult group or at the Sunday morning Breaking of Bread service, or in a public setting, or on the street at a Saturday morning outreach, people often said to me, "You're going to go into full-time ministry someday!" How I amen-echoed that thought with my best humble, "Aw shucks, gosh … I don't know … Gee, maybe someday when I'm worthy …" But people saying things like that really didn't help my patience very much at all.

Of course, I had no Bible knowledge to speak of. I was only three years old in born-again Christian years and language and had no formal training of any kind. I only had a burning desire, a knack for connecting with people, and the gift of the gab.

The frustration grew, and the more I studied privately, and the more I spoke or preached, and the more I presented at Youth for Christ rallies, outreaches, conferences, and groups, the more I wanted to "*Go!*" —somehow, some way.

"Here I am. Send me, Lord!"

* * *

It sounds a bit crass, and maybe blasé, but marriage came and went and 1975 dawned soon after. We had moved into the God-given, God-ordained cottage, drove our God-provided car, and Pauline began her new God-arranged job around the God-blessed proverbial corner. And, as you know, I also accepted a job in the area with Reckitt and Colman (of Colman's Mustard fame), which was within God-blessed walking distance of our new place and the church meeting hall. The wind in my "ambition for miracles" sails began to calm somewhat. What I didn't know was that His Holy Storm was gathering over the horizon behind me, ready to sweep through my/our life in a totally unexpected way.

As much as normalcy seemed to be looming, along with a lingering discontentment about my future in ministry, God didn't forget my hunger for miracles and my efforts at grabbing all He had to offer with both hands and a full heart.

Then, all Heaven broke loose!

Miracle No. 6 – 1975: Saturday morning, January 4th—I was beginning to emerge from a better than normal night's sleep. I turned onto my right side and looked at the bedside clock. 5:52 a.m. I yawned, knuckle-rubbed my eyes and made the easy decision to close them again and dose a bit longer. Then the near tangible sense of power and, well, presence, was there … ***very there.***

He spoke. Not a voice. Not audible. Not loud or soft but in my heart; in my mind.

But it was Him. You always remember your first time (or second or third).

I had never had such a clear voice-type encounter with God before. Sure, I'd read about such things and heard testimonies about God speaking to people. But I knew it was His voice—not from practical experience or the type of voice, but because of its location. It was that inner, unshakable, deeply personal, knowing-deep-in-your-knower voice.

I was totally awake and scarily alert as He "said," clear as a bell, **"Davie, what would make you the happiest man in the whole world?"**

I knew what He meant. I knew He was looking deep into my heart, very deep, in that secret pool of yearning and longing where I managed to dip my toe of true, total commitment and belief from time to time.

His question stunned me to my core, mainly because I absolutely knew what He was really asking me.

This was a big, real moment of truth and a profound turning point in my life.

"To preach and teach your word, Lord."

No hesitating, pausing, no *um* or *er*, or "Hmmm, let me think about that, Davie. I'll get back to you …"

No, just, *"Done,"* He replied with absolute matter-of-factness and eternal finality.

I was blown away!

Utterly gob-smacked, I lay there on the bed with a silly grin on my face wanting to sing in tongues and worship. I raised my hands, my heart bursting, my face and pillow now drenched from my tears. I settled my head back into the pillow and sobbed quietly in wonder that He had spoken to me—*TO ME—AND* those specific words!

So, that was it. It was decided and ordained. This was my/our life to be. He promised it into my spirit and commanded it into existence.

I lay there basking and trembling with a mix of "wowness" and certainty. The magnitude of the privilege that was about to be our future was truly overwhelming.

A few seconds later, Pauline woke up, turned to face me, and without even saying good morning, said, "This is so strange. I don't know why, but for some reason I just need to ask you something immediately. What would make you the happiest man in the whole world?"

Tears forming again, I said, "To teach His Word."

She replied without hesitation, "Yes, I know."

⋆ ⋆ ⋆

The enormity and eternal nature of this new development was not lost on us. This was real and serious—this was to be our new life. But we needed to stay grounded, too. We discussed what all this might mean for me and for us. We had already pretty much begun to conclude that the standards for proving readiness and calling to full-time ministry were unclear in the AOG—though it was a dream, and a hope of many young guys like me.

Yet, in all of this, I was cautiously and secretly beginning to see the AOG as a religious and works-cloaked-in-spiritual-Grace terms group and that we were just as ceremony and quasi rites obsessed as the denominations we so frequently, enthusiastically, and a tad self-righteously, labeled as drowning in religiosity. After all, so we touted, we were free in the Spirit, unshackled and unencumbered from years of religious rituals and ecclesiastical hierarchy. Yea, sure.

In reality, we couched it all in more justifiable and loftier spiritual terms, using holier-than-thou King James English while we did so.

That's what was spouted and proclaimed, officially or unofficially. Look at the skeptical way, in 1974, how we viewed the public declarations of Anglican, Catholic, and other non-Pentecostal leaders who had Charismatic experiences and spoke in tongues. In fact, pretty much the whole Charismatic Movement was suspect, and not least because they clapped or lifted their hands during chorus singing and worship times, but also because of what they *didn't do*—e.g., open ministry, baptize adult believers, or even use grape juice instead of real wine (yes, something as silly as that).

It was borderline similar to the situation in Acts 10:44–46: "While Peter was still speaking these words, the Holy Spirit came on all who heard the message. The circumcised believers who had come with Peter were astonished that the gift of the Holy Spirit had been poured out even on Gentiles. For they heard them speaking in tongues and praising God."

311

But in AOG circles, it could as easily have been said with astonishment, "… the gift of the Holy Spirit was even poured out on people who baptize babies?! —a greatly misleading doctrine and church practice that has sent more people to hell than any other …?!"

There was a sense inside me that God's special early morning message to me about my life and true happiness were somehow disconnected from where the AOG was headed or expected me to go. I had already secretly snuck off to listen to Revd. David Prior (see Dedication) teach at Christ Church and was blown away by the excellence, authority, and power of what he shared and taught.

* * *

My heart was opening to the range and depth of what God was doing and could do, in spite of my own Pentecostal religious legalism and inflexibility—and ignorance—and the limitations I (and we) placed on the wisdom, power, purposes, and intentions of God.

Looking back, we were, I was, so unbelievably, spiritually arrogant, and I had managed to cultivate this persona and perspective *in less than four short years!* As I have said in other chapters, I don't recall one time when AOG leaders or teachers stated or acknowledged that they didn't know what a particular verse of Scripture meant. In retrospect, that was, or at least should have been, disturbing to me.

Another thing that was troubling me was the expectation that young men would show near blind commitment, unquestioned allegiance, trust in and obedience to only the AOG, to the Elders and to the leader of the AOG (Brother John Bond) and to the Harfield Road pastor at the time, Noel Cromhout. That said, I really did trust Noel utterly as a pastor, mentor, and friend; I think because he was so completely authentic and naturally down-to-earth and caring; there was nothing fake about him.

* * *

Some of us asked often, pushed cautiously, but yearned deeply, for that something *more* in terms of the miraculous. Frankly, I was confused by the AOG leadership's resistance to a more obvious demonstration of the Gifts. I would have thought they would encourage it and urge discovery and the practical outworking and manifestation of the Holy Spirit's power. Of all churches in the area, the AOG, I would have thought, would be first in line!

As you will see in a later chapter, our discovery of these things resulted in harsh and hurtful criticism, followed soon after by an actual ban for some of us on any ministry—miraculous or otherwise. Added to this, for me personally, was a stinging attack and comments by Brother Bond who informed me to my face that I was a "nobody in the Kingdom of God" and would amount to "nothing," it seems, because I had decided not to continue my university education at that time (but maybe it was also because he wasn't a baseball fan).

CHAPTER FORTY-FOUR

Done! – Part Two,
Miracle No. 7 & 8 (Sort of...)

MIRACLE NO. 7: Not being one to sit or rest on my Bible, and being one who was often heard, even then, telling others that we needed to get off our backsides and knees and pews and ask God how we can be part of the answer to our prayers; Pauline and I took another big, somewhat radical, step.

We had been in our new God-arranged cottage a month, and I had only been in my new job three weeks or so, when I sat down and wrote something like this on a piece of paper for Pauline and me:

*"Lord, we give **You** our lives, our hopes and dreams, our skills and talents, our strengths, and weaknesses; we give **You** our*

*possessions, our money, our jobs, and our futures. We surrender our beliefs and our presumptions and prejudices, our allegiances and even our friends—past, present, and future. We leave our wishes, hopes, and dreams—and the desires of our hearts at **Your** feet. **You** are the Lord and our Lord alone. All belongs to **You**, and we joyfully honor and acknowledge that belief together, today, in giving it all back to **You**."*

Basically, and in our heart of hearts, we knew that what we were saying was that we were willing to—and wanted to—get out of the boat and *live by faith*.

Whatever that meant.

I had preached recently on the question and subject of, "Imagine, really imagine, what it would be like to wake up one morning with nothing, absolutely nothing ... and that you needed to trust the Lord truly and completely. Can you imagine that?!" My own sermon got me thinking about how I didn't really know what I was talking about. Nothing new there.

That said, we had begun to believe that you couldn't truly live by faith if you had a whole bunch of safety nets, but at the same time, we knew (sort of) that unless God truly called us to live like that, then it would be presumption in the extreme, mixed with an attempt to force God's blessing hand. So, how do you know? In most people's minds, it would be irresponsible foolishness. We decided that we needed to lay down our money, put it where our prayer "mouth" was, and take the step.

Signature: _____

Date: _____

Signature: _____

Date: _____

* * *

We were fully convinced that we should not tell anyone what we were doing and to never mention our needs to others, not even to family and close friends. Pauline joked for some months after that that I got her to agree and sign the document while she was sleeping because not long after this we did, in fact, lose pretty much everything.

* * *

Just to give you a funny, simple but memorable example of God's favor at this time—I don't remember why or how we had a roasted ham in our pantry, but whatever the case, we were careful to not overeat or waste. We were determined to make it last as long as possible (in responsible living by faith terms).

After one, two, three meals with minimal vegetables as a supporting act and always with tap water to drink, we were eventually down to the hambone with the usual bits hanging on here and there. So, soup it was going to be, and some bread, which was our last meal with no money in the wallet or food in the fridge—at least until Pauline got paid her meagre salary.

No one else knew about our situation.

Then, my good friend and fellow part-time copastor Vernon (and best man at my wedding), and his soon-to-be fiancée, Heather, asked if they could talk with us. Marriage stuff, we assumed. Heather and I had been at UCT together, and she had also been one of Pauline's bridesmaids. Vernon shared a very similar passion and desire for miracles, for going full-time, and for seeing God work. To put it simply, we were the closest and very best of friends.

They knew nothing of our austere faith walk, and while offering to bring dessert, they basically invited themselves over for lunch. Ham bone soup and bread were all we had to offer—literally, the ONLY things we had to offer.

Funnily enough, they raved about the soup! When Vernon asked for seconds, Pauline went to the kitchen and surreptitiously poured her bowl back into the pot, took much less for herself, diluted it, and made sure Vernon got a full bowl of the undiluted good stuff. He raved some more and nearly licked the bowl clean!

Miracle No. 8: I ate almost nothing but felt completely full ... and didn't complain one bit (-ish).

P.S. By the way, just to finish where I began this chapter, I was finally ordained for ministry in the Anglican Church when I was 30.

* * *

Personal Side Note: My dear friend, Vernon Light, was a schoolteacher when I knew him. He was also an ex-Plymouth Brethren (Church), of a very conservative, and if I remember correctly, quite critical family and father—at least when it came to his leaving the Brethren Church. He was, and is, one of the most authentic, biblically sound, serious, and "helpfully questioning of all things spiritual" person I knew and know. He was very musical and one of the most loyal friends a person could want. He had a seriously wickedly fun sense of humor. He kept me balanced and sane and focused. I depended on him to keep me on the right track. He was and is a truly remarkable man of God and a very, very special friend and brother.

* * *

A quick side note while I'm reflecting back on those days. I will always remember something that occurred during an evening service once at Pinelands AOG, when we invited those who had made recent commitments to Christ to stand up and testify. After Johnny spent some time enthusiastically and rightly selling the life-altering, radical, world-transforming power of God that makes us into new, better, and different people, etc., one young girl stood up and emotionally told her story to confirm these truths.

With makeup running down her tearstained cheeks, looking squarely and sincerely into the group's collective eyes, she said, "He has made a helluva difference in my life!"

"Very cute," he says (I say) now. I nearly choked at the time.

* * *

Then, Michael Buckland showed up in our lives—all our lives!

CHAPTER FORTY-FIVE

Then All Heaven & Hell Broke Loose – Michael Buckland – Part I

OTHER THAN HELPING OUT WITH PASTORAL, teaching, and preaching duties (with Johnny and Vernon) at Pinelands Assembly of God, by early 1975, I (we) had pretty much stopped interacting with the Jesus Movement crowd, for no other reason than life took a new different turn, and our focus was elsewhere. We were still locked into the AOG.

To be closer to the AOG action in Pinelands, as I said before, I quit my job with the pharmaceutical company and took another job around mid-February that year, just around the corner from our miracle-provided flat. It was then that the Lord said, *"Done,"* as described in an earlier chapter.

Pauline's bridesmaids were Heather (now Vernon's fiancée) and Debbie. At this time, Debbie met and got engaged to Michael Buckland. Michael was Alaskan, an ex-Vietnam Special Forces Green Beret, ex-Oakland cop, ex-pilot, and now in South Africa, having been sent by his church in Alaska to minister in South Africa—and South America. He came into our lives like a concoction of whirlwind, crashing tsunami, and hurricane of fresh spiritual air—with a whiff of mischief brewing. He was articulate, well-traveled, insightful, funny, authentic, and focused. I liked him immediately.

More than that, he had answers to our hunger for miracles questions. He didn't just talk a theoretical good game: he'd been, and was, an active player.

As you know, I had begun to absorb huge amounts of written and video material on the Full Gospel, including healing of body and mind, deliverance from demonic influence, and learning that the Gifts of the Holy Spirit were available today to accomplish His work *as tools of liberation and transformation!*

But the *"what"* that was needed through our message to the world was still all that they (anyone who presented an expert take on the subject) talked about.

It wasn't the "what" that was the problem. We had a lot of theory about that. It was the practical *"how"* that I wanted to know and learn about.

For example, "Brother, God wants to give you, or you need to use the Word of Knowledge to reveal a problem in someone's life, including if they need healing or have mental or relationship problems, e.g., in their marriage!"

But *how* did the Word of Knowledge happen? *How* did I receive or have one? Did I claim it, feel it, see it, sense it, or was it given to me in a vision, a dream, a prompting …?

*What was the practical **how**?!*

I couldn't accept that God would want to use us to bring His wholeness to the world and then make what was needed to do this so unreachable or unknowable to those He chose to use or those who wanted to be available to Him—i.e., us.

The following chapter illustrates my pre-Michael Buckland search to learn more about these things. I'm not saying it was always a good thing, but it was during the days when I was listening to and reading anything I could get my hands on regarding the Gifts of the Spirit, deliverance, and the miraculous. I will return to the "*Buckland Theme*" after that.

* * *

I've admitted in other places and chapters that in and around 1972–73, I was curious beyond measure about miracles. It wasn't that I needed the dramatic and sensational to believe in Jesus or in order to help me continue to be a Christian. It was that I had become convinced and "believed in my believer" (that place in our spirit where faith and trust live, right next door to where you "know in your knower") that salvation through Christ is not only salvation for the whole world but also for the **whole person**.

He came to rescue us and make us into whole people—soul, body, mind—through salvation, healing, and deliverance in our relationships, environment, society, and families. In short, He came to bring the promise and real possibility of restoring the image of God in all creation. That was what the New Covenant promise was all about, wasn't it?

When a student at the University of Cape Town tearfully screamed at me after he heard me preach a fairly narrow, save-your-soul-only-type message—"I'm not just a soul to be saved! I'm a person! I'm not another soul-notch on your Bible sword ... I'm a person!"—it got me thinking.

How and when does He do more? What part can I, should I, play in the bigger healing or miracle or whole restoration process?

Does He even need me, my participation, for His total salvation thing to happen?

Are there practical things—words, actions, behaviors, faith choices, or other things—that I needed to know about, or learn how to exercise, to be part of it all?

I had personally been quite dramatically healed, and also had dramatically *not* been healed prior to this. I had been encouraged by being given or using or having a Word of Knowledge once (at least I think that's what it was); but that was the sum total of my experience with miracles, or miracle-ish things, up to that point. Being given the Gift of Tongues and the small miracles during our new dawn journey were amazing enough, but they also *weren't* enough.

I confess that I was quite disillusioned and impatient with the Assemblies of God where I attended and served in the youth and young adult group. We talked a good game about believing in miracles, saying that they were valid, possible, and available for today, etc., but it didn't go much beyond holy, tasty, theoretical morsels.

Other than myths, legends, and Pentecostal old wives' tales, we seemed content with tongues, interpretation, and prophecy—but only of the tame and vanilla-flavored variety. In those days, I'm not sure what a "real" prophecy or interpretation of a tongue was supposed to be but hearing the same basic themes dozens and dozens of times, from the same people, kind of makes you long for something more substantive.

Was the Holy Spirit so inactive in people's lives and so lacking in imagination?!

Sorry if that sounds a tad cynical, but a steady diet of such words from the Lord and you begin to feel somewhat spiritually ho-hum. In the heat of the *Jesus Revolution* in the early seventies, the level of the "God-is-working-today" expectancy bar was very high and getting higher.

When I say things like that, it sounds like that's the way I believed and talked or expressed my faith back then. *Not a chance!* I'm putting theological thoughts and perspective back into my head, heart, and mouth 50+ years on. I only know what my wordless heart was feeling.

While it may seem like this chapter is about doctrinal and theological issues, that's not the intention or focus, and my rather simplistic explanation below will be woefully insufficient and bothersome to some of you reading. *I get that.*

I must confess that beyond the problems raised above, I also had real problems with Pentecostal teaching that claimed two interconnected truths:

1. That Jesus not only bore our sins but also *became sin* for us on the cross (which I buy 100%); but that He also bore our sickness and disease. I couldn't get there, belief-wise. If He *became sin* for us (1 Pet. 2:24, 2 Cor. 5:21, Matt. 8:17) then, for me, it required a bit of a proof texting dance to arrive at "*He became sickness for us*" as well.

2. That God wants to heal all people—anyone who is sick— and that it was our faith that was the key that starts His miracle engine. If obvious physical healing, for example, didn't occur after someone was prayed for, then it was the sick person's lack of faith that somehow blocked, or thwarted, God's power. Subtly added to this failed healing

feedback was the image of God sitting on His thrown, tut-tutting and shaking His head in disappointment at our failure to believe correctly or sufficiently.

Here endeth that particular lesson.

As I've said earlier, Prince, Mumford, Basham and Co. broadened their teaching on the Gifts (e.g., Discerning of Spirits), to focus on demonology, but as I also said before, this crossed into tricky doctrinal territory when they said things like, "75% of all born-again Christians have a demon—at least one …"

Oh, but, as they explained it, those Christians are demonized, not possessed, and they did some impressive original Greek gymnastics to define and clarify the difference while attempting to explain being affected by or under the influence or sway of a demon. It worked for me on some level but lost me on others.

That aside, they talked about real supernatural events, **in real time**, as if to practice them or experience them—or to be used by God to bring them—was a way of life. It was not conditional upon being part of a big, hyper spiritual gathering or meeting where a big-name, spiritual guru did his or her thing.

Basically, they said (or I heard them say), "If you walk in the Spirit, and know how to be sensitive, expectant, and responsive to Him and make yourself available to Him, He will do cool, powerful, Full Gospel stuff through you for others."

"Now that's what I'm talking about!"

But therein was also the problem or at least part of it. I was back to the beginning of my dilemma.

It was the "how to" part that stumped me.

I wondered …

How does a Word of Knowledge actually work, show up, or become evident inside your head, heart, spirit, or body? And shows up in a way that is unmistakably Him saying or leading or prompting you to do or share something at that time, in that place, in that particular way, for that particular need?

In terms of the Gift of Healing, was the gift given to me to give to sick people as a ministry (anytime and anywhere)? Or was the gift given to the sick person on a particular occasion, and I just happened to be there as part of the healing transfer process and in His timing? How did I know He wanted to heal someone on a specific occasion and in a specific way? Did my simply saying so (e.g., "Be healed") somehow produce God's power?

Add to that a particular aspect of the demons and deliverance thing that intrigued me, namely, that you needed to know the demon's name; many doubts and confusion rose to the surface in my mind. Only if you knew its name would it respond to your command, in Jesus' name, to depart from the person it was inhabiting or influencing?! Asking the demon to tell you its name was part of the process and the secret to the effectiveness of this type of healing ministry—right or wrong? Seriously?!

As intriguing as it was, I didn't think it was right to spend all my time talking with a demon instead of with Jesus ... but there you have it.

Oh, how that quasi-doctrinal spinning wheel was making me dizzier and dizzier!

* * *

Humorous Sidestep: Some years later, a friend of mine was trying to cast out a demon from a guy and asked the demon to say its name. A strange voice said, "Love!" My friend challenged that! "Peace!" "I don't believe you!" "Joy!" The exchange went back and forth for a while until the entire basketful of the Fruit of the Spirit was named. When I asked my friend what he eventually found out, he said, "His name was *Liar*." He was a lying demon. Go figure.

* * *

*So, **back to the story***—other than my own brief experience of what I called a Word of Knowledge in the pastor's kitchen pantry, **not one** of those popular teachers mentioned above taught or explained the practical *how*. There were lots of stories including phrases like, "The Lord told me, showed me, led me, pushed me, asked me, blah, blah, blah …"

But *how* did He tell you, and *how* did you know the message or leading was from Him?

Anyway, maybe you can appreciate my dilemma. My discovery and learning process was quite intense, and I continued to keep Pastor Noel up to date on my thinking, questioning, searching for answers, and turning theory into practice. I guess I gave the impression that I was open and eager to learn, as well as more willing than most to step out of the boat in faith and not be too scared to try something new and look stupid while I did so.

CHAPTER FORTY-SIX

Timothy and the Scorpion

LET ME SAY UPFRONT WITH AS MUCH LITERARY PERSUASION as I can muster, the following story is absolutely true but nearly absolutely unbelievable at the same time. As in the previous chapter, here it will also be difficult for me to not come across as a bit harsh, sarcastic, and cynical about the AOG while I share. I promise I'll at least try to be a little funny while I do so—if that helps. *Names have been changed to protect the innocent.*

There was a guy connected with the AOG through several family members.

We'll call him Timothy.

Timothy was, by most social definitions, strange. He had an artistic temperament forged in the Hippie Era, erratic mood swings, sometimes bizarre thought and speech patterns, an unhealthy interest in the occult, and generally had somewhat unstable mental and emotional health.

At some point, I assumed at his family's request and prompting, he agreed to come to the church for a healing and deliverance—or some kind—of session. I assumed Pastor Noel, or others, had chatted with him about his life and struggles prior to this, and he agreed to meet specifically with them to pray that the Lord would set him free. I wasn't part of the pre-meeting discussions, actually, so I didn't even know what ground was covered or how they prepared him for the meeting, if at all.

When Pastor Noel called me to ask me to join him and two other Elders to pray for Timothy, and especially for deliverance from a demon (or two), I was spiritually scared spitless. Apparently, I was the only person in the church at that time who was even asking questions about such things as the Gifts of the Spirit (including Discerning of Spirits) and casting out demons. He told me he was including me in the hope that "… the Lord will show you something."

I went to the room at the church full of nerves and as clueless as ever, but nevertheless, I joined in when we began to pray. *Oh, my word*, how the room was soon filled with long-winded, King James English prayers! Plus, tongues of all kinds—praise tongues, message tongues, rebuking, binding and loosing tongues, and intercessory tongues (even though we were never taught publicly about such tongues variety). The air was alive with the sound of us properly whipping and winding ourselves up into a hyper spiritual frenzy.

In the midst of it all, I still had absolutely no idea—none, zip, nada, zilch—about how, if, or when the Lord would show me anything about anything, much less if Timothy had a demon or some other problem!

I did not know how the Lord even communicated such things!

A vision, a voice, a special spiritual seeing inside Timothy's heart, observing the demon through his eyes like they were windows into his soul; a distorted image or face, or, or, or … **WHAT?!**

I was driving myself nuts!

I paced and paced (and paced some more) around the room, trying very hard to get *me,* Dave Lutes, out of the way, to remove any mental blockages, and to rightly whip myself up by earnestly and maturely speaking in tongues.

I was waiting and waiting for something to happen … not conjuring up something while trying to conjure up something!

Huh?!

Pastor Noel kept glancing at me quizzically, his look questioning if my demon radar was turned on. Periodically, others in the room would lay hands on Timothy and either speak in tongues or dramatically bind or loose Timothy—whatever that meant. (I know there were obscure Bible verses that sort of referred to doing this, but **I never did find enough Bible to justify that particular deliverance practice or methodology—then or since**).

All the while, while still pacing, I was becoming borderline obsessed and convinced that *I* had to know the demon's name, of course, assuming there was one there.

It wasn't long before everyone was exhausted; we'd been at it for over an hour, and I thought at one point Timothy had nodded off to sleep. I was trying ever so hard to allow my mind to simultaneously sift through any picture-thought that came into my head, like a slow-motion film with a new image or snapshot on each frame—while hoping the film would pause long enough so that one of them might supernaturally flash or jump out at me. *And at the same time,* to not let a stupid or weird thought or image be uncovered or surface from deep within my pre-Christian, extra-vivid, horror-film-saturated imagination.

* * *

A picture of a scorpion appeared in my head, sort of … I think.

I wasn't sure. Was it? A *picture* is not really the right word. Then, maybe not … but then maybe it was—*yes, it was a black scorpion!*

Davie, you're not looking for a thing or an object; Timothy doesn't have a scorpion inside him!

Haven't you been reading Derek Prince?! Yeah, sure, I realize that Luke 10:19 refers to "treading on scorpions," but isn't that what we are trying to do now, to take authority over … whatever?!

Besides, the demon scorpion doesn't have a name! Does he? Maybe his name IS "Scorpion" (nah, that doesn't make sense). Or maybe it's "Blacky" or "Stinger" or "Curly Tail" or "Scorp!"

*Was the message, the picture, if indeed it **was** a message or picture, even from God? Was it about the color, type of insect, poison, creepiness, people's fear of bugs or insects, or about the way it stung or what results one could expect when playing with scorpions?*

Hells bells, I didn't know! Sheesh!

No, no, no … Davie! This ain't right!

The tangle of thoughts I had were rapidly becoming untangleable.

You see my problem.

The mental and emotional gymnastics I was going through caused me to sweat profusely. If I said "scorpion" with a question mark then that would surely be a lack of faith, or at minimum telling it (the demon, if it was actually there) that I was uncertain, and it would just laugh at my so-called spiritual authority.

My memory flashed to the story of the Sons of Sceva trying to ineffectively cast out seven demons (Acts 19:11–20). ***"Jesus, we know, and Paul we've heard about, but who the hell are you?!"*** said one of the seven demons mockingly (my paraphrase).

*I really needed a name **in a hurry,** or this was going to become more than a fiasco!*

Just to help you relate to how crazy our imaginations can get (mine, at least), in the middle of all this, I thought, *If you play the Beatles' song "Revolution 9" backward, it says "Paul is dead." Now, that's weird and spooky! Aaah! That's it! What is Scorpion spelled backward? Noiprocs?*

Nah! Focus, Davie, focus!

Aaah! The thought hit me: *Maybe the demon's name IS Scorpio!*

I whispered in Pastor Noel's ear, "Scorpio."

His face and mouth copied each other. *"Huh?! What?!"*

"I think that's the demon's name."

"No, it's not! Why do you say that?!"

"Umm … well, I… erm, I don't know … just a thought. Let's ask him."

"Ask who? Timothy or the demon?"

I shrugged, a really well-practiced, sarcastic spiritual shrug.

So, Pastor Noel stood in front of Timothy and asked no one in particular, *"Are you Scorpio?"*

Abruptly, Timothy looked up, his eyes wide with surprise.

I thought, ***Ah ha! Now, that's a good sign!***

He said, "Hey, man, yes, I am! My birthday is on the 1st of November. How did you know that? Why do you ask?"

Unsurprisingly, the session ended shortly after that. We said a polite, tightly-seal-this-session-shut prayer with a rousing "Amen!" and we all went home.

So much for my foray into the deliverance ministry!

I guess I'll just head back to the guru books and tapes.

Timothy, for the record, cried a bit, confessed some stuff, repented of some things, and felt a bit better for the session, I believe.

We—Pastor Noel, the Elders, and I—didn't regroup or compare notes afterward, so who knows what we really learned or accomplished, if anything.

Over the next year or so, Timothy went on to get some seriously good professional therapy, and with the help of some bipolar-type meds and a lot of sympathetic understanding and prayers from family and friends, he turned into a really gifted artist and quite a nice guy—in my opinion.

But I still couldn't shake the sad thought, *Could Paul really be dead?!*

CHAPTER FORTY-SEVEN

Then All Heaven & Hell Broke Loose – Michael Buckland – Part II

PICKING UP WHERE WE LEFT OFF IN CHAPTER 45 about the radical breeze called Michael Buckland—

> *What was the practical "how and when" when it came to receiving or being used in the Gifts of the Holy Spirit?*

Michael knew what the tools were, but more importantly, he knew *how* and *when* to use them. I was so tired of hearing the stories from the good ol' days at the AOG about miracles that were only enshrined in the memories of the few veterans.

Maybe I was being obsessive, but my *"show me now!"* nature was ready *to do.*

I don't think I have even known such a spiritual high as I did then or since. Without having all my doctrinal or theological ducks in a row, or the right collection of words to describe what I was seeking, I simply believed that the Gospel **MUST** be more; **MUST** offer more, than simply getting saved and the baptism of the Holy Spirit and speaking in tongues.

I believed the Lord wanted to touch the whole of a person's life— soul, mind, body! He wanted to put people back together again— completely and totally—spiritually, mentally, emotionally, relationally, financially, even "careerly." In other words, He wanted people to be in the right relationship with Him, with each other, with the world around them, and in a right relationship with their futures. To me, that was "being in the Image of God."

> *He needed us and our openness and willingness to be available to work with and be led by Him to do this.*
>
> *We needed to be equipped for proactive service in the world in which we lived. We needed His tools and to know how and when to use them.*

Michael changed our thinking and our vocabulary. The Gospel now equaled or incorporated **salvation, healing, and deliverance.** Healing didn't just mean physical; it also meant mental and emotional. Deliverance didn't just mean being set free from old habits and sinful practices; it meant identifying and removing (casting out) an actual demon or breaking the power of demonic influence in someone—not just in their life generally, but inside them specifically.

This was a tricky one, not least because the huge looming question still was, *"Can a Christian have a demon?"*

If someone could have a demon, how would I know this, or how could someone identify it in order to cast it out? And if it was driven out, how could it be prevented from returning?

But what does *having* a demon actually mean?

But first things first—

* * *

Michael's guidance was fairly similar to my own guesstimating, and simple. If we open ourselves up to the miraculous, and if we make ourselves available to Him, and if we are willing to learn and be fools for Christ, He will do real, powerful, cool, and eternal stuff in people's lives.

Simple, right?!

He will include us in whatever He does, while He does it. What an awesome, terrifying privilege and responsibility. This is about people's lives; it isn't a church ritual or an occasional special service. It is eternal transformation.

He will teach us slowly; within the range and limits of our personal walk and the spiritual light we have received up to that point. (I write like I actually said it like that back then—*not a chance. Not even close!* Those words are wholly and completely retrospective.)

Then, simply look for and know how to recognize His guidance clues. Take a step of faith, speak words in faith, and step out of the boat and onto the water in faith. If you are truly, humbly, and totally committed and available to Him and want what He wants for someone —whatever that was—then you will have the mind of Christ. Your thoughts will be His thoughts, your words will be His words.

Easier said than done.

Later I will quote Michael, but I truly, truly do not want anyone to get the wrong idea or in any way misconstrue his or my meaning. He said in our interview with him for this book: "David's sincere question of, 'But how do you know what God wants you to say?' was answered with the simple instruction: 'You just trust the Lord to guide you while you make it up, David.' But you have to do it reverently and without pride pushing in. Speak what is in your heart and mind at that time, with no ego or other agenda in the way ... and no preconceived plan ..."

Based on the guidance above, the key is to be open and available and trust that He prompts, gives words, and shares meaning with the receiver of the message; opening up the conversation and interaction for clarity and impact. The tough part was trusting and submersing pride, and to some extent, logic.

I just spoke what came to mind when ministering to Timothy. I didn't guess or presume or probe for hints like a psychic medium. I didn't even think about it or analyze it and then say it. I spoke what immediately entered my head-mouth with full acceptance that I could be waaaaay off track. Which I was ... completely. But I tried.

Reflections by Michael Buckland – "Just Because It's David's Book":

To set the scene for this book that David is writing, I had come to Christ in 1969 while in the US military and undergoing Special Forces selection and training at Fort Bragg, North Carolina. Having been raised Catholic, I had turned to atheism at age 15 and followed that path for three or so years and was later part of the Special Forces Group (Airborne), which was stationed in Vietnam. Specifically, we had volunteered for something called the "Special Projects." I would spend well over two years conducting special operations missions into Laos and Cambodia. I, and the guy who led me to the Lord, were both wounded while there. Later, I became an Oakland, California, cop.

When I went to Cape Town in 1975, spiritually as it were, this was the tail end of the Jesus Movement, in which enormous numbers of young people turned to faith in Jesus who, however oddly, was happy to save the souls of folks who failed to dress "properly." So, large numbers of new converts to Christ were being produced, but the established Evangelical churches often did not know how to deal with them, and far too often, the new believers were made to feel unwelcome and uncomfortable.

Add to the mix, the huge Charismatic renewal that was underway; all too often, Charismatic Christians were not really welcome in the somewhat calcified Pentecostal establishment, which largely had reduced the Spirit-filled life to just speaking in tongues with only scant instances of the other Gifts of the Spirit.

When I went to Cape Town in 1975, I was commissioned by the church where I was a leader, Christ's Chapel, to minister the Gifts in both South America and Africa. So, I hardly was a renegade or a spiritual Lone Ranger when all of the fun got started.

Returning to Cape Town to be with Debbie, she had arranged for me to stay with a lovely South African couple by the name of Ollie and Helen Claussen. Meanwhile, Debbie had two close girlfriends with whom they'd attended school—Pauline Lutes (who had, however rashly, married the hero of this tale, one David Lutes, and Heather, who would soon marry a fellow named Vernon Light).

Looking back, the Lord had brought me, a young man (25-26 years of age) who was deeply immersed in the American Charismatic Movement and ministry to Cape Town. There I found myself surrounded by three men: David Lutes, Vernon Light, and Ollie Claussen, all of whom happened to be seriously hungry to see the power of God unleashed in their daily lives.

And so, an odd and somewhat eclectic little band of brothers "accidentally" coalesced. The late David Prior, Rector of Christ Church Kenilworth (at that time) later would take delight in referring to me as "The Guru." Though not by plan, I found myself teaching and discipling the three men (and to some extent, the four women) in the theology and practice of the still powerful Charismatic Movement. David and Vernon had been devouring whatever tapes they could on the subject already, since the Assemblies of God in South Africa weren't seeing much happening in the way of God moving immediately and powerfully in their midst. Thus, this small four-person ministry was taking shape at God's instigation, but—horrors!—without the specific blessing of the Assemblies of God.

As for the emergent "Guru-led Gang of Four," the Lord had chosen the right people to be in it. Two of the men were South African: Ollie was quite the Afrikaner, though he chose not to emphasize it in his work as a senior lecturer at the Cape Technical College. Vernon was of the English-speaking heritage and originally from the Plymouth Brethren [and] was a schoolteacher who prized an orderly and well-regulated life, bless his soul. Toss in a young American who believed in getting things done, and you have a recipe for considerable cultural conflict when it came to the extant South African religious authorities.

Enter now, per God's perfect plan, one David Lutes. David was a cultural hybrid, having spent some of his formative years absorbing the South African cultural values and attitudes, plus no small measure of their accent. He was the ideal God-arranged, cross-cultural hybrid to help the American arrival grasp the nuances of South African culture.

Again and again, David would be able to explain to me, "Well, these folks just don't do things that way, you see. In fact, they may have heart attacks at doing things like that in any way at all because everything in their world needs to be kept firmly in hand by the authorities."

338

I found this fascinating, since these Pentecostal "authorities" who required their full control over the ministry of the Holy Spirit appeared to know not much at all about God's supernatural doings.

"Yes, no, they really don't," David would patiently explain.

But they wanted to be able to regulate all of it, even though they didn't really know much about how such things work. If God does things that they can't control, it makes them very anxious and upset.

I am paraphrasing some of David's invaluable cultural instruction in the mysterious ways of the South African religious mind (Pentecostal version), since God used his deep understanding of such issues to minimize potential conflicts with the Assemblies of God religious structure.

Ollie and Vernon, being proper South Africans, were careful and cautious as they approached the walk in the Spirit but still saw some very pleasant and spiritually rewarding results. They, however, wanted to start in the shallow end of the pool and work their way out toward the middle, which was fine. David, however, had that American brashness, even if it had been half smothered by the South African cultural pillow. He flat wanted to see God move and work in the biblical manner, and his stance was slightly less cautious.

"Well, Michael, you've told me pretty clearly how this swimming thing works," quoth he, "So, is there a problem if I just jump into the deep end of the pool and see whether all this works for me?"

And rather than wait for me to reply, into the deep end of the pool Mister Lutes leapt. Fortunately, the described lessons on Charismatic dog paddling did work. But there was no question at all that the Lord would use His servant David in the deep ends of various theological and cultural pools.

A word here about what kind of raw material young David Lutes was. It seemed to me that he'd been given two particular spiritual gifts, though they weren't yet well developed. He evidenced the gift of Discerning of Spirits, which too often is seen mostly as having "demon radar," when really, it's a God-imparted sensitivity to the human spirit and its nuances and pathways, as well as situational discernment as to angelic activities (of both good and bad angels). That was really important because it enabled David to work with people while discerning serious, but hidden, issues and motivations of the heart and thus to edify believers to whom he ministered. It also allowed him to trust what he was learning because he could tell that what was being taught was coming from a heart that wanted to glorify and exalt Jesus, even if imperfectly done at times.

He also evidenced the Gift of Prophecy, or a version of the Word of Knowledge, which happens to be more about "forthtelling" than it is about "foretelling." It is being willing to let the Spirit of God speak through oneself to say what the Lord wants to have said or done in a given circumstance. Yes, it can be a blessing if used in formal prophecies given in a group setting. But it's so powerful when utilized in personal, or sometimes in small group ministry.

David's sincere question of, "But how do you know what God wants you to say?" was answered with the simple instruction: "You just trust the Lord and make it up, David, but you have to do it reverently and without pride pushing in."

Where Ollie and Vernon were much more cautious in such matters, numerous believers in Cape Town soon found themselves blessed and edified by being D. Lutes-ed with drive-by "truthings." Some astonishing things happen when you let the Spirit of God speak through you, and David soon was jumping into the deep end of the Charismatic pool, with amazing and miraculous results.

These two gifts blossomed out into the Word of Knowledge and the Word of Wisdom (knowing and the wisdom—the skill—knowing what to do with the Word of Knowledge that the Lord just gave) and to the Gifts of Healings and of miracles.

But I saw the first two as being the keys to wide-ranging ministry in the others, at least for Dave. Sometimes he and I would head into Cape Town, with no other agenda but to see who in the city the Holy Spirit wanted us to minister to through His leading and Grace. Some very wonderful and blessed things would happen as the Lord led us to this person and that, and it was David who was willing to do that sort of thing with me. I'm not minimizing what Vernon and Ollie did and learned; I'm just saying that God uses different servants differently.

– Michael Buckland, January 2022

CHAPTER FORTY-EIGHT

Hunger for Miracles – Part 2 – Then There Was William

IT HAD GOTTEN TO A POINT WHERE I PLAIN WANTED to stop talking hypothetically about them and actually discover how miracles happen and what place or role I could play in the God-process of doing them. It wasn't that I was seeking thrills and amazing stuff. I truly and simply (and passionately) wanted the Full Gospel, the full message, of salvation for the whole man and the whole of humanity to be part of our life and ministry as the Church.

We talked a good game, but other than witnessing on the streets or in big meetings or at work, it seemed to me to be more words than action, more claims and promises than reality. I'm not knocking or minimizing or reducing the amazing, eternal miracle of salvation. Being born-again in Jesus isn't insignificant. *Not at all!*

Sharing the Gospel and salvation message was, and is, the highest, most awesome privilege and responsibility we could have.

But we also claimed that we believed in the Ninefold Gifts of the Spirit (1 Cor. 12), but, in reality, we seemed content with tongues, interpretation, and prophecy, along with blessed myths and legends that ol' Brother So-and-So heard about or saw back in the good ol' days "… when the Holy Ghost really moved powerfully. Ja-Nie, I remember those blessed days!"

In the previous chapter, Michael Buckland told of how he came into our lives and guided us in our journey and discovery of not only the reality of the Gifts of the Holy Spirit for today but the practicalities of how to partner with God and be moved and guided by the Holy Spirit in touching and transforming people's lives.

I won't say much more here (Michael already shared his thoughts on this), but suffice it to say, my good friends Vernon, Ollie C. (now passed on), and I became kind of an experimental team, daily discovering supernatural aspects to our Christian lives that we never believed were possible, and we were mentored, as it were, by Michael. Our education began in early 1975, and we very quickly discovered a whole other world of spiritual awareness and sensitivity. I guess we felt we had a safe place to learn to step out in faith with the young Pinelands fellowship crowd, and we began to experience some more public "miracles" (our word), such as Words of Knowledge leading to prayer for someone's healing or inner victory, which led to a lot of joyful, godly noise.

I admit, some things were, and still are, difficult to explain, and we were too caught up in this new thing God was doing to analyze it much.

For example, when we were having a time of worship, it was not unusual for me or Michael or Vernon to have what the AOG "theory-logically" called a *Word of Knowledge* (… to know something about someone or some situation that was not learned in a natural way but was supernaturally revealed and communicated to a person …).

Usually, we would be given words or a picture (revelation) or a sense or an impression in our mind and heart or even a physical symptom that someone needed prayer for something specific.

Speaking only for myself, I would frequently sense or feel that there was someone who was suffering anxiety or who had a pain or illness in some part of their body or was struggling in some specific way. Sometimes I would experience a physical pain or sensation, which would suddenly appear and, just as suddenly, stop. If I had the courage to make an ass of myself in public, I would speak up and ask if there was someone in the gathering experiencing the felt situation, problem, or discomfort or pain, and to, "Please let us know, and we will pray for you."

Quite frequently, people would stand up and own the problem or need described, and we would join together and pray for them publicly and trust God for the miracle they needed. Faith was lifted and stimulated, especially as it seemed like God was purposefully finding someone and telling them that He loved them and wanted to touch and help them. Sometimes no one would speak up, but someone would come to us after the meeting and share that the Word of Knowledge was for them, but they were too shy or scared or whatever to say anything publicly. So, we prayed for them then.

Thank God we never laid the "It's because of **your** lack of faith" guilt trip on them, along with the "Because **you** didn't have enough faith, God didn't heal you!" or some other nauseating, manipulative cop-out like that. The Word of Knowledge, the more specific the better, made a huge difference in activating personal and corporate believing.

Physical, emotional, mental, and relational issues and other problems in people's lives came to light in this way, and frankly, we were wary and worried that this phenomenon might become the reason why people attended. Admittedly, it became a fairly regular occurrence and had a magnetic-like quality, and word began to spread as these things continued to happen.

Fortunately, as the miraculous was combined with solid teaching, consistent pastoral care, and the unselfconscious freedom to make mistakes, we believed we were learning to move and work with God in His way and in His timing. At no time did we turn meetings into a miracle show and make the gathering all about the supernatural. We admitted up front to the group that we were learning as we went, never creating the impression or sense that we were special, mystical, miracle gurus.

I'm so glad we didn't.

The three of us leaders (Johnny was also a leader but wasn't part of the smaller group being mentored by Michael) were young and inexperienced. We didn't really know how the miraculous was supposed to work in practice, but we tried to honor God with the gifting that we believed He was beginning to give us, along with this new, small church. I have to admit, for me personally, I was as chuffed as I ever thought I could be. God was making His presence, love, and power known and real in people's lives. This was very cool.

The problem was that we needed to understand that the Word of Knowledge was the tool, and the Word of Wisdom was the skill with which to use the tool correctly—sensitivity, care and timing. This took practice and making mistakes. We did … often, but God seemed to honor our willingness to let our trust and faith all hang out there. *Hence, the title of this book:*

Guidance, Goofs, and Grace.

* * *

The other problem was that the AOG senior leadership didn't like us talking about and doing stuff like the non-vocal Gifts; or perhaps, they were threatened by it. It's hard to know really.

Understandably, it seems they felt that these occurrences were crossing a line that the leaders didn't like or had never experienced or couldn't explain and were worried that we were going to become fanatical. Or go off the rails and lead other people astray with wild phenomenon or beliefs or experiences and neglect the sound teaching and preaching of the Word.

They rightly worried that what we taught and did was not biblical or was not within the AOG definition of a "real" miracle (if they actually had one). I don't think we did teach error and were very balanced in our style, but I can understand why they would be concerned.

The other issue was most, if not all, of the local AOG leadership (as far as I could tell) had never seen or been part of a "real" miracle. They just had amazing stories from a bygone age when the Mullan brothers or Nicholas Bhengu (or some other miracley-aware, spiritual giant) did something "wowifying."

* * *

Author's Note: I don't know if this falls in the category of missing God's timing, sign, moment, calling—or my stubbornness and youthful stupidity. Nicholas Bhengu came to Harfield Road AOG once. At the time, I was contemplating returning to the US to go to Bible school or a Christian college to prepare for ministry someday. Actually, my best friend, Vernon, and I were thinking of going together. I had done some research on Christian schools and Houghton College in Illinois arrived at the top of preference list. I thought, *Why not ask the Black Billy Graham for his opinion?* It seemed he was aware of what was going on all over the world. I went to him after the service and posed the question about what university he might recommend. Without hesitation, he immediately said Houghton College. I said thank you and then never did anything about it.

Go figure.

* * *

The following example illustrates where Johnny, Vernon, and I were at the time with the challenges and issues surrounding the Gifts and the AOG's concerns.

One evening, Johnny and I attended a kind of home group thing at a young couple's cottage in Kenilworth.

During the evening sometime, when things were winding down, the wife-host (V) was with a young woman (Carol), maybe 19–20 years old, trying to help her experience the baptism of the Holy Spirit and find some freedom in her spiritual life. V had picked up on the fact that there was some kind of blockage, and that Carol wasn't making much progress and needed to probe some more to find out what was really going on. V took her into the other room to chat and pray, the hope being she could lay hands on her and pray for her to receive and find some release in the Spirit.

It wasn't going so well, apparently, so Johnny and I learned later. Actually, we had never met Carol or her boyfriend (William) or knew anything about them until that evening.

William was, a bit oddly, also very upset and unusually stressed out about this thing going on with his girlfriend; so Johnny and I took him into the kitchen, along with another guy, to ask him what was up. He explained to us that his girlfriend was trying to receive or be released in the Holy Spirit but that she was having problems; that she had some kind of blockage.

> *"Yes, there is something wrong with her. She's not being obedient to God or something," he mused.*

As he spoke, the thought came into my head that *he* was the problem.

OK, the odds were pretty good that a dumb boyfriend was messing with his girlfriend's head or heart; there was no genius or miracle in me thinking like that. Been there, done that—myself!

What was weird and kind of jaw-dropping for me and the others in the room was when I said, "You've been going out together for just under six months, right?"

Gulp. "Yes … but, but, but how did you—"

I interrupted and added, "And you have been trying to have sex with her, actually, trying to force her to do it, and she doesn't like the idea—is that correct?"

His eyes opened wider as I continued, "She has even begged you to stop, to pray with her more, right? You've actually been a bit of pig about it."

William started to cry. Whispering, he said, "Yes, yes, yes … I have been forcing myself on her and trying to push her to have sex."

Johnny and the other guy with us were as gob-smacked as I was.

I continued. "She has been resisting you, is becoming more distant. You've been fighting and arguing with each other more and more, and you have threatened to leave her, to 'throw her away'—those were your words, right?"

Dumbstruck, silence followed as he slowly nodded his head.

How I knew these things is still a mystery to me; I just did. The thoughts were in my head, and I heard the words coming out of my mouth. It wasn't like I was unable to control my tongue; it was more a matter of the words were in there somewhere and simply *had* to come out, otherwise they would be stuck in there forever.

I can't remember all of the details of the conversation that followed, but I do recall that I shared with him more precise, very personal, and specific, details about his relationships with girls, his family, his work, and with God, as well as about the battle that was raging inside his own heart and mind (and hormones).

It was like God had given me—no, briefly entrusted me with— the awesome, terrifying responsibility to peel layers off a young onion's soul and life to get to the true heart of things.

As he cried and as he confessed and as we encouraged him to repent and to admit to his error and sexual addiction, we prayed with him to be forgiven and to give himself more fully to the Lord. We learned later that his girlfriend in the other room was being prayed for at about that precise moment.

She received the Holy Spirit and according to V., "... erupted with joy-filled laughter and tears and began to speak in tongues."

Now you can call it excessive Pent-up-costalism if you want to. You can say the chances that all the garbage and sin in that young couple's relationship were typical and not particularly unusual; and you could go on to say that claiming the things we shared as being supernaturally revealed is a bit of a stretch. Some have even said to me that I used a showman's mind reader or a paid psychic's trick or technique to get him to reveal the truth.

Oh well ... whatever. I can only say that that's what happened, and I'm just telling you as it was. I do know that two lives were changed that evening. I trust, for the better, permanently.

If I'm honest, and not to overstate it too much, I was absolutely awestruck, dumbfounded, spiritually drained, over the moon, and thrilled that God would use me to help someone in that way. As exciting as it was, the terrifying sense of responsibility was really sneaking up on me big time.

CHAPTER FORTY-NINE

Banned by the Assemblies of God – Part 1

THE AOG LEADERS AT HARFIELD ROAD became more intensely and quite aggressively bothered by the things we—Vernon, Michael Buckland, and I—were preaching, teaching, experiencing, and leading others into. For example, as mentioned elsewhere, during any of the weekday or weekend meetings at Pinelands AOG, God would reveal a need in someone's life—physical, spiritual, emotional, relational, etc. The need was sensed or felt (Word of Knowledge), publicly shared, and the person was encouraged to admit the need by raising their hand and coming forward, and we would pray for them.

We weren't particularly wise about bringing the need out into the open sometimes, but God was more gracious and forgiving than critical, we felt. We were learning the spiritual ropes, discovering the "how," and now also, the "why" and "when." Blurting something out about someone's life could be embarrassing for both the giver and the receiver and for others listening in or watching.

People began to come to us privately, and increasingly, there were manifestations of evil stuff, and even people in serious bondage or emotional and spiritual blockage. As Michael Buckland shared earlier, when he and I were just hanging out casually or socially, it became quite commonplace for God to reveal to us a serious spiritual need in someone who was just crossing our path—who, after prayer and sharing with them, were helped, or set free. Talking about this sort of thing, therefore, became easy sharing—almost daily-normal.

Expectancy that God was going before us, preparing people to come across our path, was on the rise. The need to suppress ego and bury presumption also grew, and a healthy fear of screwing things up by just being Dave Lutes was at the forefront of my mind.

And to spend more time in prayer.

With that introduction, I will preempt your conclusions by saying upfront, yes, the AOG leaders weren't happy and wanted to seriously restrict our activities. In short, to ban us.

* * *

Not the First Time I Was Banned

Before I share more specific details leading up to the AOG leaders taking more decisive action toward us in 1975, I need to say that it wasn't the first time I was put under a ban and restricted from ministry.

Back when K and I were still dating (circa December 1973), and she was in her final year of high school, the annually scheduled Matric Dance (US equivalent, Senior Ball) was going to take place. We really wanted to go and went to a lot of trouble to get the right dress and color coordinate my tuxedo and tie, along with the corsage I got for K. I arranged to borrow a cool car from a friend, and we allowed ourselves to get excited about having a good time.

Unfortunately, we weren't aware of, or we ignored, the fact that the AOG not only frowned on dancing (to any kind of music), but they also forbade it. I can't remember how the pastor found out about it (probably when I said I wouldn't be at the Saturday night young adult group), and he quite emphatically expressed his displeasure.

He gave us (me) an ultimatum. If we decided to disobey, I would be banned from sharing in any way—preaching, leading, outreach, sharing in Breaking of Bread open ministry, etc.—for one month.

"Dave, you need to decide and choose."

After a couple of days, we did. We decided to attend the dance.

It was a lot of fun. We were THE couple there, we could tell: a hint of lavender, color synced, dressed to the nines, very classy, and very admired. That said, ironically, we danced only once, and when we sat down, a friend of K's came to sit with us. She said, "I know you are both Christians. Everyone does. Can you tell me how to give my life to God, too? Is it difficult? What would it mean?"

Thus began our evening. We never danced again and shared for several hours with many people about Christian things, counseling, challenging, encouraging, and sharing the plain Gospel message. The next month flew by.

Ban, what ban?

* * *

Back to 1975

A few events that happened during the first six months of that year are worth sharing to show a pattern of experience that pretty much propelled us out of the AOG's good graces, not only from the leadership's perspective, but also from our own. We felt increasingly that we couldn't stay, and truthfully, they probably didn't want us to stay. We were causing too much trouble.

A good example of things going on outside of the AOG:

Brian Helsby led a YFC youth rally with 200-250 teens and young adults at the Community Center, Fish Hoek, Cape. I was the guest speaker, and Paul West (see Dedication and extract from him earlier) was the guest chorus leader and musical item singer. By this time, Paul was also part of our little group of Michael Buckland learners and had been schooled a bit in how to recognize demonic activity or influence— as well as in the use of the Word of Knowledge.

Several things were a bit weird during this rally—*and funny*. Paul had done his songs, and I was standing center stage ready to speak. The lights were dimmed, and a somewhat dramatic red spotlight shone down on me.

When I opened my Bible to share something that Jesus had said in one of the Gospels, it dawned on me quite obviously that I had a red-letter Bible—and that all of Jesus' words were in important red text. I couldn't read them. I was twisting and contorting my Bible, raising, and lowering it, squinting and squizzing, and trying to focus on the words I wanted to share. Slightly panicked, Paul joined me on stage to see if he could help. He couldn't.

We did a kind of duet, verse quoting from memory (-ish), and I was seriously, seriously panicked and disheartened, not least because I had blown a chance to share His salvation message very well. I was dreading the altar call, expecting only maybe a handful of rededications but no real salvation first responders.

* * *

Brian Helsby made the altar call, and **God being His amazing Self,** dozens of teens streamed forward to give their lives to Christ for the first time! There were so many people that there were not enough YFC-appointed counselors to help them.

Paul and I were roped in, gladly, but for some reason, we both decided to counsel one guy together who was about 20 years old (we'll call him Robert). We sat in front of Robert and began to ask him some questions about what he was thinking and feeling and why he felt the need to respond and come forward—the hope being we could help him pray and give his life to Christ, of course.

He shared some of his heart, and we told him that Jesus loved him and could help him and give him victory, forgiveness, and peace. As we said this, his eyes rolled strangely, his face contorted oddly, and his voice changed into a guttural, deeper tone. Then he suddenly went back to normal. Startled, Paul and I both looked at one another and silently mouthed, *"Uh, oh!"*

While Paul placed his hand on Robert's shoulder, I said to Robert, "I'm not going to speak directly to you now, I'm going to speak to something inside you, to something that is bothering you. I will instruct it to stay silent. You must try to listen to my voice with your heart. Trust me."

To be honest, I was pretty much just trying to use the deliverance formula that Michael Buckland had given us, almost to the point of a script. We could have just as easily said, "I am no longer speaking to Robert, I am speaking to you (the demon), and I command you to come out of him in Jesus' name." But I didn't. It actually seemed a little theatrical.

There was no messing around with finding out the demon's name, or pleading the blood, or screaming that we rebuked or bound or loosed it —not even speaking in tongues to confuse it, the person, or ourselves— no wasted spiritual energy.

I won't go into all the details here (it wouldn't be constructive), but suffice it to say, Robert began to writhe and shake in apparent agony when I spoke, to open his mouth to let out a scream that didn't come— and then to collapse into Paul's arms in tears. We prayed with him to give his life to Jesus, and after making sure YFC got his details for follow-up, we watched a smiling, peaceful Robert virtually dance out of the room.

* * *

Christ Church – Kenilworth, Cape

As mentioned in Chapter 29, I had secretly attended Christ Church for a series of weekly Bible studies in Colossians that Revd. David Prior was doing in 1974. I say secretly because if the AOG knew about it, I could have, would have, been accused of consorting with a denominational enemy who sent people to hell by baptizing them as babies and thus giving false eternal hope. Or something like that. Not even my closest friends knew I attended the six weeks of teaching.

The Holy Spirit was really moving in the Anglican Church at the time, and the Charismatic bug had bitten Christ Church and St. John's Parish profoundly. Word on the street was that Christ Church was wide open to the Gifts of the Spirit, God setting people free, and generally entering the realm of God supernaturally putting people back together —body, soul, mind, and life.

I can't remember exactly how it came about, but *first,* the Lord gave Michael Buckland a special word (a prophetic Word of Knowledge) for David Prior that, unbeknown to Michael, included a Bible reference that had very special meaning and significance to David. The word quite dramatically struck home and spoke very powerfully to him. The message confirmed something about his calling to the ministry that Michael could never have known about. David was stunned and was propelled forward into a new, dynamic phase of spiritual power and growth.

The *next* thing that happened was that we, as a team (Michael, Vernon, Ollie, and I), expressed a desire to be more connected with and to support Christ Church in whatever way the Lord might be leading. In short, to disconnect from Harfield Road AOG more purposefully.

The *third* thing that happened was when the leaders of Christ Church called us to a private meeting to talk about the expanded, more comprehensive, and fuller Gospel of salvation, healing, and deliverance —and our possible role in sharing it. They weren't skeptical of God's ability to do miracles or to put lives more totally back together by the power of the Spirit, but they were skeptical of us and our motives.

This was completely understandable. I would have felt the same way if I was in their shoes.

Jesus Is Lord!

What transpired was quite special. First of all, in line with 1 Corinthians 12:3, they read out to us, "Therefore, I want you to know that no one who is speaking by the Spirit of God says, 'Jesus be cursed,' and no one can say, 'Jesus is Lord,' except by the Holy Spirit."

Then, as a kind of test, they asked each of us, one by one, to state out loud and directly that "Jesus is Lord."

Each of us did, after which they smiled, and we sat and talked. During the time of sharing, and later during a time of prayer, God gave both Michael and me a few Words of Knowledge (I'd call them personal words of insight) about several of the leaders.

They weren't vague or generalized or symbol-laden insights, but very specific, personal, and apparently timely and poignant messages. The men were struck to their core, as were we.

There was no way we could have known in advance what we would share, and God very clearly and powerfully showed these amazing leaders that He was not only present at that moment but was very much with them in the work they were doing and hoping to do. He confirmed His hand was on them and that He would equip them with powerful love and wisdom to move the ministry forward.

I mention this because it was really the first time God did something quite remarkable that was life and ministry shaping, among a small group of highly respected, strong, and gifted leaders and not just with an individual, privately—out of the limelight. It wasn't a show, and we weren't looking for approval or validation.

But it did confirm that what He was doing in those days, at that time, was very real and historical. That evening not only touched and further shaped David Prior's ministry but also carried Christ Church further forward as a leading light in the Anglican Charismatic Movement.

* * *

A Growling Bear

I'm very aware that, if you haven't written me off by now for being a totally weird, religious fanatic, this next account will push me off and over your edge.

Pauline and I were in our 6th month of marriage. As described earlier, we had committed to try to live completely by faith as we tried to discover God's calling to minister the Full Gospel—somewhere, somehow—all the time—as a lifestyle. The more we reaffirmed our desire to serve Him, the more amazing was the way He touched lives through the Word of Knowledge, healing, and various forms, or levels, of deliverance. But as much as the blessing of God increased and was more evident, so the enemy was more active, too.

I'll summarize so as *not to give* the devil any credit.

First, Pauline had a weird dream about an eye, just one evil eye, looking at her and into her soul. Then plates, photographs, or knickknacks began to fly off shelves in ways that could not be attributed to vacuum cleaner vibration or wall bumping or earth tremors. Nothing was broken, but it did absolutely grab our attention. Pauline was becoming increasingly stressed out and nervous.

We prayed together, of course, and as I laid my hands on her shoulders, she began to growl and snarl—kind of like a bear. I was completely startled. Pauline was one of the most dedicated and committed—and Spirit-filled, soft, and gentle—Christians I had ever known. Growling, or anything remotely like it, was not in her temperament or personality—acting or otherwise.

I tried to pray for her using what I had learned about deliverance from Michael Buckland. It didn't work. She stopped growling, but clearly, she wasn't free or at peace. Pretty much unaware of what had just happened (and I didn't tell her everything that had taken place), she still had a troubling sense that something was very, very wrong. She just couldn't explain it, though she tried quite tearfully.

We got in the car and drove to Ollie and Helen's house where Michael Buckland was staying. It was still early morning. We didn't call ahead (we didn't have a phone), and our knock on the door woke everyone up. While he rubbed the sleep from his eyes, we told Michael what was going on.

Without any fanfare, he sat Pauline down, asked her to look at him, and as tears began to roll down her cheeks, the growling started again. Michael simply and undramatically said, "Come out of her now, in Jesus' name, and never bother her again."

The growling stopped immediately, she shuddered, and a relieved smile came to her face along with a lot more tears. She looked at me with a face that said, *"I'm free! I'm free!"*

We gave everyone a hug and went back home to bed.

* * *

Knowing Things That I Didn't Really Want to Know

Part of me was excited about being used in helping people see, face, and deal with the conflicts and need for healing inside them, but part of me also dreaded what I might see or know. We had been taught, and discussed in depth, that the Word of Knowledge was the tool one needed to find and reveal an inner problem or need, and that the Word of Wisdom was the skill needed to use that tool. Discerning of Spirits was about identifying the influence of demons (and even angels) in some way, at some level or other. That idea was very scary and carried with it awesome responsibility.

A friend of Ollie's (we'll call him Charles) had a physical disability, a degree of paralysis, loss of function, in one leg and arm. I seem to remember he had had polio when he was a child, but I can't be sure. Not a handsome guy by the world's standard and measure, but he was a gentle soul, kind, and highly intelligent, and he loved teaching and helping others. We (Michael and I) were asked to speak with Charles and his wife (June) about some issue in their marriage—I don't remember what it was exactly—but I seem to remember it was about their desire to have children.

What I do remember is that June, a very strong personality (who herself was no beauty queen by the world's normal measure), completely unloaded her anger and hurt and frustration (filled the room with it, actually). She turned angrily toward Charles and said, *"You! It's your fault!"* Charles flinched, but she didn't allow him to reply.

The pained look on his face told us something more was going on— not really what June had been sharing. We agreed to pray, but as we began, I found myself speaking without thinking (again), or let's put it this way, without analyzing and preparing or turning the thoughts into words (i.e., spontaneously). Looking directly at June, words began to tumble out of my mouth. I spelled out to her in VERY explicit, non-symbolic terms that could not be misconstrued—that she was in the habit of mocking Charles' inability to perform sexually.

I pointed out to her that she didn't just complain, she teased and ridiculed him for his "disability" and not just his leg and arm. She had been pointing out how unattractive he was to her, how she found him disgusting and unappealing. On and on I described her weapon of choice—totally unkind, poison word daggers—with an insight that I had no way of knowing about her and them.

Only June was more shocked than the rest of us about what I said. Then, as we laid our hands on her shoulders, she was knocked backward into a chair and wailed in unbelievably deep sorrow—and then repentance. She confessed it all to be true and begged Charles to forgive her. Tears flowed freely for some time, at least thirty minutes. Charles embraced June with a fierce, forgiving hug, and we all prayed together and asked God to bring healing and restoration and peace—and so much more.

Not that kids are always the means to, or the outcome of, a happy marriage, but we learned a few months later that June was pregnant.

CHAPTER FIFTY

Banned by the Assemblies of God – Part 2

IT'S TIME TO EMBARRASS Michael Buckland (sort of)…

Soon after Vernon and Heather Light were married, a young guy (we'll call him Jack) came to us for help. He shared openly that he had sexual addiction issues along with a number of other problems. He seemed genuinely committed to getting the help he needed. We were in Vernon and Heather's apartment in Rosebank, and while the three girls (Pauline, Heather, and Michael's fiancée, Debbie) looked on through an open serving hole between the kitchen and living room, we gathered around Jack who was kneeling on the floor facing us—with me on his left, Vernon on his right, and Michael in front of him.

Michael told him to confess Jesus as his Lord. He didn't. He sidestepped. He began to shout and to stand on his feet quite aggressively, beginning to thrash about. His face became contorted, and his voice changed to a guttural-type snarl. Michael spoke to whatever was inside him, in Jesus' name, to stop. Jack fell backward onto his side and then onto his back. He stopped thrashing and was silent.

Glancing back at the girls watching gob-smacked and terrified from the kitchen, we looked at Michael and asked simply, "Now what?"

As we collectively took our next breath, Jack began to raise himself up. Michael quickly climbed on top of him and instructed Vern to hold down his right arm and me to hold down his left. Jack continued to thrash and snarl and to display considerable strength. Michael rebuked the demon and commanded it to leave. Jack relaxed. But just when we were about to say, "That's it?!," he began to push up against us again.

I was utterly startled by what happened next. While Michael sat on his midsection and Vernon and I put all our weight on each arm, Jack lifted me with one arm nearly off the floor and then, also Vernon. We couldn't hold his arms down, and we weren't lightweights or unfit by any means, nor was Jack particularly well built. Michael rebuked the demon again … and again … and again. But Jack continued to raise us up with his arms and display unbelievable strength.

Nothing Michael, or we did, helped. When we were about to get up, run away, and rescue the screaming, horrified girls from the kitchen, Michael (a highly trained, Special Forces, Vietnam veteran) shouted, "Come out of him in Jesus' name!" and then right-hand karate chopped him in the left side of his neck, knocking him unconscious.

Vernon and I nearly wet ourselves in sanctified, smiling shock.

The story from Acts 19 about the Sons of Sceva trying to cast out demons without true Jesus power came to mind. Matthew 12:24–28 also came to mind (but I could have told you only a portion of the verses back then). Jesus said to the Pharisees, "And if I drive out demons by Beelzebub, by whom do your people drive them out?"

Answer: With a karate chop!

To end on a positive note, when Jack came around, he seemed fine and spoke normally, but a bit correctly, about his desire to serve the Lord. We prayed for him to give his life again to the Lord, but behind closed doors, we secretly admitted that we didn't hold out much hope for him to find freedom, not least because he didn't really seem to want to change. He wanted a quick fix on his terms.

I'm not sure what I learned from that experience—maybe a need to attend martial arts classes?

* * *

Why Am I Telling You These Stories?

I mention these accounts by way of a build up to the AOG leadership's ban on our ministry and to demonstrate something of our efforts to discover and be part of God's total ministry to those in need. There were dozens of other wonderful moments—some big, some small) where God did some very special and amazing things in people's lives. People came to Christ, and lives were touched for good—eternally.

Just to note, the ministry to William (Chapter 48) took place at the home of the leaders of the young adult group and was a regularly scheduled, official AOG meeting. In short, more than likely, word got back to the AOG leaders about what took place.

* * *

Summoned to Appear Before the AOG Leadership

Michael, Vernon, and I were summoned to meet with the AOG leadership at Harfield Road, which also included, of course, Noel Cromhout, the main pastor (who had also invited me to try to help cast a demon out of Timothy— see Chapter 46).

They spelled out their displeasure in very, very strong terms regarding our doing miracles and casting out demons and getting people all worked up, confused and worried. They explained that we were teaching things outside mainstream doctrine and teachings of the AOG. What is a bit ironic is that one of the Elders who was present had asked us to minister deliverance to his brother in recent weeks, but he didn't mention that—and neither did we say anything to drop him in it.

They castigated us and were quite brutal in their attack. I think what hurt the most was their extremely negative and dismissive view of our hearts, especially Vernon's and mine. They knew us, I thought, as sincere, dedicated, and humble young men of God who had a heart only for His Kingdom and His Glory. They basically labeled us as misguided, evil heretics.

Without much of a chance to get a word in edgewise, they finally asked us to explain some things, but honestly, we all sensed it wouldn't matter what we said. We didn't debate the theology of healing or the Gifts of the Spirit (the "what") with them, but they bristled at our explanation of their use (the "how"). Other than tongues, interpretation, and prophecy during Breaking of Bread services, none of them had any real experience of much more, or at least, they didn't feel free to share it then. I'm quite sure they had a vicarious collection of stories about Nicholas Bhengu, Paul Lange, and the Mullan brothers, or other famous Pentecostal celebrities.

Skeptical looks turned positively angry when I told them about Pauline's bear growling and liberation experience. That settled it. We were fanatics. I guess I understood their point of view.

One of the Elders carefully but emphatically explained to us (probably what had already been decided) that we were now under a ban; that we had been deceived, blinded, and led astray by the enemy and our own rebellious egos. We were restricted from preaching, teaching, ministering, sharing, speaking, or discussing, well, anything—with anyone. Total silence and subjection. Total verbal and public lockdown. No secretly or quietly flying under the radar. No exchange of ideas, thoughts, or views. Silence and obedience—agree or leave and be assured of public blacklisting if we continued otherwise or elsewhere—for three months.

We (at least Vernon and I as dedicated AOG members) were shamed and stunned into unspeakable silence—and agony in our souls. We had given our hearts and support for the AOG work, and God's work generally, over the years. We only wanted to be obedient to Him. It felt like an eternal wound that might never heal.

We submitted.

* * *

There is another reason why I'm sharing this here ...

I'm using hindsight when I say this now. It's almost a contradiction to what we claimed to believe was important for the church to become and the wholeness ministry we are called to carry out in the world.

So much of what we were doing, hoping to do, and training to do was, sadly, focused on healing or miraculous moments in time—done by individuals (us) ready to be bold while being available to be used by and in the power of the Holy Spirit. Looking back, the *sad thing* about our karate chop deliverance session with Jack described previously, was that we weren't plugged into a body of people who would understand what he went and was going through and could provide for him the follow-up care and support he needed. We did our "deliverance thing" as if that was enough in a moment or afternoon in time. We breezed in and then walked away.

Sure, we were moving in the Spirit but true, biblical salvation, healing, and deliverance—wholeness ministry—must take place within and through the body of Christ. Sure, we were caught between the proverbial rock and a hard place because of the AOG ban and yet the Lord seemed to want to use us to do some special and amazing things in spite of the ban. It would have been really great if we could have brought people we'd ministered to into a family of support, further healing, and wholeness to help put them back together again—a group who welcomed the transforming work of the Holy Spirit in all its manifestations.

We were caught up in doing our thing—humbly and not arrogantly or egotistically—I truly believe this. But it was still wrong—educational, transformational, yes—but wrong and unfortunate because it was done in isolation. We should have been ministering from within and with the support of a fellowship. The challenge was, we didn't know a body or family of believers who saw this as their mission as well.

* * *

Michael Buckland's Final Thoughts:

This solid chunk of recollections and thoughts of that long-ago period is still somewhat magical in my memory when the Lord moved in Cape Town. David, we were blessed to live and minister for Christ in the seventies, when many believers were foolish enough actually to believe God's Word. These days, I probably know more and understand less than we did back in the day, and that somehow seems right. It was God's good story.

To this day, I have no apologies to offer about the things that we did together for the Lord. I can say with a clear conscience and sincere heart that we were not rebellious in attitude or in spirit to the church (AOG) authorities. They were given a chance to harness a wonderful move of the Holy Spirit and chose instead to bludgeon it as completely as they could.

Over the nearly half-century since then, I have witnessed church discipline being used against various believers, some of whom did really grievous things, such as stealing another person's spouse and so on.

But in no case have I ever seen as draconian a punishment meted out as the Harfield Road AOG Elders doled out to us back then. I had little respect for those men then, and even less now, viewed through the lens of many decades. I believed it to be the will of God that we silenced their nonsense by submitting obediently to their banishment, but my honest assessment of their action is simple: "Considering themselves to be wise, they became fools" (Rom. 1:22).

– Michael Buckland, September 2021
Shared with Sanet Stander and Dave Lutes

CHAPTER FIFTY-ONE

Spiritually Diagnosing My Own Heart Problem
But Not Knowing It Was Me (Huh? What?!)

AS I'M SURE YOU'VE REALIZED BY NOW, during the first half of 1975, we were on a bit of a self-appointed and directed *How to Be Used by God in Miracles* tour. I was learning new things every day, and with Michael Buckland's mentoring and guidance, the mistakes were being kept to a minimum (I think; I hope).

Banned or not, word got out, apparently, and I was asked to share at a Sunday afternoon picnic with a small congregation—a so-called "Colored" church (non-AOG)—somewhere southeast and not far from Cape Town near an area called the Strand. It was a completely outdoor event, and after we had the braai, I was asked to share some teaching and to encourage people from the Word. Pauline was there with Michael and Debbie. The three of them were sitting on lawn chairs off to the side from where I was standing before the small crowd.

The group was sitting on a slight incline of grass, relaxed, and drinking soda or water while they waited for me to share. Preaching mini sermons (and not so mini) was something I had done often and loved, and by many accounts, I did a halfway decent job of connecting with and encouraging people. To be honest, any chance to preach was a chance for me to do what I truly loved—to be a pig in mud—holy mud and a kosher pig, of course.

As for the miracle stuff, especially the Word of Knowledge, I was still very green. A novice. A beginner. Knowing the difference between a random thought, a specific insight, or the sense of a physical need (e.g., for healing) was, for a beginner like me, *really hit and miss.*

That said, to underscore an extremely important and critical fact in my fictional *Genuine Beliefs Manual,* when I stood up in front of this group, or any group, I fully and completely believed and expected that *if* God wanted to do something miraculously special on that day, at that time, He could and would.

There was no doubt in my mind or heart that He was in the business of making people whole and restoring and anointing people for His purposes. If I could but make myself available (attitude, humility, willingness to be a fool for Him, etc.), He might, by His Grace-purposes, allow me to be part of it. I didn't exactly say it like that in those days, but that's what I basically thought and believed.

As for doing it in practice, to step out in faith and be a tool or instrument in His hands, well, I was *borderline clueless.*

Which is why I was glad Michael was there. He knew how to do this stuff.

It was a casual sharing affair, relaxed and personal, with some laughter and interaction. After I had shared from the Word and encouraged people for maybe twenty or so minutes, Michael stood up, came over to me and whispered in my ear. Everyone was watching but, apparently, no one seemed bothered.

He whispered that there was somebody sitting there who had a problem with a physical ailment or injury. I can't remember now what he told me, only that he was not at all specific.

Somewhat skeptically, I thought that it was sort of like saying, "The Lord has shown me that someone here has a toothache!" Yes, it was that vague, and by the way, what are the odds?! Vagueness didn't help me much in my communication with the group, and then, Michael sat back down.

I continued speaking, and a minute or two later, I told the group essentially what Michael had said—not that the Lord had told Michael and that Michael had told me and now I was telling them. I said it more spiritually with it than that.

With no embellishment, I made it very clear that it was one person, and they were sitting among us and that they would probably respond immediately in their heart and mind to what I was saying, knowing that it was them I was talking about. I asked the person to identify themselves so we could pray for them.

A person raised their hand, didn't elaborate on what the problem was, and some people in the group near them stood up and prayed for them—and then sat down. It most definitely was not about me being the healing guru, which was fine.

That said, as I continued to share, Michael came up again and whispered in my ear, this time something more specific. We prayed. God did His thing. Michael did it again. We prayed. And again ... 2–3 more times! Whisper, announce, acknowledge, stand, pray, sit, preach.

Lather, rinse, repeat.

But it had got to the point where people didn't really know what was going on or who was getting the revelation (Word of Knowledge). If they were thinking it (which would not have surprised me), at no point did someone say, "If God is telling him (Michael) about someone who needs prayer, why doesn't he (Michael) say it and pray it?! What are you, Dave, the telegraph office, or the delivery boy?!"

It was sort of like spiritual Tag Team Wrestling but with healing not hurting.

We had a pretty good flow going, and it seemed to not really matter who was receiving something (revelation) from God as people were being touched, and there was a good sense of God being present and among us.

But then things really got a little weird and confusing—and funny.

At some point, Michael came up and whispered in my ear that someone had a quite serious heart and breathing problem and that it had been troubling them for some days. He went back to his seat and sat down.

By now, I'm getting bolder and more energized and beginning to feel like a true man of God—*Africa's Man of Faith and Miracles!*

Oh yeah! Hallelujah!

With some emotion and a hint of mystical insight and language (trying to *faith* things up a bit), I announced that there was somebody in the gathering that had a heart condition or problem, that it had been troubling them for some days—and that their breathing was becoming difficult. Today, right then, God wanted to heal them. I urged the person to acknowledge their need and raise their hand.

No one said a word.

No one raised their hand.

No one owned the need.

Blank stares, nervous eyes.

The more I pushed it, the more stress I felt, and I was becoming increasingly embarrassed, and my own chest was beginning to hurt. I tried one more time and described what I thought would be the symptoms, trying to encourage someone to own up so that we could pray for them. I appealed, I urged, I expressed sympathy and tried to show my understanding about any fear and possible pain they might be experiencing.

Nada.

Dry-mouthed, I swallowed hard and tried to encourage the person, symbolically and empathetically while touching my own heart as I scanned eager and expectant faces in the group.

With shock on my face, and even more shock in my voice, I said, at precisely the same time as Pauline, who shouted from her chair, *"It's me!"* (*"It's you, Dave!"*)

I had been struggling with pains in my chest and had had difficulties breathing for some weeks, and it had begun to increasingly worry me (us). I had not seen a specialist but was going to do so soon—it was troubling me that much. When Michael whispered in my ear, it never entered my head that it was a Word of Knowledge *for me!*

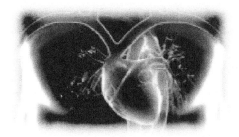

But it was, and as the leaders of the group and Pauline and Michael laid hands on me and prayed, I can without hesitation tell you ...

... I had no idea how to explain to the group what had just happened!

375

"You had a Word of Knowledge for yourself?!"

"Wow, what a spiritual giant!"

"Such an amazing supernatural revelation!"

"I think I have indigestion. Can you ask the Lord to confirm this to you, please?!"

(Under their breath and sarcastically whispering to the person standing nearby, *"Now, wasn't that convenient?!"*)

Fortunately, the group had never experienced, seen, or heard a Word of Knowledge before—so they had no basis for comparison. I could only hope that our *miracle-working show-and-tell lesson and demonstration* from that day on didn't become standard prayer or ministry protocol in their church in the future.

Good News! Whatever it was that was giving me trouble in my heart was gone. I was healed, and it wasn't for another 30 years that I actually had any real issues with my heart.

Bad News! It wasn't until I was flat on my back in an ambulance 30 years later and then, later in hospital, that I realized that for the previous 30 years I had taken His first healing for granted and hadn't looked after myself and my body.

His word to me in hospital was:

"Have I got your attention now, Davie? By the way, this next medical procedure … it's really going to hurt! But I promise you that it will be special and spiritually character building."

I'm sharing this account to illustrate two important truths:

1. We are human.

2. In spite of us, God still acts and actually has a sense of humor while He tries to use us and teach us lessons, especially, it seems, when we are trying to be part of His miracle-working activities and things.

Oh, and ...

3. Things can and will go wrong (did I mention because we're human?).

Wait, sorry, there's one more ...

4. As the old saying goes (my saying actually), "If the pudding (dessert) you design and plan for the Lord flops, He will just call it something else." (Which has temptation written all over it—if something goes wrong, "Make excuses and blame God for it.")

"Man proposes, God disposes."

CHAPTER FIFTY-TWO

God is All In! Warts and All!

DURING *THE BAN* THAT THE AOG LEADERSHIP IMPLEMENTED, our experiences and our activity (e.g., teaching, sharing, praying, etc.) in the area of the Gifts of the Holy Spirit needed to be controlled and restricted —not even monitored or developed—*just stopped*. As I wrote, we were told to "cease in the use of the Gifts of the Spirit," as the Elders described it (as if we could turn them on or off at will).

Looking back on it, it's kind of sad and a bit odd. *If* the Holy Spirit was *not* doing these things, then we would be deceived magical conjurers and manipulators of people's feelings and even misguided or deluded fanatics.

If, on the other hand, it really was the Holy Spirit's working, then how could we stop Him even if we wanted to? Granted, He needed available people who were willing to step out of the boat in faith and do or say something and be willing to make fools of themselves while they did so. But I guess I see the Elders' point in that regard.

To be told by God to take a step, reach out and touch, and speak out in His name when He indicates He wants to touch someone's life or body and then to say "no" or to turn away and to ignore Him—would be blatantly disobedient ... not to mention people who needed help wouldn't receive it.

Rock ... hard place.

* * *

I still continued to attend youth meetings and weekly activities with the young adult group back at Harfield Road AOG. I was no longer on the leadership team, and even if I were, I was restricted and not permitted to talk, teach, lead, counsel, etc. —at all.

You can imagine how awkward it was for me then when I felt a burning sensation on the bottom of both my feet while sitting during a time of worship with 25–30 other AOG young adults. It was distinct, painful, precise, and as quickly as it came, the burning pain left. It lasted long enough for me to flinch and wonder. I knew there was nothing wrong with my feet; I knew the burning was not something caused by me walking too much or by tight shoes or by any other problem.

"Ag, nie maan, Lord, nie! Oh God, please, no! Not me, not now!"

Because the physical message in my feet was so strong and unmistakable, I hesitantly asked the Lord what it was about—sort of: "Even if this is from you, Lord, I can't say anything! If you want to heal somebody's feet, get someone else to say it and do it!"

"Hmmm," He said, "but they need to know I'm right here, right now, and that I love them and that I know about their pain and that I want to take it away. I want this for them, not you. Will you help me do this?"

Why does He say things so lovingly like that?! It's really not fair when He asks like that!

"Lord, uh, you know I'm under a ban, right?"

I would really like to facetiously tell you that the Lord said, "Duh, Davie."

My mind was racing.

On the other hand, I said to myself, knowing the Lord was listening, *Why would He do this to me knowing that I am under a ban, that I could really get into big trouble for this?! Now I'm put in a position where I have to choose between being obedient to Him or being obedient to the church leaders.*

On mental paper this didn't read like much of a dilemma. *Of course,* I would place obedience to the Lord over obedience to the Elders! Uh huh, yeah, sure, really easy choice.

Did I mention being stuck between a rock and a hard place?!

That said, all these mental and spiritual gymnastics had sidetracked me away from the real issue. Someone sitting there, in that room, right then, was in pain. God wanted to show His power and love to them and heal them—most likely as part of other things He was doing in their life. I was getting all twisted up and bent out of shape with this, this—wait—there's a word for it in my unsaved vocabulary somewhere—oh yeah, sh- …-tuff.

Therein lies the added problem that would help you, dear reader, to appreciate and see spiritual risk-taking in an entirely new light. *I had to say something out loud* about someone's feet in public where everyone could listen, and everyone could see what would happen next. I guess I could have asked and trusted the Lord to show me who the person was, and when He did, go to that person privately …

Nope … I wasn't at that confident a place in this gifts thing yet. I was still learning to adjust my spiritual antenna to get the right signals from Him. I would have liked to think I knew in my knower what He was trying to say and do, but more than 50 years down the road, my heart and brain and spiritual GPS are sometimes still as jumbled as they were then. Only now, I can rationalize keeping my mouth shut much more easily.

Besides, it wasn't as if I was telling the group, lamely and safely, that there was someone in the room with allergies or that they were having problems at work or that they had a difficult mother-in-law. Those were all easy and safe options.

OK, Davie boy—speak!

So, I did.

Speaking up loud enough for everyone in the room to hear me, I said, "Someone here tonight has an infection in their feet, and it's serious, and God wants to heal your feet right here, right now. He wants to take the infection and pain away and make you whole in your feet again."

There was a deathly hush when there should have been a glory cloud of lively, joyful, exuberance-filled "Amens! Yes, that's me, Dave!"

I waited.

Everyone waited.

I, and everyone in the room, became increasingly embarrassed.

Is it getting hot in here?

I spoke again, hesitantly, "I know it's not easy to share publicly what's going on in your life sometimes. Don't be shy or embarrassed … Just trust that God has found you sitting here and that He loves you and wants to heal you. So, come on, who are you? Come on … it's OK!"

Hear a smiley, encouraging tone.

381

Getting hot wasn't even close. Stress plus anxiety plus no one speaking up and no one admitting that they were the one with an infection in their feet plus me being under a ban ...

Great Lord, that's just great! (Read: humble, cautious sarcasm.)

I wanted to crawl through the floorboards in my embarrassment. I weakly tried one more time to encourage the person, whoever they were (*If* they were?) to not be afraid, to not be scared or shy, and if they couldn't speak up now, to trust Him when they were alone ...

Cop-out ... blah, blah, blah!

Silence.

This banned, Holy Spirit-gifted dummy really wanted to die. I couldn't meet anyone's eyes over coffee; I couldn't hold a thought in my head. We couldn't get out of there fast enough. We (Pauline and I) went back home in silence. We even avoided talking about it and, in silence, got ready for bed.

* * *

Author's Explanatory Note: It's very hard to explain how to take a step of faith based upon a physical indication that somebody might be sick, injured, or have some other physical ailment. As I mentioned, it's one thing to say, "I believe that someone in this room has a headache." I mean, what are the odds? (Read sarcastic tone.) But to speak openly and publicly and precisely that somebody needed to be healed, right there, right then of something very specific, well, that required a huge step of faith, not to mention a willingness to make a complete ass of yourself (for God, of course!).

Plus, you really needed to be sure that whatever sensation you were experiencing (e.g., a burning sensation in your own feet) was actually you feeling what was going on in *someone else's* feet and was not just your own neglected athlete's foot. Then to define the cause of the burning (e.g., an infection) took things to another level of faith leap on the one hand, and risk of embarrassment on the other—not to mention God getting a bad rep or being dishonored in the process. An added problem was that there is very little biblical evidence, if any, of such a thing as a physical Word of Knowledge for healing—thin theological ice at best!

By all appearances and reasoning, someone (I) got their wires crossed and was not reading or feeling the spiritual signals right. Or I really *was* delusional and needed an embarrassing public failure like this to make me see the error of my ways and the wisdom of the church leaders' ban.

* * *

We got into bed. Then about 12:05 a.m. the phone rang. It was one of the older, married men from the meeting; he and his wife were there together. He felt that it was important enough that he needed to call me even late at night and explain to me what had happened.

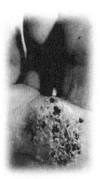

He said, "Dave, when you said someone had an infection in their feet, I didn't know what to say. You speaking out like that was kinda weird. We've never heard or seen anyone do that before. And besides, I didn't have an infection in my feet."

"O...K ...?" I replied hesitantly.

He continued, "But I have had plantar warts all over the bottom of both of my feet for weeks! It's been incredibly painful, and nothing, no treatment, seems to help. The doctor is trying, we're trying, but nothing is really helping. But when we got home tonight, I took off my shoes and socks to get ready for bed, and I discovered that I had brand-new, baby quality skin on the bottom of both of my feet, and all the plantar warts were gone. Anyway, I thought that maybe you would like to know that. I didn't have your number, so I had to find someone who did. It took a while and that's why I'm calling so late. Sorry about that."

I wept.

It seems I *did* get my spiritual antenna wires crossed, but that was OK. A lesson was learned. Remarkably, apparently reports that Dave Lutes was trying to do healing miracles again didn't reach the church leaders. I mean, after all, all I did was make an ass of myself in front of a group of people. If anything did get shared with the leaders, it was that I had botched trying to "*do a miracle,*" thus proving their point.

CHAPTER FIFTY-THREE

A White Horse, Lengthening a Leg, and Prayer Giggles

WE SEMI-ENJOYED SOME CALM for the duration of *The Ban*, which was a kind of spiritual test, regrouping of thoughts, and battery recharging (you know what I mean). We didn't talk, preach, teach, or share about anything really. We certainly didn't do or practice miracles or use the gifts of the Spirit (as if they were things we could whip out of a toolbox at will).

When the ban ended, however, in fact ***the actual day it was lifted***, we hosted basically the same young adult and student group from the previous chapter in our home. We were house-sitting for an elderly couple who had gone away for three months. This time, Johnny was there, and Vernon, as well as some other people we didn't know and some new friends and people from the church (spies?). It was quite packed.

We had begun to hear that, in spite of the ban, word was circulating that cool things, miraculous and unusual type things, tended to happen when Johnny, Vernon, and Dave ministered or were together. Some came, I'm sure, out of curiosity. We really tried to play this down.

We spent some time sharing from the Bible, of course, with some good discussion. The room was full of people and full of life. It was simply a nice, expectant vibe; very typical of the Jesus Revolution in the early-to-mid- '70s.

We decided to have a time of prayer. As we began to pray, I had a picture in my mind, clear as a photograph, of a white horse. *That was it, a white horse.* I have no idea why I was seeing a white horse. I had never seen one, ridden on one, nor had any interest whatsoever in being near one. But clear as day, there it was before my mind's eye. As quickly as it appeared, it was gone.

It was so startling clear that there was no way I could ignore it.

As Michael B. had mentioned, that sort of thing happened sometimes when God may be trying to do something special, or in Johnny's words, "God was really wanting to be very cool and do something powerful in a very real way."

Nervousness grabbed me once again. The ban had just been lifted, and now, at our first time hosting a meeting, the Lord kicks off the evening by giving me a Word of Knowledge?! At least I thought that's what it was.

But seriously, Lord, a white horse?!

What am supposed to do with that?!

What do I say? "Someone has a white horse at home with a headache or an infection in its feet?!"

Nothing more came into my head, and the image was left hanging there in my mind's eye memory.

For a moment, I thought maybe it was reference to a white horse in the book of Revelation, and I needed to share a prophetic word about the End Times. I quickly scrapped that idea. I had pretty much never read much of nor understood Revelation.

We continued to pray, as I tried to remember if I had had anything unusual to eat that day, when suddenly Johnny blurted out, "… There is someone in the meeting who is in tremendous pain in their back. More than that, it's serious spinal pain, right now! Recently you have been struggling to even walk. The discomfort for you is severe …"

This was the first time, to my knowledge, that Johnny had ever done this sort of thing (a specific revelation or insight into someone's physical problem) publicly, and it took (I know all too well) tremendous courage for him to open his mouth so purposely and precisely like that. But Johnny always was the kind of guy who let all of his faith and love and passion for the Lord and the Gospel hang out there. I always admired that in him.

Then Johnny added in his own unique way:

"Dinkum! God really, really wants to heal you right now—really —right now!"

A young woman named Sally put up her hand and said hesitantly, "Yes, it's me, I think. I hurt my back, and I am in tremendous pain, but I don't really know if that's what God wants to do. I mean, I can't tell Him what to do. How do I know it's me—that His healing, this healing, is for me? I'm not really sure about this."

I heard myself speaking before I even thought about it. **"You recently fell off a white horse, and that's how you injured your back, right?"**

The look on Sally's face was first shock, then gasping for air, followed by tears streaming down her cheeks. She looked at me, she looked at Johnny, then she looked all around the room at stunned faces with total surprise, bewilderment, and amazement on her face—and then looked back at Johnny.

"Yes, about four months ago I fell off a horse—a white horse—and now I'm suffering because of the injury. It's getting worse. The pain is unbearable. I was beginning to accept I would have to live with it."

Sally began to cry again, and those sitting next to her put their arms around her shoulders.

Johnny was really spiritually psyched now! With a huge grin and his hands raised snatching any Holy Spirit healing energy from the air that he could find, Johnny said, "C'mon Sal, let's pray. You sit in this chair, and we'll all gather around you and pray for you together."

Not to make a big deal of this again, but Johnny was truly pumped up at the thought of a semi-real-major-dinkum miracle happening that night. Vernon and I joined him, as did others, and stood around and in front of Sally who was seated in a chair. Worried that it might hurt her, Johnny then asked her if it was OK if we could raise both of her legs up, side by side and straight out.

* * *

To be honest, Johnny and I had seen other healers or had attended other healing services where people, ministers, or leaders of healing movements had asked people to raise their legs and, discovering (sometimes suspiciously) that one leg was shorter than the other—and they asked the Lord to lengthen the shorter leg. It has often been called the "leg-growing ministry." Truthfully, we had actually demonstrated once to each other how leg growing was easy to fake and was something of a joke among Pentecostal and Charismatic folks. It was easy to manipulate two legs and create the appearance of a miracle.

* * *

In any case, when Johnny raised Sally's legs up, we noticed that one leg was significantly shorter and even slightly turned in an unusual way. While she walked slowly, she didn't have a noticeable limp, yet this appeared to be a symptom of the injury, plus, the extreme pain, of course.

Johnny started to pray. In his case, you could bank on the fact that the prayer would be emotional, full of superlatives, quite convoluted, full of bad grammar, very dramatic, and even sometimes borderline cringeworthy/confusing—but coming from a place of complete love and trust in God.

He wanted this miracle *bad,* and based on his opening prayer sentence, he truly believed God was present to heal Sally. Me, too, for that matter. By the sound of the low spiritual murmur of assent, many in the room were also confident and expectant. A sanctified, spiritual winding up was going on, getting ready to release faith and power! It bothers me a bit to put it that way, but, right or wrong and people being people, that's the best way I can describe it.

Please bear in mind that this was an extraordinary moment in most, if not all, of those present. They would go home able to say they witnessed a real miracle! This sort of thing never happened in AOG church life—much less in a midweek young adult meeting.

* * *

Johnny was speaking in tongues now and holding her two legs up, side by side, with his hands under the heels of her feet. **Suddenly, he kind of gasped and paused.** I quickly looked at him, wondering what was going on. He leaned closer to my ear and whispered:

"Dave, what do I do now? Do I ask the Lord to make one leg shorter or the other one longer?"

I began to crack up laughing. Grinning from ear to ear and barely able to speak, I eventually whispered back to him, *"Good question; how the heck should I know?!"*

Not willing to lose the victory that evening, with utter calm and total spiritual seriousness, Johnny said, "Lord, please make these legs the same length, in Jesus' name!"

I kid you not, no exaggeration, no pulling and twisting of your legs or feet—or your arm—right before our eyes, Sally's legs became the same length. There were gasps all around the room. Who wouldn't have been tempted to open their eyes during prayer at a moment like that?! The look on Sally's face told more of the story: pain-free, grateful, tear-drenched relief.

Johnny smile-looked at me and said with his eyes, *"Huh, I guess that worked! So, that's how it's done!"*

* * *

Author's Note: This particular story happened back in 1975 in Kenilworth, Cape. I started writing the first draft of this book in August 2019. Early in 2020, I contacted the same Sally in this chapter to ask her if she remembered this particular incident. She confirmed that it was real and true and was a significant and amazing event in her life.

CHAPTER FIFTY-FOUR

Leaving South Africa

A Series of Cool Miracles—Small–Medium Ones—But Miracles Nonetheless

I MENTIONED CHARD BEFORE IN CHAPTER 42, "Talk About a New Dawn!" and that I believed God had clearly told me I needed to go to Chard, Somerset, England, to learn something important for my life. To be more specific, I needed to go to South Chard Full Gospel Church.

Pauline and I had also signed a *Total Commitment Promise* to God surrendering ALL aspects and features of our lives (including financial) to Him. Pauline continued to work, and I quit my job at Reckitt and Coleman and gave myself fully to the work of the ministry and to learning, under Michael Buckland's tutelage, and to discover how the Holy Spirit touches and changes every aspect of a person's life. This was truly a huge and difficult (and easy to misunderstand or criticize) decision. Breaking the news Pauline was an *interesting* moment, to say the least.

However, the AOG Ban

Because of the AOG ban, my learning curve bent toward other places and people and opportunities. It was a faith walk, not only financially, but also in terms of learning how to be led into being used in helping others. It was a tricky time and had the feel of navigating a minefield (not that I had ever done that, of course).

The Ban was still active when we reached midyear, when we had also reached crunch time to commit to going to Chard or not. We had decided to go by ship as the cheapest option, and the next voyage (13 days) was on October 3 of that year. We had three months to get our plan together without crossing a spiritual *"live by faith and not by subtle hint"* line that we had agreed we wouldn't cross—namely, telling or even hinting to anyone about our financial needs. Saving money for the down payment on the ticket was a priority, and therefore, keeping any spending to a minimum was critical.

We told friends and family that we would be leaving South Africa on a one-way ticket in October; and then on to the US to attend Bible school. In addition, I had written to the pastor of South Chard Full Gospel Church, Syd Pearce, asking if it would be OK to visit for a short while later in the year "… to hear and learn what God has in mind for us." He wrote back and extended a warm welcome!

When you read the following list, please remember, we never, ever told a soul about our financial needs. Of course, friends and family weren't oblivious, and of course, they tried very hard to respect our silence on the matter while also looking for ways to help out practically —even secretly.

Miracle No. 1: As we could no longer minister, we had to leave Pinelands, where we lived, and find something closer to Harfield Road AOG, and Pauline's family, in the Southern Peninsula. Johnny Weber, Vernon, and I remained in close touch and were so disheartened about not being able to continue ministering together. In Chapter 53, about the white horse and Sally's healing, I mentioned we were looking after an elderly couple's house. We saw an ad in the paper that they were going away on holiday for three months beginning in July. Their house was less than a quarter mile from, and on the same street as, Harfield Road AOG. When we interviewed with them to be considered as tenants, and they heard our story, they liked us and said we could stay rent free for the three months. We only had to pay utilities bills. Very cool.

Miracle No. 2: Pauline continued to work at her job in Pinelands (City Council Town Planning) until the last minute. She spent her days redrawing house, community, and road plans. She was beginning to have doubts about the idea of going to Chard along with all the changes, risks, and pressures leading up to the possible departure. I'm sure she also struggled with what she'd gotten herself into by marrying me. Too late!

Was this challenging life going to be her lot for a long time? Would she ever have a house with a beautiful garden in a nice neighborhood?

While she was puzzling and praying about the whole thing, (I'm paraphrasing) she said to herself, while looking at the plan of an amazing home in Pinelands, *Oh my, oh yes! That's perfect! Oh, how I wish…—Where is this house anyway … ?!* She looked at the street name and was stunned to tears. It was on Orchard Street. But she didn't read "Orchard," she read "*Or Chard.*" That settled it, and she left her job (not least because she couldn't travel to get there).

Miracle No. 3: See Chapter 52, "God is All In! Warts and All," which is when we were still under the ban, but He was still active and showing He was not done with us and wanted to use us.

Miracle No. 4: The Ban was lifted by the AOG leadership, and the same weekend, we held a senior young adult meeting where we were house-sitting. God stepped in and did a really cool healing miracle. (See Chapter 53, "A White Horse, Lengthening a Leg, and Prayer Giggles.")

Miracle No. 5: In the middle of an evening, actually about 9:30 p.m., a complete stranger knocked on our door at the house we were looking after and said only, "God told me to give you this," as he handed me R100 ($200) and left. We tried to find out who he was or who may have told him about us, but no luck.

Miracle No. 6: Someone bought our car for about $150 more than we were asking for it.

Miracle No. 7: A friend from the church asked me to help him out with a new product he was making and selling and paid me $150/week for one month; and I didn't need a car to do it.

Miracle No. 8: We were at the Breaking of Bread service at Harfield Road AOG, and it came time for the offering bag to be passed around. A guy sitting in front of us took a wad of money out of his pocket and was about to put it into the bag, then paused, looked back at us with a curious expression on his face, and handed me the money instead.

There were other smaller bits and pieces of money that came in. I can't remember all of them, but God clearly had a steady stream of reassurance flowing toward us.

* * *

We had one week to go now before we had to make our final payment for the ship ticket. My temporary job was finished, and Pauline was unemployed. We had made the family (in-laws) promise they would not try to pay for anything, except maybe to have us over for dinner from time to time and then, allow us to stay with them for the week before we had to sail.

Miracle No. 9: We were at the in-laws for the evening and had been fielding some considerably vocal criticism from my father-in-law to the unsubtle effect of, "How can you be so presumptuous to think God will pay your way?! I've always paid my own way! I've worked hard all my life to have a good life for my family! What a terrible husband you are for my daughter! She's made a huge mistake, I think!"

They pushed and probed, sometimes tearfully, as we tried to calmly discuss it all. My mother-in-law, throughout everything that had taken place in the past year, had given her life to Christ. She was trying to hang in there with her new infant faith. Dad was nowhere close to personal belief as far as we could tell and had a very forceful and unpredictable personality. Pauline wrung her hands and paced, tears forming. I anxiously tried to secretly put my finger in the dike of my own leaking and waning faith.

Finally, they pushed and asked how much we needed to make the final payment for the ticket the very first thing the next morning. We told them reluctantly, worried that they would whip out the money to pay the bill. We needed R100 ($200). It was around 9:00 p.m.

"^@^%$^& *son-in-law!*"

As an awkward, pregnant silence joined us in the room, the doorbell rang. It was Michael Buckland. With no fanfare, no asking to come in (from either of us), he simply said, "God told me you needed this," handed me R100, and left. What was kinda neat about it is that he had never been to the in-law's house in Plumstead before, and in those days, there was no GPS tracking. It didn't matter, he found us—God found us.

Jehovah Timex, the God of Perfect Timing …

My father-in-law was gob-smacked into silence (thankfully).

* * *

We made the final payment the next morning and prepared to leave for the UK, via the Cape Verde Islands, on the penultimate voyage of the Safmarine *Pendennis Castle* ten days later. I will tell you now, that when we finally boarded the ship, we had approximately $35 in our pocket. At least all the food and drink on the ship was included and some pretty amazing *God moments* happened during the 13-day voyage.

* * *

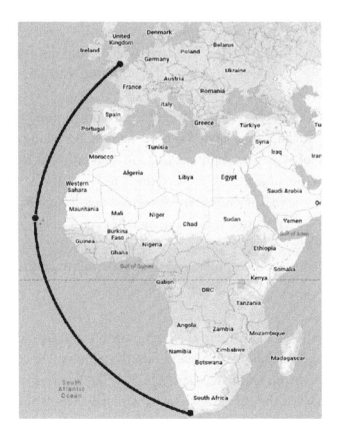

CHAPTER FIFTY-FIVE

Leaving South Africa –
The Things Only God Knew About

THE RE WERE A NUMBER OF OTHER THINGS we didn't tell anyone about. No one knew, except God.

Here are some additional and final comments that will, probably, raise some eyebrows for those reading this. You may, understandably, declare us utterly irresponsible and presumptuous in our faith walk.

You wouldn't be the first.

At no point, since we had made the faith journey commitment, did we sit back and wait for God to just pour money down from Heaven. We always took the position in our hearts, and practically in our daily lives, that we should not pray for something unless we were prepared to get off our butt-knees, or pews, and be willing to be part of the answer to the prayer. Without too obviously letting you know about our left hand not revealing what our right hand was doing, we also gave away whenever we could to anyone who had a need.

The truth is, the decision and the way the journey developed, was simply ordained by God, and sitting in or stepping out of the boat was in His hands. Sure, there were moments of doubt, but by in large, we had an inner assurance of complete reliance on Him. It wasn't easy for two hardworking, active people who most definitely were not lazy believers, to do nothing and just blindly trust Him.

But there's more to raise your eyebrows.

I mentioned briefly that Vernon and I had prayerfully toyed with the idea of going to Bible school in the US, even to the extent that I had spoken with Nicholas Bhengu about which university he might recommend (and then ignored his confirmatory recommendation). Part of our living by faith journey was that we (Pauline and I) were *still committed to going to Bible school, somewhere, to prepare for ministry.*

The original "trust plan" was to go to South Chard in the UK for 1-2 weeks (and ideally learn something profoundly life-changing) and then head to the US to study. For some reason we had sort of settled on Elim Bible Institute and College in Lima, New York, which was about 70 miles from where my parents lived and where I had grown up.

There were numerous challenges ahead.

1. We had no money to get from Southampton Seaport, UK to Chard—about 88 miles; we assumed we would go by bus or train but weren't sure.

2. We had no money to live on while in the UK.

3. We didn't know if we needed to pay rent or some other costs while staying at the South Chard Full Gospel Church community.

4. We had no money to travel—we assumed by plane—from the UK to the US whenever we were ready or wanted to do so.

5. Pauline didn't have a visa to enter the US, and we had no money to pay for it if and when we applied for it.

6. I had not enrolled at the Bible school, and if and when we did, had no money to pay to attend.

It was a bold faith plan that wasn't actually a plan.

It's OK, you can say it.

You will need to get a copy of the sequel to this book, *Guidance, Goofs and More Grace,* to know what happened … if I ever finish it.

Stay tuned!

The next and final chapter of this book will give some of the "game" away. I share it because it illustrates so wonderfully well how God had it in His plan and purpose to connect Holy Spirit ordained "dots" during my exchange year, baseball, baptism, the Jesus Revolution, the AOG ban, to our calling to Chard, and then to my family back home in the US.

Yes, we did get there but not in any way like normal.

Please read on. Thank you!

CHAPTER FIFTY-SIX

Mom, It's So Simple

I WON'T TELL YOU MUCH NOW that you don't already know but will briefly reset the clock back to the early Jesus Revolution days in Cape Town.

To recap, when I was studying at the University of Cape Town in 1972–73, I lived with a family from our church in Kenilworth, Western Cape and spent most of my spare time playing baseball and attending or participating in dozens of churches, youth groups, parachurch organizations, and related activities each month. I was 20 years old.

During this period, I discontinued my college studies, started a new job as a computer operator for a large pharmaceutical company, lay co-pastored a student-focused Assembly of God fellowship in Pinelands, Cape, while the desire in me to share a message that could change someone's world—completely and forever—*was becoming a burning passion.*

My parents, with another couple, came to South Africa at the end of 1972, which was an amazing time of reunion—only eight days, but a very special time, nonetheless. One interesting and special moment was when they traveled from Johannesburg to Cape Town on the *Blue Train* (a kind of five-star hotel on rails). We (K and I) knew they would need to stop at Wellington Train Station, which was not far from where K lived. We sat on the center bench on a nearly ½ km long station platform.

To this day, I'm not sure what we were expecting to happen, but when the very, very long Blue Train pulled up alongside, we were stunned to see so many cars and gave up hope immediately that we might see my parents. The conductor appeared in front of us and looked up and down the platform (no one was boarding of course)—and at *that precise moment* right in front of us, my father put the window down and saw us sitting there. The hugging and laughing and crying that followed prompted the conductor to invite us onto the train and to ride the 40+ miles into Cape Town for free. A very cool *God Moment.*

But during the whole time they were there, we never discussed Christianity or church stuff. I think I was too afraid to rock the family boat. I showed off my new "country," they met K and the baseball team leaders, and they went up Table Mountain. I drove them all over the Cape in my kombi. We made some good memories. It would be nearly another three years before I saw them again.

* * *

Sometime near the end of 1973, I had a dream before I woke up one Sunday morning. I dreamed about an angel flying across and then up the full length of the Atlantic Ocean to visit my mom (Phyllis) in Upstate New York. The angel very clearly, unexplainedly, and directly said to her …

"Phyllis, it's so simple."

That was it.

I guess I somehow knew in my knower that it was a Holy Spirit message, but no details were provided, just a sense that God was doing or saying something special and significant. I logged it in my heart somewhere for discovery or action later.

Now I'm not a "dreams guy." In those days, I didn't have visions and special words or experience weird stuff. Secretly, I wanted to, but I also knew my logical, prove-it-to-me nature would more than likely get in the way. So, I reluctantly accepted that *I was the problem, not God.* I was, as someone politely described me once, "sort of cerebrally spiritual."

When I got to church that morning, Jenny Mills (Avril [Mills] Meeker's sister), a good friend from the senior youth group, came purposefully up to me and said, "You know, Dave, I had the weirdest dream this morning. I dreamed of an angel flying across the ocean to speak to your mom, and the angel said to her, **'It's so simple.'** What the heck is that all about?! What on earth does that mean?!"

Jenny knew virtually nothing about my family, much less about my mom.

I was utterly gob-smacked. I told Jenny that I had had the same dream, and while we mulled, puzzled, smiled, and felt those spooky Holy Ghost Moment goose bumps, we concluded that something was going on. Duh? But being young and totally out of my depth in these matters, I could profoundly say little more than, "Something is going on… Maybe I should contact her."

I didn't.

I didn't even write to her about it. I don't know why. I guess I didn't know how to write to her only or speak only to her on the phone. My dad would want to know what was going on, and it could get dicey for my mom. Dad was one of the kindest, smartest, most supportive fathers a boy could ever hope for, but he was a total and quite firm atheist. Well, a closet atheist really. He never spoke about it to us boys, except to show some strong disdain for the church, from time to time, as an institution specifically.

Anyway, after I was married and traveled to the US via Chard, UK, I was finally home with my new wife, Pauline, whom the folks had never met. It was a very special time for our new lives in America—wherever that might be. It was not long after the new year, January 1976.

* * *

As was our very much cherished custom, Mom and I sat up late, after everyone else had gone to bed, and talked. Even before I went to South Africa, we covered all manner of subjects, and those chats were some of the most honest, open, and cherished times where Mom really shared her heart—and I felt she really understood me as well. We hadn't really talked like that since July 1971. We both missed it.

When I think about God's timing, I realized later that that evening could have been because she had a spiritual hunger, but as Dad was so anti-God, and even more anti-church, her hunger never revealed itself. But since Dad was never really very vocal, or otherwise in-your-face, about his atheism, it never really entered my mind that these feelings or latent faith was part of my mom's heart life. Actually, Dad didn't talk much and very seldom shared his feelings about anything. But as I have said for decades, he was a solid gold, utterly honest, man of amazing integrity and an incredible high school math teacher—but very quiet.

403

That evening, chatting with Mom, the subject, of course, turned to Christian things.

At some point, I looked very purposefully and honestly into Mom's eyes and said to her, "Mom, can we talk about Jesus and about this thing that has happened to me? Can I talk with you about me being born again and all that stuff?"

Her eyes looking troubled, and she said in a low, emotional voice, "I don't know if I can. It scares me. I'm not sure I can cross that line. My feelings might show, and your dad is so terribly against it. I'm worried he will sense that I'm even a little bit curious about these things again. I want to respect his feelings about that. And besides, I just don't understand it all … It's too much for me to take in, I think. I don't know *how* to believe—certainly not like you do."

I was sitting some feet away from her but still urged by my heart to reach out to her as I said, "Oh, Mom, it's all about His love for you, for me, for John and Skip … even for Dad. Mom, really, it's so simple, what I want to tell you … **It's so simple.**"

I was startled as she burst into tears. I quickly went to sit closer to her and put my arm around her shoulders.

Softly I said, "Mom, what is it? Talk to me. Talk to me … please."

After a minute or two, she composed and gathered herself together, and her voice quivered with a mixture of joy, sadness, and awe as she said in almost a whisper, "When I was in the hospital giving birth to you, I went into a coma. They thought I was going to die. Your dad wasn't in the room, not like husbands sometimes are these days, but they let him know something was wrong. He feared the worst.

"While I was in the coma—I don't know for how long—I heard an amazing, calm, powerful, unbelievably loving voice speaking directly to me: **'Phyllis, it's so simple, trust me.'**"

Tears streaming down both our faces now, she continued, "I knew at that moment, things were going to be all right. I came out of the coma, and you were born safely, healthy, and with all your parts—all 8 lb. 4 oz. of you—and here we are [smiling]. And now you come to me, 23 years later, when we are talking about God and Christian things and you being born again and all, and you say to me, 'It's so simple'?!"

The dots weren't difficult to connect.

The presence of God was very real.

"Mom, I have something else to tell you. A few years ago, I had a dream ..." and I told her the story of the dream both Jenny and I had. She was stunned into silent disbelief, and quietly began to weep again.

I sensed the time was right and suggested maybe she should pray and ask Jesus to come into her life.

"Oh, Dave, I don't know how to pray like that. I've sort of prayed for years, always for you boys and your dad, you know, but I wouldn't know what to say now. What if I don't say the right things?"

I smiled and asked, hesitantly, "Would you be OK if I said a prayer for you, as if I am you ... and if you agree with the words and their meaning, maybe you could say 'amen' when I'm done? That would be like saying, 'Yes, you agree.' And we'll just trust God that He'll turn this amazing series of events, and this wonderful conversation, into something special for you?"

"OK, yes ... I can do that."

So, I prayed something essentially like this:

"Dear God, if what my son is telling me is true about your Son, Jesus, please do whatever it takes to write it on my heart to make it real to me and to help me believe. Help me to really believe. Help me to know you are real. Help me to discover how simple it is to accept your love for me and you into my life. Amen."

"Amen."

We hugged and cried together. I shared some Bible verses with her and went to bed. That was in early January 1976. The new journey for her would *not* be that simple—I knew that. But something incredibly and angelically special had begun for her and for me. We never spoke again about that evening until late 1994. She had terminal cancer. The last conversation we had before she died was about that oh so special, and not so simple evening in 1976.

Mom died on June 12, 1995. I couldn't be by her side.

I give thanks to God for the most amazing mother—ever!

See you someday, Mom. Love you!

Could this be why God found me in South Africa, rescued me, kept me from going to Vietnam, began to transform my life there, did and didn't physically heal me there, brought Johnny, Vernon and Michael into my life, sent an angel to speak to Jenny and me, and took Pauline and me on a faith journey from Cape Town, via the UK, to home in Trumansburg, New York?

With Him, it is so simple.

COPYRIGHT PERMISSIONS AND ACKNOWLEDGMENTS

The following websites and blogs are quoted frequently or referred to in this book.

https://capetownforjesus.wordpress.com/about/

http://hippyrevival.blogspot.com/

http://margeballin.weebly.com

https://www.pinterest.com/pin/471541023487106279/

∗∗∗

Special thanks to Laurie Lamont Daly, of Ardmore, Alabama (formerly from Trumansburg, NY – my hometown) for the photo on page 5—taken on February 28, 2023.

A special acknowledgement, with huge thanks, goes to Jack Hartland, Marge (Ramsden) Ballin and Jessop Sutton whose blogs and articles are quoted extensively by us and others. All personal photographs, images, and copies of e.g., newspaper articles, are used with permission.

COMMENTS, SUGGESTIONS, CATCH-UP

Dear old friends from the Cape Town Jesus Revolution days:

If you have any comments, additions, or corrections for this book, or you want to just catch up and meet on Zoom or other video chat, please contact us!

* * *

Authors' Contact Information

David Lutes

*Wentzville, Missouri,
USA*

 +1-636-497-5617   +1-636-634-9007

 www.Under-New-Management.com

 DavidLutes@Under-New-Management.com

 Under New Management LLC

 https://www.linkedin.com/in/dlutes

 Dave Lutes@davelutes6535

 UnderNewManagementLLC

Sanet Stander

*Somerset West, Cape,
South Africa*

 +27-72-437-2644

 www.KonnectBrainProfiling.com

 Info@KonnectBrainProfiling.co.za

 Konnect

 KonnectBrainProfiling

 linkedin.com/in/sanet-stander128a5b269

Made in the USA
Monee, IL
11 July 2023

38988021R00243